Claude McKay

Claude McKay

*The Literary Identity
from Jamaica to Harlem
and Beyond*

Kotti Sree Ramesh *and*
Kandula Nirupa Rani

McFarland & Company, Inc., Publishers
Jefferson, North Carolina, and London

LIBRARY OF CONGRESS CATALOGUING-IN-PUBLICATION DATA

Ramesh, Kotti Sree, 1968–
    Claude McKay : the literary identity from Jamaica to Harlem
and beyond / Kotti Sree Ramesh and Kandula Nirupa Rani.
        p.   cm.
    Includes bibliographical references and index.

    ISBN-13: 978-0-7864-2582-2
    ISBN-10: 0-7864-2582-2 (softcover : 50# alkaline paper) ∞

    1. McKay, Claude, 1890–1948.   2. Authors, American—20th
century—Biography.   3. Authors, Jamaican—20th century—Biography.
4. African American authors—Biography.   5. African Americans in
literature.   6. Blacks in literature.   7. Harlem Renaissance.   8. Black
nationalism—History—20th century.   I. Nirupa Rani, K.   II. Title.
PS3525.A24785Z87   2006
818'.5209—dc22   2006013445
[B]

British Library cataloguing data are available

Cover photograph: Claude McKay ca. 1920s or 30s (*Library of Congress*)

Manufactured in the United States of America

McFarland & Company, Inc., Publishers
    Box 611, Jefferson, North Carolina 28640
    www.mcfarlandpub.com

I fondly dedicate this book to my mother,
K. Chandramathi Devi.
—Nirupa Rani Kandula

I dedicate this work to my parents,
K. Sree Rama Muthy and Sree Ranganayakamma.
—Kotti Sree Ramesh

Acknowledgments

A study of such a canvas that deals with exile, identity, race and ethnicity requires the support and encouragement at all levels, intellectual, physical and spiritual. From the day we began our work searching the *Who's Who* in the Andhra University library to finding Claude McKay's grave in the vast Catholic cemetery in New York City on a snowy day in January 2000, we received the help and support of many individuals and institutions. It is our duty to acknowledge their help and express our gratitude for helping to bring our endeavor to fruition.

The most exciting part of our work was a six-month predoctoral Fulbright Scholarship to Harvard University for Sree Ramesh. For that we are particularly indebted to the Fulbright Foreign Scholarship Board and the United States Educational Foundation of India for providing travel and living grants. We fondly remember the friendly support given by the USEFI staff.

We wish to convey our profound gratitude to world-renowned teachers Professor Henry Louis Gates, Professor Anthony Appiah, Professor Biodun Jeyifo, all the members of the Department of Afro-American Studies and Professor Orlando Patterson of the Department of Sociology at Harvard University in Cambridge, Massachusetts, for opening new vistas of learning and knowledge.

Without libraries and the friendly support of their staffs, the scholar is (usually) lost. We want to express our thanks to the staff at the beloved Indo-American Center for International Studies (IACIS, formerly ASRC) in Hyderabad; Widener, Lamont, and Houghton libraries at Harvard University; Beinecke Rare Book and Manuscript Library at Yale University; and the New York Public Library, Schomburg Branch in Harlem, New York City, for sharing their knowledge and resources.

We also thank our family members, especially Sirisha Sangamirra, Ramesh's wife, who extended unstinted support throughout this endeavor.

Table of Contents

Preface

Claude McKay's literary oeuvre is a unique contribution to the global discourse of black writing. It inaugurated two significant black cultural movements, the Harlem Renaissance in the United States and Negritude in Europe. McKay began his career as a British colonial subject writer, and through his life and writings, analyzed the larger problems of identity, vocation and politics of the black man in the highly racist Western society of the first half of the twentieth century. His exile, throughout his writing career in the Euro-American world and North Africa, greatly helped his ideological evolution and had a deep impact on his writings. But McKay is widely read within the context of the Harlem Renaissance and is considered a deeply conflicting literary figure. Due to his strong militant voice, critics in the United States, right from James Weldon Johnson in 1930 (*Black Manhattan*), started reading him solely from Harlem's ethos, ignoring McKay's Jamaican colonial identity. They did not consider his distinct British colonial subjectivity, whose social and identity formations were qualitatively different from that of his Harlem peers, so they tried in vain to fit him into the Harlem picture. Initially, we, too, thought that his ambiguities were the result of the peculiar social and cultural position of the black artist in a hostile American society which imposed a double consciousness—American and Negro.

But a comprehensive reading of his life and writings, and of his sensibilities and aspirations, reveals that the ambiguities that afflicted McKay were qualitatively distinct from his Harlem peers. Reading him in the light of recent postcolonial theories we understood that the source of his ambiguities was from that of a colonial subjectivity.

1

Though critics and his biographers are aware of his Jamaican origins, they did not focus on his distinct colonial sensibility. They often equated his movement from Jamaica to Harlem to the movement from the rural U.S. South to the urban North, common to many of his Harlem peers. The result is a gross misunderstanding of his emotional geography, making him a highly paradoxical figure, an *enfant terrible* in the (African) American literary scene of the early twentieth century. The same is true with McKay scholarship in the Caribbean. Though he was rightly recognized and granted the due position he holds in the development of Caribbean letters, that focus is mainly on his texts located in the Caribbean. His exile and the cross-cultural impact that informs much of his oeuvre is often overlooked. So we have attempted to relocate and reread him in his natural habitat—noting the colonial sensibility, exile and cross-cultural experiences—and thus locate and establish him as a paradigmatic Black West Indian colonial writer in exile.

This study aims to identify the influence of his traits, distinguishing the colonial strain and sensibility, and thus explain and accommodate the ambivalences in his life and writings. We will focus on his poetry written in Jamaica (*The Dialect Poetry of Claude McKay*), poetry written outside Jamaica, containing poems of America and England (*Selected Poems of Claude McKay*), fiction written in France and North Africa (*Home to Harlem, Banjo, Ginger Town* and *Banana Bottom*) and autobiographies *A Long Way from Home* and *My Green Hills of Jamaica*. After showing McKay's ambiguities as product of the colonial constellation, this study proceeds to trace his quest for identity in exile. From a colonized subject writer imitating the British literary masters to a proponent of Negritude and then as a mature West Indian writer in exile who realized his essential hybrid identity as a Third World expatriate, McKay's ideological evolution is traced.

We hope the book will be able to give a comprehensive picture of this influential author whose life spans some of the key movements in black history.

A Note on Terminology

Throughout this study, we use a variety of terms that warrant clarification. The terms African American and Afro American refer to individuals of African descent who are born in the United States, as does the term "native born black." United States is mostly "United States" but may occasionally be "America." We used the terms "Caribbean" and "West Indies" for the Caribbean region, as we use "West Indian" and "Caribbean" for those of African descent of that region who have immigrated to the United States.

Introduction

Leaving his picturesque Caribbean island, Jamaica, then a British colony, at the age of twenty-two, Claude McKay landed on the shores of United States of America in Charleston, South Carolina, in the summer of 1912. He had published two volumes of dialect poetry in Jamaica, and had the reputation of being a poet, the "Bobbie Burns" of Jamaica. Within two years after coming to America to study agronomy, McKay quit two institutes—Tuskegee and Kansas State College—and drifted to Harlem, in 1914. Even though he published a couple of poems in various magazines, it was his most popular poem, *If We Must Die*, written in the context of Red Summer riots in 1919, that established McKay as the inaugurator of the Harlem Renaissance movement. His first book of poetry in the United States, *Harlem Shadows* (1922), was the first one to be published by a black artist since Dunbar broke the ground for a new chapter in African American letters. While his strong militant protest poems became a clarion call to generations of struggling blacks, his novel *Home to Harlem* was the first fictional work to hit the best sellers list by any black writer in the United States.

Yet the harbinger of the Harlem movement spent the best part of the "Renaissance" outside the United States, remaining not only skeptical of its ideological tenets but also highly critical of its members and their achievements. Always in and out of many Negro movements, McKay was a radical at the beginning of his career but turned to Roman Catholicism at its end. A gifted, rebellious writer who packed his hard-hitting protest poems in classical European tradition, he was more at home with bohemian white intellectuals than with American Negro leadership. An early proponent of Negritude, he was a writer who openly acknowledged the influence of English literary masters. If his life and opinions were contradictory and hence confusing to his peers, the apparent ambiguities in his writings are baffling to his critics. Explaining these ambiguities has remained the central task of McKay scholarship for many years.

Every attempt remained either unsuccessful or incomplete due to the variant readings of his life and his writings. While critics in the United States frequently associated him with the Harlem Renaissance and centered their study on his American productions—poetry and novels like *Home to Harlem*—critics in the Caribbean focused on his dialect poetry and novels like *Banana Bottom*, set in Jamaica. Consequently, the former recognized him as part of the Harlem literary triumvirate, sharing the position along with Jean Toomer and Langston Hughes, while the later projected him as one of the foremost authors of Jamaica.

Beginning with James Weldon Johnson's ambitious work of social history, *Black Manhattan*, in 1930, critics in the United States were completely at home in identifying McKay with the Harlem group. Wayne Cooper, McKay's biographer, argues that McKay can be understood only within the full context of his life and career and promptly locates him in the "continuous chain" of African American literary tradition from Booker T. Washington to the Black Power movement of the late 1960s (Cooper 2–3). Though recent American critics recognized his outsider status in relation to his African American peers, they often miss the colonial and cross-cultural experiences that foreground much of McKay's writings. Stating that the Harlem Renaissance was fraught with tensions, Tyrone Tillery, despite recognizing McKay's Jamaican origins, concludes in a well-researched 1991 biographical study that more than any other Harlem Renaissance figure it is McKay who embodies these contradictory impulses. Kenneth Ramchand, Lloyd Brown and other Caribbean critics, though, focus on his Jamaican background, often overlook his exile and the cross-cultural impact that marks a substantial part of his oeuvre. Informed by the recent postcolonial theories, this study will examine the life and writings of Claude McKay from a comprehensive colonial and cross-cultural perspective not previously engaged upon in McKay scholarship. Closely assessing McKay's life and writings raises questions regarding issues of exile, identity, race and ethnicity that are dominating the contemporary literary discourse.

While the pleasures of exile[1] to Great Britain from the Anglophone Caribbean world have been well theorized, a similar study is lacking in the case of Caribbean immigration to the United States. This study examines possible differences between the interaction and maturation of Caribbean writers who emigrated to the mother country and those who emigrated to the United States.[2] However, McKay's migratory peculiarities complicate the whole process as many of his productive years as a writer were spent in constant migration to Europe and Africa, voyaging the slave trade triangle. However, any examination of McKay's work in the above context is further complicated by the fact that many early twentieth century writers went into self-imposed exile and that many African American and African Franco-Caribbean writers, too, spent time in Paris along with metropolitan writers, but for different reasons.

McKay's shifting affiliation with various contemporary political ideologies which were often poles apart also had serious implications on his writings and must be taken into consideration. Always trying to overcome the narrow constructs of race, McKay used to pick up certain "isms" and ideologies that sounded promising; yet as a writer of integrity and conviction, he never hesitated to reject the faiths and beliefs that did not work the anticipated way. After losing faith in the rationalists and free thinkers whom he admired from a very young age, McKay turned to communism in the United States. With a firm belief like many intellectuals of his age that communism could bring not only economic equality but also racial equality, McKay got involved in communist movements in the United States and in England. Educating himself in the basic concepts of Marxism in the British Museum, he took active participation in the Sylvia Pankhurst's *Workers' Dreadnought* resulting in numerous writings that carry his interpretation of Marxism in racial terms.[3] Yet McKay's optimism did not last long as he always sensed the racial prejudice lurking in the minds of British and American communists. His visit to Russia (1921) and his address to the Fourth Congress of the Third Comintern in Moscow were mainly meant to raise the issue of racial prejudice among the American communists. Though he received a rousing reception, McKay ended his "magic pilgrimage" to Russia dejected that the communists could never break free of racial prejudices.

As McKay became more and more international in his outlook, another ideological paradox took shape in his career as he unswervingly turned to black nationalism. Different from the escapist brand of Negro nationalism of Garvey and the utopian type envisaged by the communists in America, McKay's nationalism was strategic, practical and realistic, laying the foundation of the Negritude movement. It became a sort of prelude to the Black power movements in the 1960s. The impact of this essentialistic stand on his writings is another important issue, as it advanced a new aesthetic of black literature. Many of his precepts—affirmation of black identity, racial pride, celebration of blackness and black life, culture, art, music, dance, search for the African ethos, a critical stance toward Western civilization, and the development of a Third World sensibility—not only form the bedrock of black aesthetics that took root in Africa, the Caribbean and the United States, but also attests to his broader but outsider status to his contemporary African American literary tradition. The final controversial turn in McKay's life was his becoming a Roman Catholic. Why did McKay chose to become a Catholic? Was it mere opportunism— a last refuge for a battered writer—as many of his scholars concluded, or was it because of his "mystical feelings"?

The question of his migration is yet to be resolved. What were the "pull" factors of the Caribbean migration to United States, given its violent record in matters of race? At the same time what were the "push" factors that made McKay the first native writer to leave the Caribbean in a long list of artists who would eventually emigrate? Was McKay a simple black migrant and part of the great migration from the rural South to the urban North, as many of his peers took him to be, or was he part of the African Caribbean immigrant group in search of greener pastures? These questions inevitably lead to other complications involving race and ethnicity. Essentialized conceptions of "African American," "black" and "West Indian" lead to the question of how exactly race and ethnicity were related in the United States. Which preceded the other? Identity in the United States was generally conceived on the simplistic binary of black or white. This conception has historically obscured ethnic differences within the "black" race, as all black immigrants are lumped together in the conundrum of race irrespective of their sociocultural, ethnic and national background. Therefore, the routine categorization of African Caribbean immigrants as "black" or African American has overlooked numerous cultural and national differences that informed their interaction and negotiation of identities in the American milieu. This naturally leads to other basic questions regarding ethnicity. Who is an African American and who is a West Indian? Why are the two groups at loggerheads with each other, and what were the underlying reasons for ethnic stereotyping? What was the impact of "Caribbeanization," especially in the context of McKay's fellow Jamaican Marcus Garvey's influence on African American culture and politics? Risking essentialization, should one study these two groups and focus on the specific differences in their identity formation?

Very few scholars, with the exception of sociologists like Ira De A. Reid (1939) and Roy Bryce-Laporte, have recorded patterns of political, economic and cultural adaptation by the Caribbean immigrants. While George Lamming, Stuart Hall and Paul Gilroy have theorized the Anglophone Caribbean migration to the United Kingdom, a similar study is lacking in the United States. By focusing on a first-generation immigrant author's life and writings in the United States, the present study attempts to fill this lacuna regarding the colonial dispensation, forces of migration, racial, ethnic and national affiliation and cultural adaptation producing hybridized entities, thus providing a framework to study further (im)migrations.

The (im)migration background of McKay has only accentuated the complication regarding his identity. Brought up in a British colony, was not his identity marked by the colonizer-colonial dialectic? Given his colonial upbringing, was the double consciousness—that of an American and a Negro—that his peers in the United States confronted, the same that structured McKay's consciousness? What was the impact of a highly racist society like that of the United States on this colonial immigrant, in whose society the black body was not a target of specific physical abuse? Why was it that he was unable to find a "home" in Harlem and was always in search of one—in Europe, in Africa and in the United States? What was the cause for this constant migration, from one country to another and from one "ism" to another?

Then comes the question of literary tradition. The African American literary tradition has been built on certain aesthetic and rhetorical principles that reflect African American experiences like double consciousness, integration and pre-generic myths like literacy and freedom. Texts by the black immigrant writers that complied with this tradition were quickly absorbed into the canon, while texts that recorded their Caribbean or Third World experiences were marginalized. Claude McKay's popularity in the initial stages of the Harlem Renaissance, due to his strong militant voice, and his exclusion for almost forty years and revival during the Black Arts movement for his cultural nationalism and Pan-Africanism, stands as a typical example of this phenomenon. Even his two autobiographies (one recording his life in exile in the United States, Europe and Africa, and the other recording his life in Jamaica) were marginalized, as they did not address the sociopolitical as well as cultural obstacles that impede the liberation and empowerment of African Americans in the United States. As products of his exile and cross-cultural experiences they naturally belonged to a different genera. The keen distinction between "I was born in..."[4] and "I had arrived in the States from..."[5] needs to be further explored. If the original autobiographical impulse in African American literature is firmly rooted in and thus emerges from existentially pertinent historical circumstances and cultural interests of their practitioners, the autobiographical act of the immigrants springs from the most defining moment of their lives—exile and the resultant cross-cultural experiences. Therefore, the study will compare and contrast the black immigrant writer's autobiographical motive—how they arrived[6] and wrote themselves into being[7]—with that of their African American counterparts.

Even though African American scholarship is sensitive to the "dual tradition"—African and Western—it does not recognize the distinct minority voices like the Afro-Caribbean in its literary tradition. However, recent Caribbean immigrant authors like Paule Marshall, Jamaica Kincaid, Rosa Guy, and Michelle Cliff are now routinely included in the African American literary canon. Thanks to the womanist discourses, these writers could find a place in the African American women's literary tradition. However, they are yet to be read as products of two cultures and cross-cultural fertilization. The plurality of African American culture as reflected in its literature and other arts has received very little attention.[8] By relocating and rereading McKay in his natural habitation—colonial sensibility, exile and cross-cultural experiences—the present study has undertaken to address these politics of inclusion and exclusion.

The first thing that the study grapples is with the issue of colonial subjectivity. A colonial subject as inferred from the theoretical postulates of Frantz Fanon, Albert Memmi and Homi Bhabha is the product of multiple constitutions and of the inherent contradictions and overdeterminations of postcolonial ideological positions. A product of the Manichean world, the colonial subject caught between two gravitational pulls, the native and the adopted, is condemned to dwell in a limbo. McKay's writings are marked with this dichotomy, which manifested in a variety of binary units, bisecting his writings throughout his career. Nevertheless, to conclude that he is forever caught in a limbo is to be oblivious of his evolution, as the study shows, over time, as an émigré writer. Indeed, Michel Pecheux's three modes of subjectivity—identification, counter-identification and dis-identification—can be traced progressively in his career.

Reading him as a colonial writer in exile does not mean that his contribution to (African) American literature and Harlem Renaissance movement will be underrated. To read him in the right perspective is to understand the nature of his ambiguities and "recognize the intellectual baggage he brought with him to Harlem—the English attitudes, a European sensibility, and the general impedimenta of a colonial mind, cognitive elements all together unknown to most Harlemites" (Chauhan 80). Only then will McKay's contribution to the black cause, which apparently is not limited to the (African) American context alone, be appreciated. Reading him in an appropriate frame of reference, i.e. within the context of colonialism and cross-cultural fertilization, will help us understand as natural, what is now considered ambiguous and problematic.

Before analyzing his writings in detail, it is necessary to draw the larger framework of the black struggle in early twentieth century and trace the reasons for McKay's exile. As relocating McKay in his native terrain is an important aspect of this study, a grounded and historicized study of differences in identity formation between black Jamaicans and African Americans is taken up in the opening chapter, in spite of the risk involved in cultural essentialization. Identity categories need not always automatically devolve into essentialist programs but can provide modes of articulation. Further, examining significant correlations between lived experience and social location helps to focus on differences. Foregrounding the colonial background of McKay and the resultant ambiguities, the study proceeds to trace his attempts in resolving that duality, while confronting complex problems of race and its relation to the modern world. Tracing his journey through the slave triangle and his literary productions, the study will not only observe his evolution as a writer but also his struggle for identity in a world structured to marginalize him.

— 1 —

Theoretical Considerations

The problem of the twentieth century is the problem of the color line, declared W.E.B. Du Bois at the beginning of the century. The first half of the twentieth century was a momentous period for the "rising blacks" all over the globe. Dehumanized over the centuries and reduced to the status of a beast, the black man started fighting for his recognition as a human. The struggle for recognition culminated in various movements, literary, cultural and political simultaneously, in all regions of oppression, varying according to historical and geographical conditions. Giving strong impetus to a new racial awareness among blacks throughout the world was the World War I and its aftermath. It forced a re-evaluation of Western civilization and encouraged non–Europeans to esteem their respective cultures as being as valid and civilized as Europe. A new racial awareness swept across the black triangle, Africa, Europe and the New World seeking an equal place in humanity.

The struggle of the black race and its diaspora against white racism converged into mass political and cultural movements. The Harlem Renaissance in the United States, Negritude and Pan-Africanism in the Caribbean and Africa ushered in an assertive black nationalism. Africa, once relegated to the dark corners of the universe, became the unifying principle for its diaspora. It became an imaginary continent, a rallying point for the oppressed blacks. Doubly exiled, bodily from Africa in the past, and psychologically, "in the midst of the cold buildings of white culture and technics," in the present, black intellectuals and writers, especially of the diaspora, set out to search for their identity in Western civilization and to assert their races' rightful position in humanity (Sartre 12). Ironically, it was the best European educated black intelligentsia that led the cultural counteroffensives, reinforcing the growing trend among African-descended people to unify around a singular sense of cultural identity. W.E.B. Du Bois and Alain Locke in the United States, Aime Cesaire in the Caribbean, Léopold Sédar Senghor in Senegal, Africa, were some of the prominent figures who led significant cultural and literary movements in their regions. Equal citizenship for the minority blacks in America, deeply ingrained colonialism for the majority blacks in the Caribbean, and suppression of cultural and political freedom for the Africans were some of the key problems addressed by these movements.

Claude McKay is one black writer from the British West Indies whose writings had a profound influence on these movements. His life and career, spanning the most turbulent period in the history of the black race, was a struggle against all the worst manifestations of white oppression: colonialism, brutal racism and negation of identity. As a colonial subject, he had to struggle against the implanted colonial ideology, which confined him to the prison walls of British culture. As a black American immigrant, he had to struggle against brutal racism. Finally as a black man, he struggled against the common problem of his race — negation of identity. His exile in the black triangle, United States, Europe and Africa, and the concomitant quest for the identity of the black man helped lay the foundation for the Harlem and Negritude movements. Starting his literary career as a British colonial, imitating English literary masters, he evolved as one of the most significant black voices to thoroughly debate and struggle against the many complex issues that the black race faced in the first half of the twentieth century. McKay was an uncompromising personality. His life, his checkered literary as well as political career, now stands as a momentous episode in the chronicle of the black struggle in the New World.

He was born to peasant parents in Sunny Ville, a small village in the remote Clarendon Hills of central Jamaica, then a British colony, on September 15, 1890. McKay spent a happy childhood among the many streams, hills and rivulets of the picturesque island. His peasant parents, supposedly prosperous by Jamaican standards, were a second-generation peasant group that came into existence facing almost insurmountable difficulties after the emancipation in 1834. His father, who traced his ancestry to the Ashanti tribe, used to narrate African folk tales to the children,[1] which influenced McKay's reverence for Africa and its heritage in his later years. In spite of the pride in African heritage, McKay's father was a great admirer of and a strict adherent to the Anglo-Saxon justice system and was a sort of elder and important member of the local church. Unlike his fellow peasants, he was not superstitious and refused to acknowledge the power of Obeah for the many market and meteorological misfortunes the peasants faced. Indeed, he gave his children a thorough British education.

McKay attended a local school and at a very tender age was exposed to the British system of education. Even at the elementary level, where education had been extended to all classes and races, it was heavily laced with British propaganda. The British have very well utilized the education system to impose their cultural hegemony throughout their colonial rule. A fine example of the colonial education that doesn't teach what E.K. Brathwaite calls the geo-psychic aspect of the Caribbean can be found in McKay's elementary text books: "In our elementary school books we read stories of English, German and Dutch children playing in the snow. I especially remember the pictures of the Dutch children in their colored scarves and wooden shoes; but we never really had a correct idea of what snow was" (*GH* 72). The colonial education not only conditioned them from a very early age to appreciate everything British, but also created what Bhabha calls a "recognizable Other, as a *subject of a difference that is almost the same, but not quite*"[2] (*Location* 86). McKay also admitted that the educational system was so directed that they really and honestly believed that they were little black Britons. He remembers participating each year along with thousands of other Jamaicans in the celebration of the Queen's benevolent deed. They spoke the King's language, vicariously admired British power, imitated the British system of government, and learned to accept the British stratification of social classes. It was the "special achievement of the British ruling class," says Ngugi, "to inculcate someone with certain values without his realizing he has so been inculcated" (97). He quotes C.L.R. James, who rightly assessed the master's influence through education:

It was only long years after that that I understood the limitation on the spirit, vision and self-respect which was imposed
on us by the fact that our master, our curriculam, our code
of morals everything began from the basis that Britain was
the source of all light and leading, and our business was to
admire, wonder, imitate, learn; our criterion of success was
to have succeeded in approaching that distant ideal — to
attain it was, of course, impossible. Both masters and boys
accepted it as in the very nature of things. The masters
could not be offensive about it because they thought it was
their function to do this, if they thought about it at all; and,
as for me, it was the beacon that beaconed me on. The race
question did not have to be agitated. It was there, but in our
little Eden it never troubled us [97].

This educational process that concentrates and transmits European
knowledge and values continued until recently, suggesting a total
absence of worthwhile historical and cultural materials of local or
African origin, creating in the colonies a colored educated class of what
Orde Coombs calls "insidious Anglophiles" (qtd. in Rahming 109).
Reinforcing McKay's colonial school education were two important
influences that helped shape his intellectual development, his brother
Uriah Theophilus, an elementary school teacher, and Walter Jekyll, an
English man, who was at that time collecting Jamaican folklore. McKay
had access to their impressive libraries, which exposed him to English
literary masters — Shakespeare to Victorian writers — and to Western
philosophy. Encouraged by his brother and his schoolteachers McKay
came to develop great esteem for these writers. He started writing sev-
eral pompous verses at a very tender age, imitating English models.
"Old England," one of his early endeavors at poetry, illustrates his infatuation for Britain. His attempts at writing poetry brought him to the
attention of Walter Jekyll when he was working as an apprentice to a
cabinetmaker. He goaded McKay to write poems in the Jamaican
dialect. The outcome of this endeavor was *Songs of Jamaica* and *Constab Ballads,* two volumes of poetry published in 1912. While McKay's
rural Jamaica forms the basis for *Songs of Jamaica, Constab Ballads* arises
from his bitter experience in the city — Kingston and Spanish Town —
as a colonial cop. The remote Clarendon hills of Jamaica, in which he

grew up, supplied him with the material and black folk idiom for his early collections of poetry. For the first time in the history of Jamaica, a black poet captured its life, fauna and flora, in the idiom of its majority population. However, as they were written in dialect, McKay's poems were slighted when he read them at poetry societies and "Browning Clubs." McKay recollects their supercilious attitude:

> "Well, he's nice and pretty you know, but he's not a real poet as Browning and Byron and Tennyson are poets" [*GH 86*].

This had a far-reaching impact on McKay's life and literary career. It not only forced him into exile, but also made him give up the use of dialect in his future endeavors. Creole languages of Africans and their descendents that developed in the New World were conferred an inferior status as compared to the standard norm of the European languages. They were considered bizarre, aberrant, and corrupt derivatives of one or other European languages and were not viewed as natural languages with their own rules of grammar.[3] They served to categorize the population ethnically and culturally, and unfortunately further the divisive interests of imperialism. The subject colonial population came to approve the colonizer's interpretation of the languages. Alleyne validates it:

> Caribbean people have largely accepted European's views of their language behaviour as part of a more general self deprecation and negative evaluation of their cultural behaviour. The general feeling is that creole languages and dialects are defective — that they may be suitable for the expression of "folklore" (folktales, folkmusic, proverbs, swearing, etc.) but that they are quite inadequate for the expression of complex and abstract thought [160].

This has created throughout the Caribbean hostility toward creole languages.[4] Language became the most important cultural tool in the formation of the West Indian hierarchical society. Because to speak means, as Fanon puts it, not only to be in a position to use a certain language structure and grasp the morphology of a language, but above all to assume a culture, to support the weight of a civilization (*Black Skins* 17–18). A situation arose in the Caribbean where the Black man was proportionately whiter in direct ratio to his mastery of the European language. Fanon too corroborates this when he says that all colonized people, whose cultural originality was systematically annihilated, find themselves face to face with the civilizing nation's language; that is, with the culture of the mother country. The more they conform to the mother country's cultural standards the more they are elevated above their general status (*Black Skins* 18).

In the "post creole linguistic continuum" situation of Jamaica, different graded levels of speech show different degrees of approximation to (and conversely, deviancy from) a standard norm of English. These levels correspond more or less to the social stratification; that is, there is a tendency for upper-class people to speak more standard English, and for lower-class people to speak a more creolized form. The different levels of language correspond usually to the rural vs. urban dichotomy and, within the urban sector, to levels of socioeconomic stratification. Insofar as social values are attached to levels of speech, one moves from extreme negative to extreme positive, as one moves from one polar level of speech to the other.

Though McKay chose the dialect medium under the pressure of his English patron, he understood that to be recognized as a writer he should write only in straight English in the lines of his English literary models. Giving up the dialect medium, he explains, on his departure to America: "I would write poetry in straight English and amaze and confound them because they thought I was not serious, simply because I wrote poems in the dialect which they did not consider profound" (*GH* 87). As England was the sole arbiter in matters of literary taste and culture throughout the English speaking Caribbean colonies, it was imperative for any writer to be endorsed by it. To gain recognition as a writer by his countrymen, McKay should invariably get the approval of the metropolitan center, and the only route open to him was emigration. George Lamming describes this typical Caribbean phenomenon: "These men had to leave it if they were going to function as writers since books, in that particular colonial conception of literature, were not — meaning, too, are not supposed to be — written by natives" (*Exile* 27). Hence, "sooner or later, in silence or rhetoric," West Indian writers have to "sign a contract whose epitaph reads: To be an exile is to be alive" (*Exile* 24). McKay too left Jamaica in 1912, for both recognition and market, becoming the first in the long list of exiled West Indian writers. It was the need for a market for their books and the colonial's ideal of assimilation to the colonizer's ways, says Viney Kirpal, that prompted the large-scale emigration of writers from British and French colonies to the metropolitan countries (4–5). Therefore, exile for these writers is both a spiritual and a physical state, and emigration the symbol of a struggling West Indian alienated from his past and immediate world (Ngugi 128). Unlike his successors of 1950s and '60s who chose the "mother" country, McKay turned to the United States of America for exile, opening a new chapter in Third World emigration.

Discussing the issue of West Indian writers' emigration, whose orientation is colonial, Lamming thinks that there will be "certain complications" when the writer chooses for residence "the country which colonized his own history," i.e. England for the British West Indian writers (*Exile* 24). Although the new circumstances are quite different, Lamming continues, and "even [more] favorable than those he left in the West Indies, his reservations, his psychology, his whole sense of cultural expectation have not greatly changed. He arrives and travels with the memory, the habitual weight of a colonial relation" (*Exile* 25). If a writer takes up residence in America — as Claude McKay did — Lamming emphasizes, "his development would probably be of a different, indeed, of an opposed order to that of a man who matured in England" (*Exile* 24–25). True, McKay had a different experience in the new milieu, and the difference lies in his exposure to the too apparent primordial racial hatred in America, which was cosmetically covered up in England. For the Caribbean colored migrant, America remains an extension, an outpost of the Anglo-Saxon power structure, where the basic colonial relations were only more virulent and open. Hence, even if the situation of those who emigrated to Canada or the United States appears to be less problematic, the cross-cultural coordinates of their reality are hardly less contradictory, because they involve the peculiar affinity to the British value system of the former, and the complex history of military, economic, and cultural imperialism of the latter, in the Caribbean.[5]

Confronted by the overtly violent American racial setting, McKay was quickly forced to take a rebellious position as against a colonial migrant to England where the process was delayed. His reaction was evident in the angry poetic outbursts that served as a trumpet call to the New Negro in the Harlem setting. Volatile poems like "If We Must Die," though in sonnet form, broke out from his deep disgust against the inhuman racial oppression. They were later collected and published in the American volume *Harlem Shadows* (1922). The repressed Afro-America, struggling with Jim Crowism and lynching, found a fresh and strong militant voice in McKay. He was immediately hailed as the black people's poet and announced as the harbinger of the New Negro movement. Nevertheless, it is difficult to conclude that McKay joined the African American literary pedigree overthrowing the habitual weight of a colonial relation in the mighty citadel of Anglo-Saxon power on the American continent, because his collection of poems and fictional works are not always protest writings echoing specific American concerns. Race, let alone the American minority problem, was not yet the central focus of the British colonial's literary vision. He was quite consistent in pursuing the objective of becoming a "universal" poet for which he left his island colony. He reserved substantial space in his anthology for "heartfelt effusions." With themes of love and nostalgia, he published, outside Jamaica, his first volume of poems, *Spring in New Hampshire* (1920), in England. So to call him a homegrown Harlem poet jettisoning his Jamaican colonial background is to misunderstand his "true emotional geography" (Chauhan 69).

Moreover, the birth and growth of Harlem Renaissance in the 1920s actually followed McKay's departure from Harlem into exile to Europe and Africa for more than a decade. Though the violent racial setting in America had driven him into further exile, finding a solution to the specific American minority problem was not his agenda. The overt American racism only hastened and bolstered his quest for identity and home. If recognition and market were the main motivating factors for his exile from Jamaica, dehumanization and marginalization of the black race in the white world forced him to inquire into the ontological status of the black man in a world dominated by Caucasian values. The nature of this quest for identity is qualitatively different from that sought by the African American intellectuals like Du Bois and Locke, for whom identity is a resolution of their double consciousness — to be a black man and an American.

That McKay's quest is quite distinct from that of the Harlem elite is obvious from his three novels, *Home to Harlem, Banjo* and *Banana Bottom,* which are set in three different places. Only the first, as the title indicates, is set in the United States. However, McKay's conception of black manhood, the primary motif of *Home to Harlem,* is quite at odds with the bourgeois expectations of his Harlem peers. From the beginning of his literary career, McKay closely identified with the lower-class sections of society. Whether it was the peasants of Jamaica, the working class in America, or the black vagabonds on the Marseilles beachfront, his sympathies were always with the underdog. He portrayed their life vividly in his writings. He came to believe firmly that it was only the lower-class black people, who retained the "healthy primitive" values of the black race. It was only they, he thought, who could withstand the leveling onslaught of Western civilization. Naturally, he loathed the Harlem elite's agenda of promoting the middle class, who McKay believed were only bent on proving themselves to the white man.

His second novel, *Banjo,* is a description of the loose life led by black vagabonds drawn from Africa and its diaspora on the Marseilles beachfront. While the depiction of their loose lower-class life is at odds ideologically with the Negro elite, the Pan-African motif nowhere served the African American interests. Similarly, *Banana Bottom,* dealing with questions of identity and culture in the life of an England-educated Jamaican rural girl, has little to do with the problems of black American identity. McKay was not only indifferent to the ideological concerns of the Harlem elite, but also his comments on the renaissance, distant and derisive, argue against his incorporation into the movement. His two autobiographies, *Long Way from Home,* describing his exile life in the United States, Europe and Africa, and *My Green Hills of Jamaica,* describing his colonial life in Jamaica, affirm his ideological distance and distinction from Afro-America. Reading him solely in the Harlem setting, oblivious of his Jamaican background, many African American scholars have found him a deeply conflicting figure. Expressing his strong protest in European forms, taking pride in black culture but trying to gain acceptance in the dominant white society, graphically describing black life in the metropolitan urban contexts but always longing for a distant romanticized rural past, toying with radicalism but ending up in Catholicism, were some of the ambiguities that were distasteful to the American critics. They tried to explain these ambiguities in strange and unacceptable terms. Even though critics and his biographers were aware of his Jamaican origins, they did not focus on his distinct colonial sensibility. They often equated his movement from Jamaica to Harlem to the movement from rural South to the urban North common to many of his Harlem peers. The result is a gross misunderstanding of his emotional geography, making him a highly paradoxical figure, an *enfant terrible* in the (African) American literary scene of the early twentieth century.

Wayne Cooper, McKay's biographer, locates the source of all these ideological paradoxes in the "personal pathology of a personality characterized always by a deep seated ambivalence" that was caused mainly by "dependence upon a succession of father figures" (16). James R. Giles, another McKay scholar, held a similar view. Typical of the current scholarship's understanding of McKay's affiliations, Geta LeSeur in her essay "Claude McKay's Marxism" affirms that McKay "remains today part of the acknowledged literary triumvirate of the Harlem Renaissance. He shares this prestigious position with Langston Hughes and Jean Toomer" (219). Tyrone Tillery, in a recent (1991) biographical study of McKay, attributes these ambiguities to McKay's own times. He says:

> The paradox of Claude McKay cannot be reduced to any
> simple formula.... Yet these tensions, as I will show, cannot
> simply be ascribed to personal or psychological problems.
> Ultimately, they were rooted in the ambiguous social and
> cultural positions of the black artist and political radical of
> the early twentieth century [Preface].

True, the early twentieth century was beset with social and cultural ambiguities for a black writer. Nevertheless, the source of the peculiar problems afflicting McKay was from a different constellation, which only got further complicated in the new milieu. A Third World colonial expatriate from a British colony, his sensibilities and aspirations stood radically at odds with the African Americans. His peers in the United States were entirely strangers to the duality that structured his consciousness due to his colonial upbringing. Unable to realize and appreciate the ethnic differences within racial sameness has led to a gross misunderstanding of his responses, both poetic and political. Hence, as Chauhan has rightly emphasized, if one has to account for all the ambiguities and elements of his thought, one has to read him as a colonial writer who happened to stop over in Harlem on his life long quest for a spiritual home, a quest no colonial writer has ever effectively escaped (69).

Therefore, the present study has undertaken to (re)read McKay as a paradigmatic black colonial writer in exile from the West Indies, a Third World expatriate before the term existed. Reading him as a colonial writer in exile does not mean that his contribution to (African) American literature and the Harlem Renaissance movement will be underrated. To read him in the right perspective is to understand the nature of his dichotomy and recognize the intellectual baggage he carried with him to Harlem — English attitudes, a European sensibility, and the general impedimenta of a colonial mind, cognitive elements of which most African Americans are ignorant. Only then will McKay's contribution to the black cause, which apparently is not limited to (African) American context alone, be appreciated. Reading him in an appropriate frame of reference, i.e. within the colonial context, will help us understand as natural, what is now considered ambiguous and problematic.

Therefore, the study will be made under three rubrics: first, to locate Claude McKay as a paradigmatic black colonial writer (burdened by the colonial ideological baggage) in exile from the Caribbean (which amounts to contesting his appropriation into the African American literary tradition); second, to discuss the struggle he waged to overcome the colonial limitations in his literary writings, and find a viable identity for the black man, in a world dominated by Western values, within the context of his exile to the United States (as against the migration to England, the mother country, by later writers) and other Western and African nations; finally, to study how the wanderings helped him to evolve ideologically, becoming a pioneer in recording the embryonic Jamaican national identity, while contributing to the global discourse of black writing. To substantiate the hypothesis, the study begins with the supposition that McKay was a Caribbean colonial writer, while negotiating appropriate theoretical frame-works.

Arguing for a regional criticism of the Caribbean literature, Jeannette B. Allis in her essay "West Indian Literature: A Case for Regional Criticism" warned against the "dangers inherent in allowing external perceptions to dominate the evaluation of West Indian Literature" (7). She points out that cultural and sociological phenomena are often interpreted in the light of critics' own experiences, rather than within the cultural context of the literature itself. Non-regional critics, for her, often fail to recognize the subtle nuances bearing directly on West Indian life and are forced to deal with the more obvious cultural aspects (8). Given the colonial relationship, the British reviews of the immigrant West Indian writers seemed to be rather favorable and patronizing, conveniently avoiding "the harsher realities of poverty and deprivation" and above all the themes of color or race (Allis 9). In the American context, Allis treated white and black reviews separately as she found distinct critical reactions to West Indian literature. While magazines that catered usually to the white audience treated West Indian writers as naïve, the Afro-American critic's evaluation centered on the "communication of Blackness and fidelity to the observed or intuited truth of the Black experience in the United States" (14). Citing the reviews in the African American magazines *Black World, Phylon,* and *Freedomways,* she concludes that the "West Indian's measure had been taken and that he had been found wanting" (15). Even Claude McKay, supposedly the pioneer writer of Harlem Renaissance, she finds, was considered to be hampered by his West Indian limitations. She cites George Kent writing in *Black World*:

> On the one hand, Claude McKay works with a more secure
> grasp of the big picture, the sheer magnitude of the problem

> of black soul than did most writers of the Harlem Renais-
> sance; but, on the other, his peculiar sensibility, com-
> pounded of his background and sustained commitment to
> romantic individualism, create an obstacle course over which
> his Blackness must run.... In the light of his poetry and
> fiction, it is possible to see that he was without certain
> significant resources derived from the situation of the Ameri-
> can born Black writers [Allis 11].

Not only does the preoccupation with black expression tend to prejudice the Afro-American critic's perspective, but also the position of a
black person within American society tends to cloud his view. W.
Lawrence Hogue confirms this attitude when he says that "Afro-
American critical studies ... identify Afro-American literary traditions,
canons, and myths which establish a critical matrix that receives Afro-
American texts more favorably, by defining the worth of Afro-American literature within an Afro-American cultural context" (21). This
means that the writings of West Indian or other ethnic groups will be
analyzed in terms of the Afro-American's own cultural references.[6] A
case in this point was the reception of McKay's novels and poetry.
While his protest poetry was favored, poems dealing with his nostalgia and other romantic topics were not appreciated. Similarly, *Home to
Harlem* received much critical attention, while *Banjo* and his last novel,
Banana Bottom, were neglected. Though the non-regional critic,
according to Allis, recognizes and works within these limitations, producing meaningful assessments, "only the regional critic can provide
the vital cultural connection between a writer's works and his society"
(16–17). However, Allis should not be misunderstood as encouraging
an exclusivistic attitude, debarring non-regional critics from interpreting West Indian literature. In fact, Lloyd Brown has helped to clarify
the issue when he pointed out that "a desirable 'regionalism' may be a
matter of perception, a clear understanding of the area and its literature rather than the mere matter of geographical origin" (West Indian
Literature, 4). A regional criticism, based on a contextual cultural and
historical knowledge, in interpreting West Indian writers reinforces the
objective of reading McKay as a colonial writer from British Jamaica.
Recent advances in modern linguistics, along with developments in

semiotics and Michel Foucault's concept of discursive formations that eroded many of the assumptions and presuppositions traditionally associated with literature and criticism, only strengthens it. They have not only undermined the proposition that the writer is the "creator" of something "original" but also challenged the assumption of the text's literariness — that is, that the text possesses certain qualities that place it above the matrices of historical conditions.

So these advancements have not only produced critical and theoretical options for reading marginalized texts whose formations are different from or exist outside established definitions of the literary experience, but also strengthened the premise that literary production in the colonies is strongly influenced, even determined, by the experience of colonialism as well as racism and sexism. Hence, a close relationship between real-life experience and writing, between writer and text, motivation for writing and message of the text, and written word and intended audience cannot be ignored. The denial will miss the basic political texture of the literary project in a postcolonial environment and denigrate the text to a mere intellectual play.

Therefore, the source of the meaning of the text is to be found in the triangle between the author, his or her real life experience, and the text; i.e., the context or site of its conception, rather than merely in the linguistic material of the text. As textual production is intricately bound up with historical and political forces, this study adopts as a fundamental principle the inevitable conclusion that its product can only be understood within a larger framework of social reality. This takes the study into the framework of postcolonial critical theory echoing Marxist concepts of art. However, emphasis on extra-textual reference and the political dimension of postcolonial writing does not imply that its artistic merit was of minor importance. On the contrary, the present study is very much a cultural and even cross-cultural reading firmly grounded in the literary analysis of McKay's writings. The study proceeds with the firm conviction that authorial, historical, and cultural contexts play an important role in determining the reader and critic's success in gaining access to the texts and their overall textures and meanings. They are indispensable dimensions to critical inquiry as they contribute substantially to and reinforce the literary expressiveness of the text itself.

A recent study of theory and practice in postcolonial literatures places the body of texts and criticism at the crossroads of various contemporary critical discourses. Apart from extending literature beyond its traditional boundaries to include the multi-disciplinary territories of history, politics, sociology, and ideology, the relationship between colonizer and colonized and the consequent subject formation is the area in which the inputs from Marxist ideological criticism (Althusser and Michel Pecheux) been significant. Their theoretical postulates, along with those of Albert Memmi, are of particular relevance in the problematic study of the relationship between the colonizer and the colonized and between language and literary practice and to the problem of constituting identity within the division between Self and Other imposed by imperialism.

However, this does not mean that the present study goes whole hog and adopts everything Marxist or bases its analysis on a single theoretical perspective. As Allis's study has revealed, the usually unadapted application of Western critical methods and literary tradition as measures of evaluation in the context of West Indian literature is likely to be a major obstacle in the critic's interpretive endeavor. Wole Soyinka too feels that the application of European critical theory "derived from the apprehension of their world and their history, their social neuroses, and their value systems" to African texts (even with the best of intentions) is ushering in "a second epoch of colonization" (Preface x). These critical tools sprung from specific cultural and historical constellations and developments, and cannot always accommodate those "other" realities and experiences of postcolonial societies, which are characterized by a different historical and cultural background. They are likely to fall short of their analytical promises, if adapted uninterrogated.

How, then, should the critic of postcolonial literature position himself or herself with respect to the dominant theoretical and critical tendencies, as they are grounded in and developed from the specifically Western culture and historical traditions? Answers to this question may be found in the debate concerning "decolonization"—what it implies and how it should be achieved. For some critics, decolonization can be achieved only by recuperating precolonial languages and culture. Colonization for them is only a passing historical feature, which can be shed once the colony becomes politically and hence culturally independent. For others, recuperation is impossible, and cultural syncreticity is as valuable as it is inescapable. For these critics syncreticity has reinforced the strength of postcolonial societies, giving new creative energy. Though the former is politically attractive, syncretic critics consider it problematic. For them, even a text written in the indigenous language in the postcolonial society is a cross-cultural hybrid.

These questions were intensely debated even in the Caribbean context, where the fusion of culture was implied in the use of European languages. Edward Kamau Brathwaite, "a poet of total African Consciousness," as the Ghananian author Kofi Awoonor has called him, along with Chinweizu and other writers, has regarded a return to African roots as crucial to contemporary West Indian identity (*Microsoft Encarta Africana 2000*).[7] Soyinka in the African context and Wilson Harris in the Caribbean, on the other hand, espouse a cultural syncretism without denying ancestral affiliations. For Wilson Harris, the mixed ancestry (Amerindian, African and European) is "symbolic of a possible synthesis to overcome polarization" (*E.A. 2000*). Afro-Caribbean destiny, for these writers, is inescapably enmeshed in a contemporary, multi-cultural reality.

Essentialist movements such as Negritude or Black Power and Black Arts figure as milestones in the development of distinct African and African American cultural and literary traditions and aesthetics. At a certain time, and within a certain context, they served to map and secure a territory for cultural manifestations, opposite the dominant tradition. Despite their contributions to the formation of a distinct sense of ethnic or national identity, and their often-successful challenges to the old order, in hindsight, it can be recognized that they are caught in direct relation to the very systems they challenged. It can also be suspected that their own ideological limitations have more often than not turned out to be inhibiting the artistic potential and the possible communicative functions and effects of creative expression. Thus, essentialist stances have come to be recognized as important and necessary but ultimately inadequate (because exclusivist and thus replicating imperial paradigms) and therefore merely transitional stages in the struggle for liberation from the cultural patronage of the colonial past.

Just as the wholesale application of Western critical methods is inept and ultimately culturally hegemonic, it seems equally inadequate by now to base one's analysis in indigenous essentialism, on abstracted nativism, denying thereby the influence of the colonizers' traditions. Ashcroft, Griffiths, and Tiffin's suggestion seems to be appropriate:

> Nationalist and Black criticisms have demystified the imperial processes of domination and continuing hegemony, but they have not in the end offered a way out of the historical and philosophical impasse. Unlike these models, the recent approaches have recognized that the strength of post-colonial theory may well lie in its inherently comparative methodology and the hybridized and syncretic view of the modern world which this implies. This view provides a framework of difference on equal terms within which multi-cultural theories, both within and between societies, may continue to be fruitfully explored [36–37].

Hence the impulse to create or recreate an independent local identity and postcolonial literary tradition yields the most fruitful results, it seems, whenever infused with considerations about the complementary interaction of the European or North American (colonial or neocolonial) and the local, indigenous traditions in postcolonial settings. Along these lines literary criticism and theory of writing by colonial and postcolonial "subjects" have arrived at foregrounding both the need for and the appropriateness of a syncretic approach that recognizes the plurality of traditions, which have shaped the literature from these areas. In applying a Marxist ideological critical approach, the present study will be guided by the principles of pragmatism, eclecticism and appropriation, which will allow it to be informed by available theories and approaches. Because discursive formations are not hermetically sealed — they overlap and intersperse in ways that may be fruitfully and reflexively utilized — postcolonial discourse may appropriate what it requires from European theory (Ashcroft et al. 168). Hence, the use of Marxism in this study is from a Third World perspective, in terms of ideological construction of the Self and the Other, imperialism and exploitation, rather than merely the mode of production. Albert

Memmi is right when he argues that Marxism's emphasis of the economy in all oppressive relationships is not to the point. To the question of whether the colonizer-colonized relationship is not basically economic, one can't but agree with Memmi: "maybe — not certainly" (xii).

The concept of "ideology and ideological state apparatuses," deriving from the work of Louis Althusser, focuses on subject formation, which helps to establish McKay as a colonial subject writer from the Caribbean — the primary objective of this study (140). Althusser defines "ideology" as a "'Representation' of the imaginary relationship of individuals to their real conditions of existence" (162). As Kavanagh elaborates, ideology is less tenacious as a "set of ideas" than as a system of representations, perceptions, and images that precisely encourages men and women to "see" their specific place in a historically peculiar social formation as inevitable, a necessary function of the "real" itself (310). "Reality" here is arbitrary because ideology has a way of obscuring the real conditions of existence by smoothing over contradictions in its attempt to present a coherent picture of that world. Social institutions, which Althusser calls ideological state apparatuses, support and reproduce these ideological practices.[8] The aim of these apparatuses' diverse operations is to construct people as subjects without their ever being conscious of it, because it is so obvious and commonsensical. The British colonial institutions which nurtured McKay were part of a network of power responsible for fixing him in that position of total acceptance. This brings in the central idea of Althusser that "ideology interpellates individuals as subjects" (170). Althusser's use of the interpellated subject is not only the grammatical subject "I," center of initiatives, author of and responsible for its actions, but also a subjected being who submits to the authority of social formation. McKay, born and brought up in a colonial society where the dominant ideology was British, and consciously perpetuated through their ideological apparatuses, was molded as a colonial subject without his ever realizing it.

The theory of discourse put forth by Michel Foucault also has a similar function in forming individuals as subjects. Post-Freudian psychoanalysis privileges language over consciousness as the constructor of identity. This concept of the primacy of language over subjectivity, developed by Lacan, decenters the individual consciousness as the origin of meaning and knowledge. A child, in the mirror phase of its development (the imaginary), has no sense of identity until its entry into language (the symbolic order) when it becomes a full subject, able to differentiate itself as "I" (self) from "you" or "s/he" (others). Subjectivity, in short, is a subject-position that is linguistically and discursively constructed. Discourse, as a domain of language use for Foucault, involves certain shared assumptions, which appear in the formulations that characterize it (i.e., its rules and conventions), which are already inscribed (always-already-there) in the discourse, even as it is uttered or written. Hence, discourse is best understood as a system of possibility for knowledge. It is related to academic disciplines and social institutions that authorize, legitimize and endow it with the power to form and shape humans as "subjects." Discourse makes possible disciplines and institutions, which in turn sustain and distribute those discourses. As these discourses are linked to social institutions, which have power, they can control bodies and actions.

Thus, it constitutes entire domains of action, knowledge and social being, by shaping the institutions and disciplines in which, for the most part, individuals largely make themselves. Hence, there is no place for any one to stand outside of it. The colonialist discourse is a good example of how the West has transformed mere representations of the "Other" colonized races into forms of knowledge, describing, authorizing, teaching, settling and finally ruling. These "realities" are then given validity and coherence by the various institutions (Ideological State Apparatuses) of Western society, through its historical and archaeological research, linguistic codification and academic scholarship. They are finally circulated with all the power of discursive authority and military strength behind them. In this context, the West Indian colonial becomes the cultural child of the colonizer in a double sense: first, the colonizer has created the former's subhuman image by the power of discourse, and second, the colonized substantiates that image by acquiescing in the cultural ideology of the mother country, perpetuated through its ideological apparatuses. McKay, along with other West Indian writers, is no exception to the question that E.K. (Edward Kamau) Braithwaite faces: "How can we as Caribbean writers come to

31

terms with our experience, how can we retrieve a sense of history in spite of and beyond the metropolitan English education we were given?" (23). Hence, the question of decolonizing or continuation of the culture seems to be problematic in the highly hybridized and syncretic West Indian context. This is the basis, says Lamming, for the West Indian community's complacency in demanding absolute freedom.

Thus both the colonized and the colonizer, operating within the imperial ideological framework and colonialist discourse, aided by the repressive and ideological state apparatuses, were frozen into a hierarchical relationship by the assumed superiority of the colonizing society. This posits another problem as to how McKay, the colonial subject writer once shaped by (imperial) social institutions (Ideological State Apparatuses), was able to extricate himself from the ideological predispositions of his age to challenge the dominant culture. How could he conceive, let alone organize resistance, after coming to consciousness within a language that is continuous with the power structure that sustains the social order? This leads to the subversion/containment debate, to which Althusser has pointed a way out. For him, if the goal of all ideology is to produce social subjects, the attainment of this goal is never assured; the struggle in and for ideologies is perpetual. Though the "ruling" ideology is "realized in the Ideological State Apparatuses" it is not done unilaterally or without struggle as these ISAs are also sites of contestation. Althusser says:

> This last comment puts us in a position to understand that the Ideological State Apparatuses may be not only the *Stake*[9] but also the *site*, of class struggle, and often of bitter forms of class struggle. The class (or class alliance) in power cannot lay down the law in the ISAs[10] as easily as it can in the (repressive) State Apparatuses, not only because the former ruling classes are able to retain strong positions there for a long time, but also because the resistance of the exploited classes is able to find means and occasions to express itself there, either by the utilization of their contradictions, or by conquering combat positions in them in struggle [147].

Developing Althusser's idea, Michel Pecheux says that Ideological State Apparatuses are not merely "instruments of ruling class, ideological machines, simply reproducing the existing relations of production" but also "constitute simultaneously and contradictorily the site and the ideological conditions of the transformation of the relations of production." *Hence the expression "reproduction/transformation"* (97–99). This is because "the class struggle traverses the mode of production as a whole, which, in the region of ideology, means that the class struggle "passes through *the complex set of ideological state apparatuses*" contained in that social formation at a given historical moment and for a given social formation (99). He observes:

> In fact, this is where the contradictory connection between the reproduction and transformation of the relations of production is joined at the ideological level, in so far as it is not the regional ideological "objects" taken one by one but the very division into regions (God, Ethics, Law, Justice, Family, Knowledge, etc.) and the relationships of *unevenness-subordination* between those regions that constitute what is at stake in the ideological *class struggle* [99].[11]

This concept is particularly relevant to show how the Ideological State Apparatuses (education, religion, arts, trade unions, etc.) in colonies have initially become the means for imposing hegemonic ideology and at the same time sites for struggle of the colonized against the colonizer. The Church and trade unions played an important role in the liberation struggle of the West Indies. The relationship of art to ideology as propounded by Althusser is also relevant in this context. Works of art (English literary masters) were used as raw material for ideological practices in colonies under the garb of "educating" and "civilizing" the "natives," but they also revealed to the subject population the contradictions in the avowed ideals and its practice by the colonial power.

Similarly, contaminated as they are by the imperial ideology, the writings of the colonial subjects, by *internal distantiation,* allow the reader to "perceive," make visible (critically) *from the inside,* the very ideology from which they emerged. Art can become the matter of ideology (as in the colonies), just as ideology is the matter upon which aesthetic practice works (Sprinker 271). That means art gives form to the materials of ideology. Though they do use ideologies as their materials of construction, they do not simply replicate the ideological material of a given epoch (Sprinker 270). Althusser asserts:

> What art makes us see, and therefore gives to us in the form of "seeing," "perceiving" and "feeling" (which is not the form of knowing), is the ideology from which it is born, in which it bathes, from which it detaches itself as art, and to which it *alludes* [222].

Discussing culture, Stephen Greenblatt emphasizes that "great works of art are not neutral relay stations in the circulation of cultural materials. Something happens to objects, beliefs, and practices, when they are represented, reimagined, and performed in literary texts, something often unpredictable and disturbing. That 'something,' is the sign, both of the power of art and of the embeddedness of culture, in the contingencies of history" (230–231). Althusser's discussion of the Brechtian drama in terms of this concept helps us to focus on the colonial subject's struggle to subvert the dominant ideologies in his or her writings. As Michael Sprinker interprets:

> On Althusser's account, the ideological power of Brechtian drama resides precisely in its aesthetic distantiation of existing ideologies, its production of dissonance between its ideological materials and the development those materials undergo in the action of the play. A Brecht play is a certain product of ideology, but it is, as well, the production of a new ideology [281].

Partha Chatterjee arrived at a similar thesis in his study of nationalist thought, which for him, while it recognizes the inherent contradiction of its reasoning within a framework of knowledge serving a structure of power it seeks to repudiate, is concerned to establish its *difference*: "Its politics impel it to open up that framework of knowledge that presumes to dominate it, to displace that framework, to subvert its authority, to challenge its morality" (Chatterjee 42). Claude McKay's exile writings, as the present study argues, act as battlegrounds of his struggle, to produce a black identity, different from the one imposed by the white power structure. Even his early writings (*Dialect Poetry*), written under the constraints of imperial patronage and ideology, subvert and challenge that authority. In this context, it is understandable if the West Indian scholars read Claude McKay's West Indian writings as early texts of Jamaican nationalism. This is possible, even though McKay used the language and literary forms of the colonial master for his rebellious writings. Because meaning, for Pecheux, does not reside in language itself (i.e., in its transparent relation to the literal character of the signifier), but linguistic meaning has a material character produced by the position of language as a signifier in social, political, and cultural struggle. In his view, "*Words, expression, propositions, etc; change their meaning according to the positions held by those who use them,* which signifies that they find their meaning by reference to those positions," i.e., by reference to the ideological formations in which those positions are inscribed (111). These theoretical postulates show that a colonial subject is the product of multiple constitutions, and of the inherent contradictions and overdeterminations of postcolonial ideological positions, and that these positions are always negotiated and negotiable, in addition to the fact that ethnic and cultural differences are sites of articulation.

Michel Pecheux lists three modes in which subjects are constructed. They help to chart the ideological evolution of McKay as a writer. The first mode is that of "good subject" that results from "identification," i.e., free consent (in Althusserian terms) to the deterministic discursive formation. This is achieved by the "superimposition (a covering) of *the subject of enunciation and the universal subject*" such that the subject's "taking up a position" realizes his subjection in the form of the "freely consented to"; i.e., the subject suffers the determination blindly, he realizes its effects "in complete freedom" (156–157). McKay's fascination for the metropolitan literary forms, language and literary masters in his colonial days reflects this position. Even though he used dialect for his early writings, *Songs of Jamaica* and *Constab Ballads*, it was only under the pressure of his colonial patron. His natural inclination was to follow if not imitate English models and achieve "universality" in art. His identification with the colonizer is so complete that he even echoes the colonial master's opinion regarding black race and Africa, in some of the poems of the former collection. Only in *Constab Ballads* does one sense his growing uneasiness with the dominant power structure after being painfully instrumental in perpetuating social and racial injustice as a constable in the colonial police force.

The second mode is that of "bad subject," "in which the *subject of enunciation* (colonized subject) turns against" the universal subject (the colonizer) by taking up a position which now consists of separation (distantiation, doubt, interrogation, challenge, revolt) "*with respect to what the 'universal Subject' gives him to think*": "a struggle against ideological terrain on the terrain of that evidentness, an evidentness, with a negative sign, reversed in its own terrain" (Pecheux 157). This subject (trouble maker), the result of "counter identification," swings to the other extreme and not only totally rejects the image offered to him, but also throws it back to the giver, a phenomenon characteristic of nationalist and racist criticisms. Terdiman calls it the technique of "re/citation," where the subject seeks to "surround the[ir] antagonist and neutralize or explode it" (qtd. in B. Parry 88). For Pecheux, though this is an important and radical mode, it is finally limited, because this counter-identification implies the danger of counter-determination; that is, it may inadvertently support what it seeks to oppose by confirming "symmetry" between the two. Ashcroft, Grifiths and Tiffin find an example to this in the Negritude movement. McKay achieves this stage during his exile to the United States after experiencing first hand brutal racial discrimination. It manifests in some of his angry poetic protests in the United States and quite explicitly in his major fictional works *Home to Harlem* and *Banjo*. Indeed, Aime Cesaire and Senghor acknowledged McKay's *Banjo* as an early influence in their development of the Negritude concept (71).

The third mode results out of "dis-identification" (159). Here the subject (colonized) comes to terms with the political and discursive forces working on him and is determined to exploit this awareness to work "on and against" the hegemonic (colonizer's) ideologies. This amounts to accepting the inescapability of dominant ideologies but believing in their transformability. "Disidentification," says Pecheux, constitutes a *working* (transformation-displacement) of the subject form and not just its abolition. McKay's literary career, as will be discussed in the subsequent chapters, shows his struggle to reach this "dis-identification" position. This ideological evolution is realized in his last work, *Banana Bottom*. Realizing the inescapability of Western influence, he works out a compromise by proposing a syncretic identity.

However, reading McKay as a colonial writer from the West Indies leads to contestation of traditional McKay scholarship in America, which treats him solely as a Harlem writer. To understand McKay's distinctiveness, a thorough exploration of the differences in identity formation in black West Indians and African Americans is imperative. The way England and America went about colonizing their black populace had its impact on both the self-image and self-esteem of the black people in the respective countries. The plantation (sugar in the Caribbean and cotton in the United States) is the basis for any understanding of social and identity formations in black people. They are not merely large-scale production units but happened to be crucibles for fashioning generations of men's lives. The specific differences in controlling these plantations showed its effects differently in the respective countries.

The end of seventeenth century saw the establishment of large sugar estates in Jamaica employing hundreds of slaves with each estate resembling a small town. In contrast to the continental slave population, the typical plantation on these islands was double the norm in terms of slaves and usually held around 200 slaves per unit. The American South, by contrast, was neither overwhelmingly white nor overwhelmingly black: slaves formed a large minority of the population (in some areas, of course, they formed the majority), and despite regional variations, most slaves lived on small and medium-sized holdings containing between 5 and 50 slaves. As whites greatly outnumbered the slaves, it did not give much scope for open armed rebellions. Moreover, a substantial revolt presupposes the formation of ideology and leadership. These components were far more possible in the Caribbean and in Brazil with a large slave labor force and small white population. Only under these conditions could a positive group identity and nationalistic ideologies, which promote resistance, be easily developed.

In the United States, on the other hand, half the slaves lived and worked in groups of twenty or less with a majority of the other half living and working on plantations in groups of fifty or less. In most cases, these relatively small units were closely supervised, not only by white planters, but also by non-slaveholders who supported slavery. This explains the absence of maroon societies on the American mainland like those in the Caribbean and Latin American countries. Catching runaway slaves by non-slave holders, making it a community affair in the American South, has deeper ontological reasons explaining American Africanism. William J. Wilson rightly captures the reasons:

> One of the remarkable paradoxes of United States history is that although only a small percentage of whites enjoyed the social prestige and economic benefits of slave ownership, slavery received overwhelming support from white Southerners. To some extent, this is a testament to the power of the slaveholders — they were able to influence and direct patterns of thought among whites. Their characterization of slaves as either uncultured savages or inferior human beings in public discussion helped to strengthen the sense of group position among whites as well as to secure both formal and informal support for slavery. Even the poorest white non-slaveholder derived some psychic benefit from his identification with a "superior" caste.... As long as both slaves and freed blacks were denied the privileges enjoyed by the white caste, the nonslaveholder was assured a position above the bottom of the social ladder [86].

In her attempt to prove that black presence is central to any understanding of the American identity and American national literature, Toni Morrison in her monumental book *Playing in the Dark: Whiteness and Literary Imagination* also focuses on this issue. Morrison explains that the contrastive, radical binary opposition of blackness and whiteness in the U.S. most likely arose from the white immigrants' immediate concern to define themselves in Crevecoeurean fashion as "new men," i.e., first and foremost as "Americans." For the white American immigrants the flight from Europe to America was generally a flight from oppression and limitation to freedom and possibility. Whatever the reasons, Morrison says, the attraction was of the "clean slate" variety, and American colonies offered "opportunity not only to be born again but also to be born again in new clothes, as it were. The new setting would provide new raiments of self" (34). The black presence has given unimaginable psychic satisfaction to the white immigrants. As European sources of cultural hegemony were dispersed but not yet valorized in the new country, the process of organizing American coherence through a distancing Africanism became the operative mode of a new cultural hegemony (8). The need to establish difference stemmed not only from the Old World but also from a difference in the New. She observes:

> It is no accident and no mistake that immigrant populations (and much immigrant literature) understood their "Americaness" as an opposition to the resident black population [46–47].

Blackness — the Africanist presence — has become the central, albeit negative, reference point of identity; and the primordial violence in American race relations can be understood to be a product of that constellation. Hence, under the pressures of ideological and imperialistic rationales for subjugation, an American brand of Africanism emerged: strongly urged, thoroughly serviceable, companionably ego-reinforcing, and pervasive (8). So Morrison concludes:

> For in that construction of blackness *and* enslavement could be found not only the not-free but also, with the dramatic polarity created by skin color, the projection of the not-me. The result was a playground for the imagination. What rose up out of collective needs to allay internal fears and to rationalize external exploitation was an American Africanism — a fabricated brew of darkness, otherness, alarm, and desire that is uniquely American[12] [38].

The result is an Afro-American representing a *difference*, an Other — a level of human experience that the dominant society denies. James Baldwin puts it quite poignantly in his interview with Studs Turkel: "To be a Negro in this country ... is never to be looked at. What white people see when they do look at you is what they have invested you with. And what they have invested you with is agony, pain, anger, and passion and torment, sin, death, and hell in which everyone in this country is terrified. You [the Negro] represent a level of experience which Americans deny" (qtd. in Hogue 23). Unlike the English colonists in the United States the planters in the Caribbean usually left their estates in the hands of the white overseer and went over to Britain along with their families. They sought to make quick killings on their planting ventures and then retire to a life of leisure in England. Hence, estates began to be articles of commerce rather than plantations to be managed personally. To put it in the words of Parry and Sherlock:

> Except among merchants, shopkeepers, and a handful of
> professional men, the ambition of most White West Indians
> not born to property was to manage an estate, then to own
> one, and ultimately to retire to Europe on the proceeds. The
> general disinclination to reside continuously in the West
> Indies was attributed to many causes: the unhealthy climate
> (a much exaggerated cause); the lack of cultured society and
> entertainment (though this was as much a consequence as a
> cause of absenteeism); the lack of educational facilities for
> children [153].

The European colonizers of the West Indies, who were never bent on settling down (Caribbeanization), by and large did not seek a new identity but had a more profane interest: to get rich off of these tropical lands. Therefore, they had no comparable need for contrastive identity formation vis-à-vis the imported African slave population; therefore, the racial discrimination in the West Indian colonies (as savagely and reprehensibly as it, no doubt, has manifested itself throughout colonial history) developed a different background from that of the United States. Another feature of Jamaican society, which distinguishes it from the U.S.A., is the fact that the vast majority of the population is black or colored, because, unlike the United States, which came to replenish its enslaved population by natural production, Latin America and the Caribbean relied upon continuous large African imports, up until their various dates of emancipation.[13] Hence, the particular problems of the American black community, as a minority group, are rarely found in the Caribbean context. The constant physical threat that the minority African Americans feel before an overwhelming white majority is not felt in the Caribbean colonies. George Lamming elucidates the difference in belonging to a majority group in his criticism of James Baldwin, when the latter feels lost in the face of Western achievements:

> But there is a great difference between Baldwin and a comparable West Indian. No black West Indian, in his own native environment, would have this highly oppressive sense of being Negro. That may be all to the good; but there are definite reasons. It has to do with the West Indian's social and racial situation. The West Indian, however black and disposed, could never have felt the experience of being in a minority. For the black faces vastly outnumber the white or expatriate white. This numerical superiority has given the West Indian a certain leisure, a certain experience of relaxation among white expatriates; for the West Indian has learnt, by sheer habit, to take that white presence for granted. Which is precisely his trouble. At the other extreme, Baldwin is haunted by that white face, and the historic and cultural meaning of its achievement for him as a writer. To be black, in the West Indies, is to be poor; whereas to be black (rich or poor) in an American context is to be a traditional target for specific punishment. Racism is not just an American problem. It is an element of American culture [*Exile* 33].

As the West Indian societies developed as extensions or outposts of the European colonial metropoles, the ideological mechanisms of "othering" were governed by economic and demographic considerations, rather than by ontological and psychological needs, as in the United States. However, the luxury of belonging to the majority group in the Caribbean was undermined by the development of a peculiar color class system. The population pyramid was made of three divisions. At the apex stood the planters or, later, rich whites concentrating all the economic and political power in the society. In between the whites and the majority blacks, stood the colored class, as a sort of buffer zone between these groups.

The progeny of inter-racial liaisons were classified as colored and were consciously granted preferential treatment by the whites, creating a division between the colored and the black classes. Unlike the whites the social grading within each of these groups was determined not only by occupation or income but by actual skin color and features. Those nearest to the whites in appearance were accounted superior to those whose appearance were more Negroid, and so down to the full-blooded Negro. Prosperous whites not only recognized their colored offspring by freeing them from slavery, but also often educated them in England and left them property in their wills.[14] Some historians are of the opinion that at least in this respect West Indian slavery is less severe than in North America (Floyd 60). The early mixes were so easy to identify that precise terms were used to denote the gradation of mixing:

> Mulatto — offspring of Negro and White
> Sambo — offspring of Negro and Mulatto
> Quadroon — offspring of Mulatto and White
> Mestee — offspring of Quadroon and White
> Mestefeena — offspring of Mestee and White [Floyd 58].

The mestefeena were regarded as white, and free by law, which helps to explain why terms of racial crossing are important, prior to emancipation (Floyd 58). Within this hierarchy, whiteness had the highest social and therefore political value. The predominance of this white ideal penetrated the entire society. The lesson for the nonwhite population was to strive to become whiter, whether by producing whiter offspring (by their choice of mate) or by "behaving" white. Thus, the entire society could look to the redemption of the nonwhite, even if on a distant timetable.[15] Even though social prestige was associated with color, it does not mean that poor whites enjoyed higher social status. As their economic position was little different from that of the Negro, they were recognized by the society as the social equals of the Negro. McKay too notes in his autobiography that a black man places much more value upon the friendship of a light-colored person of the wealthy and educated class or of a black prosperous peasant than he would upon that of an undistinguished poor white (LW 36). This explains the Caribbean nonwhite population's easy and uninhibited relationship with the whites.

As lesser degrees of color brought special privileges in education and employment during the colonial period, the colored class viewed the black masses as a threat to their privileged position. The black masses too were more suspicious and envious of the colored class than they were of the whites. The animosity between these two groups was greater than it was between the black masses and the whites. However, the general discontent among these groups in the Caribbean rarely found open expression, partially due to the imposition of an English class system that cosmetically covered over the racial motives behind the social and economic structure in Jamaica.[16] Mulattoes had no special privileges in the United States and were lumped together, legally and socially, with their dark brethren. Black blood was like original sin and stained a man and his heirs forever in the United States. In the Caribbean, it was possible to pass from black to white in three generations. The color class system, and identification with and emulation of the British systems and language, have combined to create a peculiar but complicated colonial situation in Jamaica.

Moreover, unlike in the United States, emancipation in Jamaica was a bloodless affair, due to the huge compensation paid by the British Parliament to the slave owners. This measure reduced the associated grudge and had its influence on future racial attitudes. In the course of the succeeding post-emancipation period, the relationship between the ruling minority whites and the black masses gradually shifted in the West Indies and, consequently, increasingly differed in its sociopolitical and psycho-cultural implications from the situation in the United States. Race relations, during the nineteenth century British imperial era, became more habitual and congenial, not least of all though the implementation of liberal education programs. However, in the nineteenth century United States, discrimination and disenfranchisement of the black population continued with utmost brutality. The British strategy of providing the local population with a European education allowed for considerable social and political integration of the former slaves and the free colored people in most of the island societies. This strategy succeeded in fostering an atmosphere of favorable inclination towards the colonial power while creating a faithful middle class. This integration nurtured the illusion among members of the emerging West

Indian middle class of being bearers of the British values. McKay's father was a fine example of this phenomenon. Hence, Lamming affirms that colonialism was "the very base and structure of the West Indian's cultural awareness"[17] (35–36). The West Indies was the only modern community in the world, concludes Lamming, where the desire to be free, and the ambition to make their own laws, and regulate life according to their own impulses, was dormant (35).

If identity is defined as being oneself and not other, then from the very beginning, the black identity in the Caribbean entailed being oneself and another. For, as Fanon says, not only must the black man be black, he must be black in relation to the white man (Black Skin, 110). It is a world cut into two — a Manichaean world. The colonial subject writer is caught in it and the result is a split consciousness: a fragmented and alienated being straddling two worlds — one of its origin, the other of its adoption. The result of this dichotomy is vacillation and alternating preferences for the native culture and the metropolitan, pull between the pastoral and the urban, attachment to the simple rhythms of the native world and fascination with the metropolitan systems. Politically too, the colonial's sensibility, values and attitudes derive from, and oscillate between, the two antagonists: the victim and the victimizer. A creature of the colonial experience, the subject colonial writer is condemned to dwell in the indeterminate state of the imagination of the colonized, never able to state a clear-cut preference. His consciousness is forever anchored in the imperial-colonial dialectic. This informs the bipolar tensions that underlie the conceptual design of Claude McKay's literary productions. An analysis of McKay's writings will be made within the context of his colonial subjectivity, while his quest for identity and the subsequent ideological evolution will be examined within the context of his exile and the resultant cross-cultural experiences.

— 2 —

The Colonial Subject:
Poetry under Patronage

McKay's literary career started in his native island colony. He was the earliest black West Indian to use his native island dialect as the primary poetic medium. Written by a budding black artist, his poems of dialect can be read as social documents of historical value, and as linguistic and artistic creations of pioneering importance in the development of modern West Indian literature. However, like texts written in the second stage of literary production in the development of postcolonial literatures by the natives, his work is subject to the political, imaginative and social control involved in the relationship between the colonizer and the colonized (Ashcroft et al. 5). Writing doggerel verses imitating English writers, he came to the notice of Walter Jekyll, an English folklorist./A dedicated student of Jamaican dialect, Jekyll had published in 1907 *Jamaican Song and Story*, a collection of Annancy stories, digging songs, dancing tunes and ring tunes, supposed to be a classic in its field. He took McKay under his "protection" as he found it "interesting to meet a Negro who was writing poetry" (*GH* 66). Jekyll persuaded McKay to write in the dialect medium capturing the lives of Jamaican rural folk, which McKay did quite reluctantly. A colonial conditioned to esteem the metropolitan literary writings, McKay's reluctant initiation into dialect poetry is quite interesting. He narrates it in his autobiographical work, *My Green Hills of Jamaica*:

> All these poems that I gave him to read had been done in
> straight English, but there was one short one about an ass that
> was laden for the market — laden with native vegetables — he

had suddenly sat down in the middle of the road and
wouldn't get up. Its owner was talking to it in the Jamaican
dialect, telling it to get up. That was the poem that Mr.
Jekyll was laughing about. He then told me that he did not
like my poems in straight English — they were repetitious.
"But this," said he holding up the donkey poem, "this is the
real thing. The Jamaican dialect has never been put into literary form except in my Annancy stories. Now is your
chance as a native boy to put the Jamaican dialect into literary language. I am sure that your poems will sell" [67].

Though McKay was not very enthusiastic about this proposal, as "the
Jamaican dialect was considered a vulgar tongue," he began to think
seriously about it later, and "decided to do *some*[1] poems in dialect"
(*GH* 67). As the "Englishman had discovered beauty," McKay "too
could see where" his "poems are beautiful" (*GH* 69). The relationship
that McKay developed with Jekyll early in his career seems paradigmatic of that existing between many "colonials" and metropolitan elite
"patrons" in which the patron desires the writer to create "authentic"
and "native" art that differs from metropolitan codes. The admoni-
tions of Charlotte Osgood Mason (the often tyrannical bestower of
artistic largesse nicknamed "Godmother")[2] to both Langston Hughes
and Zora Neale Hurston, and Arthur Symons and Edmund Gosse's
encouragement of Sarojini Naidu[3] in the Indian colonial context to
depict the "native" or "folk" is underlined by similar dynamics. By
making McKay redirect "his instinctive predilection for the use of standard Literary English," McLeod feels that the patronage system is enter-
taining a "nefarious" design (125). As there is no legitimate literary
market among the black rural folk, the intended audience comprises
the British and Jamaican elite. The European readers and the Jamaican
elite — users of standard English — can replicate Jekyll's response and
be amused at the endeavors of the colonial native.

Though it is difficult to judge Jekyll's intentions, as he made sincere efforts in recording Jamaican folk songs, still, however benevolent
might be the patron, the relationship between the patron and the
patronized in a colony invariably operates within the parameters of the
colonial dialectic. The efforts made by the patron to promote the poems

and the response they received in Jamaican elite circles only confirm it. McKay corroborates it:

> The wealthy near-whites and the American and British Residents all wanted to know me. Mr. Jekyll trotted me out. Wherever I went, I read my poems in the dialect and they all caused great amusement among the upper-class people because they were all about the common life of the natives. Words they had heard but never believed could be put into poetry were now in poetry, and they liked it [*GH* 77].

Jekyll's patronage of McKay suggests a need on the author's part to negotiate between his own desire to be a "real poet" by writing in the traditional British forms and the expectation that he would be an "authentic" Jamaican poet by writing in the native or peasant vernacular. A product of imperial education, McKay was drawn to standard nineteenth century British literary models and themes, like his predecessors creating a unique linguistic tension in his dialect poetry. Hence, McKay's dialect poetry and even poetry written outside Jamaica should be analyzed with a demonstration of how its structure and tone can be explained only with reference to his colonial heritage. However, to a degree greater than earlier West Indian poets, he clearly revealed in his dialect poetry the intellectual, social and cultural ambivalences that faced a prospective black artist in a British colony. Moreover, McKay in these poems developed certain basic themes and stylistic tendencies that persisted in all his subsequent endeavors.

The first volume, *Songs of Jamaica* (1912), was a collection of fifty poems portraying various aspects of Jamaica rural life that McKay knew as a son of a black peasant. Reflecting mostly the hard realities of peasant life, some of his poems also reveal his intellectual convictions and commitments at that time. The mask of native idiom in some poems gave McKay scope for subversion. Yet, his fascination for British romantic poetry has ensured some love poems in the collection that are neither original in content, nor style. *Constab Ballads*, his second collection, published in late November 1912, records McKay's experiences and impressions as a constable in the colonial police force — the repressive arm of the imperial government. McKay revealed his best when he tried to capture the every day life of the peasants in their own idiom. However, he represented well the suffering of the common man in standard English. Nevertheless, his poems often suffered from a bisected consciousness, divided between the native peasant rhythms and lyrical traditions of England. Linguistically too the conflict is too apparent to ignore.

That Mckay's loyalties were evenly divided between the imperial homeland and Jamaica was evident, when the loyal son of Jamaica dedicated a poem on "de homeland England" along with a poem on his "Native Land." The poet who writes that "Jamaica is de nigger's place" and that "Dere is no land dat can compare" with it, in his "My native land, my home" (DP 84) has "a longin' in" the "dept's of heart" ever "since" he "could form a t'o't" to "sail athwart the ocean" and visit "de homeland England" (DP 63). Only a colonial writer has the "advantage" to owe allegiance to both the mother country and the colony. At the same time, true to his colonial legacy, his loyalties seem to be at conflict even within these two poems.

A loyal colonial pilgrim,[4] the poet speaker would visit England and see all "de famous sights dem 'bouten which dere's so much talk" like "Saint Paul's Cathedral" and "Westminister Abbey," "immortal Milton an' de wul'-famous Shakespeare, / past'ral Wordswort', gentle Gray" and finally "de lone spot" where "Rests de body of ... Missis Queen, Victoria de Good"(DP 63–64). All these sights, which he was longing to see, will "impart" a "solemn sacred beauty to a weary searchin' heart" and "rest glad an' contended in" his "min' for evermore" after he sails "across de ocean back" to his "own native shore"(DP 65). The young colonial, who was rapturous about the mother country, seems to realize that England cannot be his homeland as he reaches the final lines of the poem. Considering McKay's dialect poetry better than the American school, Mcleod says:

> Unfortunately, this type of verse is to be found in the literary first fruits of most of the Commonwealth countries; and in Nigeria one of the poets, Dennis Chukude Osadebay, produced doggerel much worse in his *Africa sings* as recently as 1952 [127].

In, "My Native Land, My Home," the poet speaker declares, "Jamaica is de nigger's place," which gives "life an' nourishment" growing "all o' t'ings" in its "fertile soil" to "full de naygur's wants" (*DP* 84). "Dere is no land compare" with it "in all de wul' none" fair to his "native land" his "home" (*DP* 84). The speaker seems to be very assertive that Jamaica is the "naygur's" home, denouncing the white colonizer who declared "dem" "no-land race" (*DP* 84). Traces of early nationalism appear in this poem when the poet speaker resents the colonial master's presence and his rule in Jamaica. Even though the speaker's "native land" "hab all t'ings fe mek life bles" the "buccra 'poil de whole / wid gove'mint an' all de res" (*DP* 85). The volume lacks another such a poem which portrays, so openly, a high degree of nationalism:

> E'en ef you mek me beggar die,
> I'll trust you all de same,
> An' none de less on you rely,
> Nor saddle you wid blame [*DP* 84].

Yet, the poet's confused affiliations curtail that fervor when the poem reaches its final lines. There can be a "time when" the poet speaker "...'ll tu'n 'gains" his country when it "can't give" him "grub" leaving to winds his earlier assertions (*DP* 85). This could be possible because the poet speaker, a colonial, has the "comfort" to choose an alternative "homeland." It may even be a justification to leave his "native land" in the future, as it cannot provide him "good opportunities." In fact, Claude McKay was the first in the long list of West Indian writers to migrate to the metropolitan centers.

If McKay's dialect songs of nature and romance like "Ione," "School-Teacher Nell's Lub-Letter," and "Lub O' Mine" are inconsistent in form, sentimental and unconvincing in content, his poems on racial or social themes are decidedly more impressive. It is true that Claude McKay did not register candidly a strong social protest in this volume. Still, his dialect poetry, composed in the shadow of a colonial patron, along with his own preference for the master's language, is not lacking in subversive potential. However affected, there are some poems in this volume where McKay's dialect was powered by a social consciousness and anger that increases its impact and authenticity. A close study reveals a nascent Jamaican identity and a faint West Indian awareness taking life throughout this volume. Nevertheless, how could McKay, a colonial, and subject of imperial ideology and patronage, achieve this?

Works of art do use ideologies as their materials of construction, but they do not simply replicate the ideological material of a given epoch. The poet's subversive potential is facilitated by the inherent contradictions (contradiction-unevenness-subordination between its elements) that are a part of the political mythology the dominant culture perpetuates in order to justify its own ascendancy. Moreover, "the artist," Louis Montrose contends, can achieve a "relative autonomy" in order to affect cultural change (5–11), "fashioning and refashioning consciousness, defining possibilities of action, shaping identities, and shaping visions of justice and order" (Fox-Genovese 222). In a fine monologue, "Quashie to Buccra" a peasant laborer good-humoredly undertakes to explain to "Buccra," that life on a farm is not so easy and is filled with lot of hardship. The black peasant's understated bitterness at the white landowner's entrenched privilege is subtly brought out in the opening lines:

> You tas'e petater an' you say it sweet,
> But you no know how hard we wuk fe it;
> You want a basketful fe quattiewut,
> 'Cause you no know how 'tiff de bush fe cut [*DP* 13].

The sweetness of the sweet potato, which the buccra enjoys, is contrasted with the hard work of the black peasant which "Is killin' somet'ing for a naygur man" (*DP* 13). He has to work in "De sun hot like when fire ketch a town" while he "caan' lie down," in the "temptin'" "shade-tree." McKay employs folk proverbs and the associated humor as a rhetorical mask for his social satire (Brown, *West Indian Poetry*, 49):

> You see petater tear up groun', you run
> You laughin', sir, you must be t'ink a fun [*DP* 14].

Brown says that employing the hyperbole in the sentence, "you see petater tear up groun', you run," not only "celebrates plenty and gives voice to the speaker's vitality," but the specific phrase "tear up" implies both the welcome crush of abundance and the impact of social inequalities which allow buccra the exclusive prerogatives of a comfortable shade-tree existence (49). Brown continues:

> The sweetness or vitality of Quashie's spirit is both a
> reflection of his actual bouyancy in the face of adversity
> and the smiling mask which he offers to ridicule and
> satisfy buccra's guilty expectations. This mask, the mask
> of language, excites buccra's laughter because he is unpre-
> pared to accept the bitter hardness of the sweet potato
> as a fact. And quashie's rhetoric exploits the advantage of
> this mask as a covert protest against privilege and injustice
> [49].

Employing of words like "buccra" for the white man and "naygur" for the black peasant gives a sharp edge to McKay's subversive tactics, because meaning, as Pecheux considers, does not reside in language itself (i.e., in its transparent relation to the literal character of the signifier), but linguistic meaning has a material character produced by the position of the language as a signifier in social, political, and cultural struggle. By using "naygur," the dialect word for the negro peasant, the poet is defiantly reversing the insulting racial stigma into a sign of ethnic pride. Similarly, employing its dialectical counterpart "buccra," the poet is subtly mocking at the omniscient white man. McKay could thus subtly make this poem a vehicle for exposing the economic injustice of the whites. The hilarious poem ends with a sad note about the peasants' helplessness in getting a good price for their produce:

> You tas'e petater an' you say it sweet,
> But you no know how hard we wuk fe it;
> Yet still de hardship always melt away
> Wheneber it come roun' to reapin' day [*DP* 14].

McKay shows the powerlessness of the peasants over the economy and the tragedies that can strike them in a full-length poem "Two-an'-Six" when a peasant comes to sell sugar on the market day. A poor peasant who "thinks" only about the "seben hungry mouths fe feed" "Neber dreamin of his own" goes "wid joyful face / Till him re'ch de marker place" (*DP* 88). Then the news "Sugar bears no price te-day" welcomes him (*DP* 88). McKay then brings out the pathetic situation of the peasant as he remembers his family and the financial obligations he has to fulfill:

> As de market is so bad;
> 'Pon him han' him res' him chin,
> Quietly sit do'n thinkin'
> Of de loved wife sick in bed,
> An' de children to be fed —[DP 88–89].

McKay movingly depicts the perseverance of the peasant family in the face of adversity:

> But de sick wife kissed his brow:
> "Sun, don't get down-hearted now;
> Ef we only pay expense
> We mus' wuk we common-sense,
> Cut an' carve, an' carve an' cut ... [DP 90].

In yet another poem, "Hard Times," he not only depicts a similar resilience of the peasant but also expresses the resentment felt by them when working for a lazy, white landowner who knows nothing of the crops, their cultivation, or the efforts they put into its production — and yet who finally benefits while the poor peasants gain nothing. The poem exposes the perils of a plantation economy where the peasant works "like a mule / while buccra, sittin' in de cool, / Hab 'nuff nenyam fe waste" (DP 53). In "Fetchin Water" McKay rebukes white tourists who enjoy the sight of poor peasant children at their daily chores in the hot sun. He contrasts the cool comforts of the outsider with the hot, tiring drudgery of fetching water. The very presence of the white tourists reinforces the imperialism that keeps these children fettered to lives of poverty and oppression.

"Cudjoe Fresh from de Lecture" mirrors the deep distrust of the colonial population about the theories of racial inequalities spread by imperialism. Cudjoe, a shrewd semiliterate man, is enthusiastic to share with "cous' Jarge" the lecture on evolution that he heard just now, which strengthened his skepticism on the traditional Old Testament view that "de whole o' we are clay" (DP 56). Hence, his excitement about the evolution theory arises from its basic tenet that the entire humanity has the same origin: "For ebery single man, no car' about dem rank / Him bring us ebery one an' put 'pon de same plank" (*DP* 55). It relieves him from the clutches of religious theories that spread and reinforced the imperial theory that the black man is cursed and hence inferior:

> No 'cos say we get cuss mek fe we 'kin come so,
> But fe all t'ngs come 'quare, same so it was to go [*DP* 56].

At the same time the evolutionist's viewpoint that Cudjoe believes, "Yes, from monkey we spring," has, as Brown says, been fraught with distasteful implications for blacks (*West Indian Poetry*, 45). It was the imperialist's opinion that the Negro is a stage in the slow evolution of monkeys into men (Fanon *Black Skins* 17). As the evolutionist's "we" assumes wryly-ethnic significance, the speaker's semi-literate enthusiasm acquires an unconsciously subversive naiveté (Brown, *West Indian Poetry*, 45). Ironically, the subversive quality becomes counterproductive when Cudjoe's opinion about Africa and Africans run parallel to the imperialist's notion:

> Seems our lan must ha' been a bery low-do'n place,
> Mek it tek such long time in tu'ning out a race....
> Talk 'bouten Africa, we would be deh till now,
> Maybe same half naked — all day dribe buccra cow,
> An' tearin' t'rough de bush wid all de monkey dem,
> Wile an' uncibilise', an' neber comin' tame [*DP* 57–58].

The above lines replicate Hegel's notorious theory that Africa is a dark continent and that the Negroes are "out of the historical process" in his *The Philosophy of History*:

> Africa proper, as far as History goes back, has remained —
> for all purposes of connection with the rest of the world —
> shut up; ... the land of childhood, which lying beyond the
> days of self-conscious history, is enveloped in the dark mantle of Night.... The Negro as already observed exhibits the
> natural man in his completely wild and untamed state [qtd.
> in Gilroy 41].

Cudjoe's slurs on Africa reveal the self-hate and self-deception that imperialism has inculcated in the black people. Cudjoe's image of "uncibilized" half-naked Africans, driving the white man's cow, over-looks the fact that in his own "blessed" Jamaica, blacks do drive the white man's cattle. The influence of imperial education on the grate-ful colonial can be gauged when he condones slavery and his removal from Africa:

> Yes, Cous' Jarge, slabery hot fe dem dat gone befo':
> We gettin' better times, for those days we no know;
> But I t'ink it do good, tek we from Africa
> An' lan' us in a blessed place as dis a ya [BP 57].

This passage echoes Hegel's opinion that slavery has been the occa-sion of the increase in human feeling among the Negroes. The dises-teem for Africa is balanced by Cudjoe's allegiance to "blessed" Jamaica, which Brown counts as McKay's nationalism (West Indian Poetry, 45). The poem also reveals the immense belief of McKay in the rational-ism of Western science to underscore the essential irrationality of West-ern racism.

A prostitute's tongue-lashing in the poem "A Midnight Woman to the Bobby" turned into a good opportunity for McKay to attack the abuse of power (by the police and law courts) and the poverty perpet-uated by the colonial system. The harsh rebuke of the policeman by the prostitute in dialect reveals many sad facts of both their lives — the poverty that has driven them from the countryside into the corrupt-ing influence of the city. That the police force in the colonies was never considered as a law enforcing agency but a repressive state apparatus in the hands of the white man is clear from the woman's lashing: "You come from mountain naked-'kin / An' come join buccra police force" (DP 75). In her warning to the police man about the dismissal of his earlier colleagues: "Yet whe' dey all o' dem te-day? / De buccra dem no kick dem 'way?" McKay is subtly indicating the high-handedness of the white police officers (DP 75).

The corruption of the "Country Girl" in the city is the subject of a full-length poem. In pleading with the girl to give up her evil pro-fession in the city McKay unveils to the readers the darker side of their rural life and their eventual fall: "Fed, it was horrid de lone country life! / I suffered — for sometimes e'en hunger was rife" (*DP* 119). These poems reveal the formative influences on McKay, and serve as introduction to nearly all the themes — city versus countryside, the attachment to the simple rhythms of the native world, and the fascination with the metropolitan systems, which would constitute his major concerns hereafter. "Harlem Shadows" in his American collection runs almost parallel to the theme of this poem.

It is evident from the poem "Strokes of the Tamarind Switch" that McKay is most convincing when he expresses his social protest in his "own" tongue — "straight English." Written after McKay joined the colonial police force, the poem expresses his genuine rage at the barbarities sanctioned in the name of law. It tells the story of the whipping of a young man by the police. As he explains it in his note, the subject of the poem

> ... was a lad of fifteen. No doubt, he deserved the flogging administered by order of the court: still, I could not bear to see him — my own flesh — stretched out over the bench, so I went away to the Post Office near by. When I returned, all was over. I saw his naked bleeding form, and through the terrible ordeal — so they told me — he never cried. But when I spoke to him he broke down, told me between his bursts of tears how he had been led astray by bad companions, and that his mother intended sending him over-sea. He could scarcely walk, so I gave him tickets for the tram. He had a trustful face. A few minutes after, my bitterness of spirit at the miserable necessity of such punishment came forth in song, which I leave rugged and unpolished as I wrote at the moment [*DP* 113].

McKay's "spirit" is "filled with hate," at the "depravity" of men who could whip a young boy of his "own flesh," until his legs looked like "boiling bark" (*DP* 111). The intensity of the poem results from the depth of affinity that McKay feels with the actual speaker, that is, with himself. He makes the reader feel his sorrow, his hate, his shame, and his compassion. Ironically, his rage finds its expression through the master's language, the language with which he had very deep affinity.

But Brown thinks that "the use of standard English here is fundamental to the ironic design of his art: the brutality of the established order and its essentially non-civilized approach are exposed through the very medium — its language — which it holds up to illiterate (non-white) world as the norm of civilized existence" (50). However, there is enough reason to question whether McKay's use of standard English is indeed intentionally ironic. A product of the colonial educational system, his use of the "cultivated tongue" reveals his own concession to the ruling systems that subjected the adolescent to such abuse.

McKay's use of standard English in this poem indicates the ambiguities and tensions evident in the relationship between a white Western value system and the black rural poor in the dialect poems. Overall, the poem "Strokes of the Tamarind Switch" acquires a special position in this collection precisely because it was written in McKay's own voice, which is integral to his poetic consciousness. The magnitude of the sensitive colonial's rage and compassion, added to his confusion about his relation with the victim and the victimizer, gives this poem of intense emotion a special place in this volume.

McKay's next volume of poetry, *Constab Ballads,* reveals his conflict as poet and policeman. As a sensitive poet, he was sympathetic toward his oppressed race, but as a middle class colonial educated in Western values he was unable to identify with the peasants and their language. As a black Jamaican and victim of the colonial oppression and racism, he was unable to identify with the white ruling establishment. Unfortunately, as a cop, he was a representative of the oppressive white power structure against his "own flesh" (*DP* 113). He "confess[es]" in the preface to the book, "I had not in me the stuff that goes to the making of a good constable; for I am so constituted that imagination outruns discretion, and it is my misfortune to have a most improper sympathy with wrong doers" (*DP* 7). He never "openly rebelled; but the rebellion was in" his "heart, and it was fomented by the inevitable rubs of daily life." Deeply steeped in Western values, McKay can never "openly" rebel. His "rebellion" is always stifled within the language, forms, and clichés of the metropolitan. In the poem "The Heart of a Constab" he laments that he lost "De frien's dat ... used to hold dear?" "Becausen de red seam" he now wears (*DP* 62). He regrets joining the police force and grieves that his people will not love him again:

> Tis grievous to think dat, while toilin' on here,
> My people won't love me again,
> My people, my people, me owna black skin,—
> De wretched t'ought gives me such pain [*DP* 63].

Hence his life in Kingston city as a constable, which he very much disliked, created in him a nostalgia for the peasant life in the remote hills of Jamaica:

> I'll leave it, though flow'rs here should line my path yet,
> An' come back to you an' de soil....
> Then oh for de country, de love o' me soul,
> From which I shall nevermore part! [*DP* 63].

The antithesis between city and the countryside (the city is always the metropolitan center of the white civilization) became a permanent aspect of his poetry, as he became an urban exile later on. The whole of Jamaica became a pristine pastoral image from the distance of the urban centers of New York and London. McKay also brings out the high-handedness of the colonial police in poems like "The Apple-Woman's Complaint." A street hawker complains that the "de head-man fe de town police / Mind neber know a little peace, / 'Cep' when him an' him heartless ban' / Hab sufferin' nigger in dem han" (*DP* 57–58). McKay makes it clear that poor "niggers" are suffering a lot in the hands of the white police establishment in many of his poems in this volume. This recalls Fanon's grim comments on the colonial police force in his book *The Wretched of the Earth*:

> The colonial world is a world cut in two. The dividing line,
> the frontiers are shown by barracks and police stations. In
> the colonies it is the policeman and the soldier who are the
> official, instituted go-between, the spokesmen of the settler
> and his rule of oppression [29].

By their immediate presence and direct action, the soldier and the police officer maintain contact with, monitor closely, and advise the colonial by means of rifle butts and napalm. Even the judicial system doesn't seem to come to the succor of the oppressed people: "But how judge believe policemen, / Dem dutty mout' wid lyin' stain?" (*DP* 58). McKay brings the helpless woman's plight very touchingly when she finally appeals to God:

> We hab fe barter-out we soul
> To lib t'rough dis ungodly wul';—
> O massa Jesus! don't you see
> How police is oppressin' we? [DP 58].

The constable's identification with his own people comes out in the poem "The Bobby to the Sneering Lady," when the narrator of the poem asks a white woman not to report him for his refusal to arrest a servant girl who is accused of stealing. The girl has already been whipped and the policeman thinks the punishment is enough for her crime. The racial injustice of the police force is subtly exposed when the narrator policeman worries that he cannot always go hard against his own people:

> Ef our lot, then, is so hard,
> I mus' ever bear in mind
> Dat to fe me own black 'kin
> I mus' not be too unkind [*DP* 67].

That McKay became the instrument of oppression seems to have made the conflict more acute as he demonstrates it in his "Preface" and the poem "The Heart of the Constab." This volume anticipates the fierce racial and social satire of the American Harlem years even while betraying poignantly his mind divided along two axes. McKay's dialect poetry is often compared in the United States with the dialect poetry of African American writers like P.L. Dunbar. James Weldon Johnson, like many critics, thinks that McKay had the peculiar freedom, which he was able to exercise in the use of this medium in *Songs of Jamaica*:

> [T]hey are free from both the minstrel and plantation tradi-
> tions, free from exaggerated sweetness and wholesomeness;
> they are veritable impressions of Negro life in Jamaica.

Indeed, some of these dialect poems are decidedly militant in tone. It is of course clear to see that McKay had the advantage of not having to deal with stereotypes. He found his medium fresh and plastic [163].

Only a close linguistic study reveals how McKay has put to use his "fresh and plastic" medium. Critics usually distinguish McKay's dialect poetry from Dunbar's which, they argue, lost its efficacy when he wrote in a dialect tradition that had been used by sentimental Plantation School white writers. Dunbar's dialect more closely resembled the words of these authors, which is often used to ridicule and demean black, than it resembled the actual African American speech. George E. Kent also attests Johnson's opinion that Claude McKay's use of dialect in poetry reflected an artistic freedom which was not meaningfully available to most American black poets until such writers as Langston Hughes and Sterling Brown could make a sufficient disassociation from the sensibility enforced by white American culture (The Dialect Poetry, 39).

Contrary to African American critics' opinion that McKay's Jamaican background provided him with a source of sensibility, which gave him certain advantages over American born black writers, his poetry is actually weighed down from the set poetic pieces, phrases or abbreviations and clichés from metropolitan English. It is evident from the effective bisection of his poetry between formal English and Jamaican dialect that McKay was caught up in the colonial dilemma. In common with all the writing done in colonies, his work seems linguistically to be a hybrid product. Two gravitational forces pull him, the one of his native tongue, the other of the language of the colonizer. A product of the British education system, McKay, who learned to scorn the dialect as vulgar, has admitted to this linguistic tension in his American volume of poetry, *Harlem Shadows*:

> The speech of my childhood and early youth, was the Jamaican dialect ... which still preserves a few words of African origin, and which is more difficult of understanding than the American Negro dialect. But the language we wrote and read in school was England's English [xix].

Hence, the "cultivated" tongue of "straight English," which interrupts the mood and tone of the dialect, is now accepted as McKay's voice. This is in spite of his sincere "apologies" to the "immortal spirit," Robert Burns, for "making him speak in Jamaica dialect" (Preface *DP*). But Lloyd W. Brown in his excellent chapter on McKay, in his more general study of West Indian poetry, argues that the "intermingling of forms enforces the poet's perception of the duality that is inherent in his literary heritage (English and Afro-Caribbean) and in his cultural milieu" (*West Indian Poetry*, 42). This kind of objective, he asserts, conforms very well with McKay's preoccupation with a sense of aptness, "in choosing the diverse forms and cultural structures which were available to him" (*West Indian Poetry*, 42).

At the same time, Brown also acknowledges that such "intermingling merely creates a sense of jarring incongruity" but that this "marked unevenness results, in part, from the insecurity of an inexperienced poetic imagination" (*West Indian Poetry*, 42). However, a close study of his dialect verse shows it to be limited, less by a conscious effort to wrestle into one form the two aspects of his literary heritage, than by an inherent struggle raging within the young poet himself, to reconcile his warring British and Jamaican identities. The dual versions of the language, like those of the island culture, internalized during the period of his cognitive development, shadow McKay's work to the very end and affect its tone and texture in various ways.

"Out of Debt" provides an excellent example of how McKay struggles for mediation between the two voices — Jamaican peasant and British intellectual — which characterize his dialect poetry. A good dialect stanza, depicting the happiness of a peasant who is out of debt for this Christmas, is immediately followed by stanza written almost in standard English:

> No two bit o' brater
> Wid shopkeeper Marter,
> I feel me head light sittin' down by me wife;
> No weight lef' behin' me
> No gungu a line fe
> De man who was usual to worry me life [*DP* 38].

Here the vernacular grammar is at work, full of native expressions.

The author even helps the readers with his notes, without which it is difficult for non-native readers to understand. Purely native grammar and expressions mark the first two lines. They mean that shopkeeper Marter and the peasant speaker "are no longer two brothers": meaning, the peasant speaker "is not always going into his shop, and so keeping in debt" (*DP* 38). Though the third line sounds standard English the vernacular usage of "me" for "my" saves that line. The remaining three lines are good dialect constructions with native phrases and grammar. By employing the native expression "no gungu a line" (friends plant their gungu — congo peas — together, and in picking the crop, are not particular about the line between their properties) McKay catches the rural Jamaican spirit very accurately. It means the peasant speaker is "to have no truck with" the shopkeeper as they cease to be friends (38). Such a stanza is immediately followed by a stanza written almost in standard English, betraying McKay's uneasiness with the dialect:

> We're now out o' season,
> But dat is no reason
> Why we shan't be happy wid heart free and light:
> We feel we are better
> Dan many dat fetter
> Wid burden dey shoulder to mek Christmas bright [*DP* 39].

The first line uses only standard English and the second line is almost the same with the unlikely insertion of "dat" in place of "that" which leaves the reader uncertain about the form the poem will take. Except for dialectal "wid" for "with," "Dan" for "than," and "dat" for "that" the third and fifth lines along with the fourth are written in standard English. The sixth line follows the same pattern with dialectical insertions of "wid," "dey" and "mek." As the poem progresses, these discrepancies continue both in language and in structure. This is the case with the majority of his poems. The intrusion of formal style and language into dialect verse seems to occur throughout *Songs of Jamaica*. Although the collection was proclaimed dialect poetry, there is some thing besides dialect at work. Stanza eleven of "Ribber Come-Do'n" is another glaring example of this linguistic tension. Out of the thirteen stanzas of the poem, the first ten are in dialect. The tenth stanza:

"Ebenin', cousin Anna,
Me deh beg you couple banna,
For dem tarra one is berry hungry home;
We puppa ober May, ma,
We mumma gone a Bay, ma,
An' we caan' tell warra time dem gwin' go come" [*DP* 118].

Such a good dialectical continuity is suddenly snapped as McKay switches to formal English in the eleventh:

The kind district mother thought
Of her own baby far away,
An' wondered much how he fared
In a foreign land that day [*DP* 118].

Hansell in his essay "Some Themes in the Jamaican Poetry of Claude McKay" comes to an unconvincing conclusion that the district mother is white and that may be the reason for McKay to switch from dialect to formal English. He says:

Since in these poems of Jamaica all officials above the lowest ranks are white, one assumes this woman is.... The narrator's style changes from a very pronounced dialect to almost formal English when he relates the woman's thoughts,... then returns to dialect to describe the results of her charity [129].

In "Nellie White," which is actually a reply to the preceding poem, "School-Teacher Nell's Lub-Letter," the dialectical "lub" and "lubbed" which he uses in many of his poems is replaced by the standard "love" and "loved" even though the speaker is a peasant whose speech is supposed to be vernacular. If a full stanza interrupts the flow of the dialect, as in the examples discussed above, there are poems where just a few words or phrases reveal McKay's evenly divided lexical loyalties. In "Whe' Fe Do?," McKay repeatedly juxtaposes words that are pronounced in standard English using a soft "th" with similar words that he records as being pronounced with a hard "d":

We happy in *de* hospital;
We happy when *de* rain deh fall;

We happy *th*ough *de*[5] baby bawl
Fe food dat we no hab at all; [*DP* 28].

The reader will be left questioning why the formal "*th*ough" is used instead of the dialectical "dough" when "de" for the formal "the" is used alongside. Many such inconsistencies can be noted within a stanza. For example, in fourth line of stanza four in the poem mentioned above he uses a perfectly good English "that" but in the eighth line of the same stanza he reverts to the dialectical "dat." Walter Jekyll, McKay's patron, tries to explain these inconsistencies in his preface:

> In these poems *the, they, there, with*, etc.; are not always written *de, dey dere, wid*, etc.; and the reader is at liberty to turn any soft *th* into *d*, and any *d* into soft *th*. And here let me remark, in passing, that in one breath the black man will pronounce a word in his own way, and in the next will artic-ulate it as purely as the most refined Englishman ... and for fear of confusion with well known words, *though, those* are always written thus, although generally pronounced *dough, dose* [7].

Even if one agrees to a given number of alterations in order to remain clear to the reader, they do not follow the set order. The reader is left questioning why certain dialectical words, as "that" for "dat," are used, when they are linguistically comparable. Moreover, consistent use of dialect terms will not hinder the reader's comprehension. Jekyll's contention that McKay is forced to make changes "for fear of confusion" underscores McKay's dependence as a patronized writer both on Jekyll and the intended audience — the elite of Jamaica and the reading public of England. The rural Jamaican folk upon whom McKay draws for his personae do not talk in this way. Their ability to speak both versions of the language with ease has specific purpose. As Louise Bennett[6] says, "[T]he speaker in Jamaican dialect, uses or refers to the 'grand' style of standard English, with an underlying irony that lends itself to a barely straight-faced imitativeness or to outright laughter — while being able to function with serious fluency in standard English whenever the occasion demands it" (qtd. in Lloyd W. Brown *West Indian Poetry*, 43).

McKay's linguistic irregularities, which do not occur in an identifiable pattern, along with the structural inconsistencies, raise the question of whether he or his patron fully trust the dialect to convey accurately the meaning the author intends to express. His tendency to insert "cultivated English" into dialect poetry testifies his implicit acceptance of the supposed superiority of the British aspects of his colonial education.

The subtle invalidation of the vernacular, combined with the intrusion of McKay's formal voice, results in an uneven and unconvincing volume of poetry. The two volumes reveal that the colonial lacks that empathetic personality in his art which would allow him to assume in their entirety both the folk language and the modes of perception which it embodies. The deep-seated conflict within McKay's own artistic personality can be attributed only to his colonial upbringing. As McKay, the black poet peasant, seeks to embody the Jamaican peasants' life in their own speech, McKay, the British educated, middle class intellectual, is allured by the idiom of the Master, revealing the colonizer's sway.

The title "Bobbie Burns" of Jamaica and a silver medal for the volumes did not encourage McKay to continue with the dialect medium. The Browning Clubs confirmed to the aspiring colonial writer that to be recognized as a "real poet" he should write like his metropolitan masters, Browning, Tennyson, Keats and Shelley. As the mother country is the sole arbiter in matters of literary taste, the colonial writer to be recognized as a writer in his own country has to get the approval of the headquarters. Therefore, McKay had to give up his dialect medium, which he reluctantly chose. He embarked on a journey to the metropolitan centers firmly resolved to show the Browning Clubs "something" in "straight English" (*Green Hills* 87). This he achieved in his expatriate collection by writing in "straight" English and using European forms, although the volume, like his dialect poetry, is bisected on aspects of race, radicalism, and nostalgia in the new milieu.

— 3 —

The Colonial in the United States: Anger and Ambiguity

Within two years after coming to America, McKay quit two institutes — Tuskegee and Kansas State College — and drifted to the Negro mecca, Harlem, in 1914. His experience at these institutes — where his performance was less than satisfactory — confirmed that he was unsuitable to agronomy, for which he joined them. The disciplined life of academia seems to be incompatible with "the spirit of the vagabond, the daemon of some poets that got hold of" him (*LW* 4). However, the harsh realities of American life did not give him the luxury of an easy bohemian life like his British models. He had to work as a porter, fireman, bar-boy, houseman and waiter on the Pennsylvania railroad. During these years, which he considers a training period, McKay says that he accumulated much experience to "graduate as a poet" if not "graduate as a bachelor of arts or science ... writing out of" himself, "waiting for an audience" (*LW* 4). Finally, McKay turned to New York, which could not have been a more logical move for a black poet in 1914.

Harlem in New York City was slowly emerging as the cultural and intellectual center for the African Americans. Waves of blacks swarmed into the northern cities driven by extreme poverty and racial bigotry in South, making it the Great Migration in American social history. As European migration was cut off, the blacks filled in the war industries' labor needs. In addition to these, thousands of blacks came from the West Indies looking for opportunities in the industrial North, especially New York. Great numbers of blacks, says Huggins, seemed to mean new power. Conscious of this, Harlem steadily evolved into the biggest and most elegant of black communities in the Western world. This community was not peasant but urban within the most urbane of American cities, which was just feeling its youthful strength and posturing in self-conscious sophistication (Huggins 14). Naturally, Harlemites shared this strength and felt that it should be the capital for the race, a platform from which the new black voice would be heard around the world. As Harlem became the intellectual center of the "New Negro," it symbolized the Afro-American's coming of age.

West Indians too flocked to Harlem but found it difficult to assimilate into the mainstream (black) American life.[1] They were profoundly at odds with white America. Their conflict with the larger society was the result of the pervasiveness and virulence of racial discrimination and their own social and cultural background. Coming from a socially ranked color class system, these nonwhite immigrants abhorred the prevalent brutal racism of the United States. They openly resented being called "George" or "boy" by whites (Reid *The Negro Immigrant*, 107). Moreover, the cultural baggage they brought from the West Indies prevented them from assimilating into mainstream African American life.[2] Priding themselves on being British citizens, these black West Indians affirmed that racism did not exist in their islands. Even McKay used to assert that no race problem existed in Jamaica. In a letter to James Weldon Johnson he remarked, "In my village, I grew up on equal terms with white, mulatto and black children of every race because my father was a big peasant and belonged. The difference on the island is economic, not social" (qtd. in Tillery 15). So comparing their "homeland" to America, the immigrants "seldom had a pleasant word to say about American society, while they were hardly critical of the West Indies" (Holder 58). Hence home remained for them, though naturalized, or for those who remained unnaturalized, not New York, nor America, but some island in the Caribbean under the control of one of the European colonial powers. It was "home," unlike America, which would offer them respite from racism. Hence, many looked forward to settling at home in their twilight years. Of course, most never left the city, but died and were buried in the country they disliked. McKay's life is a classic example of this pattern.

Even though the primordial racial animosities that mark American race relations were absent in the West Indian societies, it is "simply untrue," as Bryce-Laporte says, "that the average black immigrant has come out of a nonracist situation" (39). Laporte says that the average black citizen of these countries was made to believe that their country was free of racism. McKay was no exception to this belief, and the class explanation that he gave was not tenable because, even in terms of class, they suffered, at any rate, disguised inequalities.[3] In order to emphasize their distinctiveness these immigrants used exotic apparel, displayed heavy accents, and avoided contact and association with black Americans (Bryce-Laporte 40). The British Jamaicans' distinctive accent and the grammatical correctness of their English is a point in this argument.

It is also generally agreed that these West Indian immigrants were more successful than their American counterparts in their enterprises or professions. Perhaps, one of the probable factors for the West Indian immigrant's success was that he was pushed more by the socioeconomic conditions of his home country than by the subtle racism there. As economic advancement and social mobility have higher positive valence, these immigrants were highly disposed to run risks, and engage in sacrificial, persistent and ingenious activities. America for the black immigrants, like their white counterparts, represents a personalized, predefined frontier. Bryce-Laporte's observation, regarding the immigrants' social behavior in the American context, is important to understand McKay's ease with the bohemian white radicals:

> As a foreigner, the black immigrant would have come to this country with less inhibitory socialization either in terms of self pride and self-confidence or previous exposure to de facto or de jure prohibitions about public conduct vis-à-vis whites. Unknowingly, he breaks barriers and demolishes stereotypes by his unrehearsed aggressiveness, naïve open-mindedness and, thus apparent easiness in the presence of whites. He forces his white adversaries to accept him as a man, which they often do by redefining him as exceptional to the extent that is possible and attributing that exceptionality or competence to his foreign background [47].

Triggered by their urgency to establish quickly, these immigrants moved with much aggressiveness, competing with their fellow American blacks in jobs, creating tension between the two. To aggravate the matter further they refused to be grouped with African Americans, whom they considered less cultured. The conflicts and misunderstanding between native and foreign blacks even extended to cultural and political matters.[4] Factors contributing to the conflict were usually differences in folk culture, colonial orientation, attitudes toward whites, and exposure to metropolitan life styles. Consequently, some stereotypes were formed.[5] If the African Americans were "clowns" to the West Indians, they in turn were "monkey chasers" to the American blacks. McKay says that their general opinion of American Negroes was that they were clowns more or less: "All those that we saw in Kingston on the street were the happy-go-lucky clowning types who sang 'coon' songs for the white men and they seemed to like it.... Our Negroes even though they were very poor would not sing clowning songs for white men and allow themselves to be kicked around by them" (*GH* 85).

In addition to these notions, the West Indians did not share the African Americans' perception of race. While race was synonymous with color for the African Americans, the West Indians, brought up in a color class system (oppressive as it was), did not view race as the defining problem for all people of color. Hence, the race conflict was more acute between the black British West Indians and African Americans. Whenever the British West Indians faced racial discrimination, they turned to the British embassy and not to American authorities. In fact, many never renounced their British citizenship as they felt that they had the support of a powerful nation that made them immune to certain forms of racism (61).[6]

Even as a writer, McKay could not overcome some of these illusions and prejudices. Lonely by instinct, McKay's personality would always remain a major impediment to his establishing a close relationship with African Americans. His West Indian origin only complicated the matter further. Many a time in America, McKay and Marcus Garvey led themselves into awkward situations when they openly displayed their dislike for fair-skinned Negroes.[7] McKay's early life in New York is a classic example of the West Indian immigrant's behavior. He tried his hand at business in New York but, unlike his fellow West Indians, McKay failed in both business and marriage. Nevertheless, failure seems to have helped him to pursue his sole objective in life — writing.

McKay never mingled with the black middle class intellectuals in Harlem. Instead, he joined freely with the serving class of African Americans, while working at various odd jobs, absorbing their nightlife in Harlem. This was the time when a new political agenda advocating racial equality in the African American community, particularly in its growing middle class, was evolving. Black intellectuals like W.E.B. Du Bois and white liberals like Spingarn championed that agenda. Projection of the positive self-image that black men were also artists, thinkers and intellectuals, the young Du Bois believed, would remove the inequities. Art and culture would bring the warring races on to the common ground and reform the brotherhood in a common humanity (Huggins 4). Signs of a new literary movement appeared within the black community with its emphasis on African American racial heritage. McKay, the artist with a colonial mindset from the West Indies, did not fit into this scheme. He was very much against the aspect of promotion in art. McKay never experienced the urgency felt by African American intellectuals to project the race as equally talented (talented tenth of Du Bois) through its achievements in art and literature. For not advocating the race, some of his poems were even rejected. They even questioned his use of sonnet form. Disillusioned, he wrote to W.S. Braithwaite: "[T]his has set me wondering whether Fine Art is not beyond nation or race — if one's mind can be limited to one's race and its problems when Art is as sublime as he who gave it to man" (qtd. in Tillery 31).[8]

Racial issues did not inspire McKay. He himself declared after World War II that he never considered himself a Negro poet. He believed that literature was independent of race and nationality. Hence, James R. Giles concludes that a great deal of his poetry cannot be classified, directly or indirectly, as black protest (42). Even his most popular poem "If we must die" does not speak of race. Though the 1919 race riots were the immediate context for its creation, years later he denied its racial objective (*LW* 31). He even pointed out the universal quality of the poem when he affirmed that it was written for all men who were being "abused, brutalized, and murdered, whether they were black, brown, yellow, or white Catholic or Protestant or Pagan, fighting against terror"[9] (qtd. in Tillery 34).

Its universal quality was more than confirmed when Sir Winston Churchill quoted it at the conclusion of his speech before the American congress urging America to involve in World War II — making it a classic example of the mother country incorporating the colonial's challenge.[10] Ironically, the poem was made to reinforce the same political apparatus that it denounced. Finding a parallel in Henry V's famous "St. Crispin Day" speech to this poem, Keller says:

> McKay's use of these materials constitutes a mutual appropriation of materials by the alienated minority artist and the power structure. Shakespeare's work constitutes the conservative European cultural traditions that are recuperated by the marginalized artist for the purpose of transforming the dominant culture. In turn, the government apparatus would recycle and reform the revolutionary potential of the art work, employing it to strengthen its power structures and, thereby, guarantee the continued persecution of minorities [450].

The poem for which McKay became the literary hero of the New Negro movement was first published in the *Liberator*; a white radical publication read less by the black community. McKay, the poet aspiring for "universal" acclaim, must have intended a wider audience. However, numerous Negro magazines soon picked up the poem and it became a sort of tribal litany for the cause of the black people. It announced with a bang the arrival of the New Negro. No other black writer could so deftly combine what Frank Harris called "authentic fire and blood," satisfying the deep hunger in the hearts of American Negroes (*LW* 32). Such is the impact of the poem as a harbinger and symbol of transition in black letters that it continued to influence even the next generation. Nevertheless, McKay, on whom the title a poet of his people was thrust for this poem, was never comfortable. To be cast in the role of a race poet representing the African American was not the objective for McKay. He was not appreciative of being indented in the narrow groove of race, at the cost of his universal outlook. Hence the lukewarm response:

> And for it the Negro people unanimously hailed me as a
> poet. Indeed, that one grand outburst is their sole standard
> of appraising my poetry [*LW* 31].

This ambivalent attitude perplexed many McKay critics. Citing this poem, many of them tried to explain these contradictions, betraying only their bewilderment. Aware of "the many vicissitudes in his life and career," John Hillyer Condit agrees with Wayne Cooper's thesis that McKay's literary significance can be understood only within the full context of his life and career. He concludes that "at any given moment or in any given work," McKay was "striving to balance his universalism with his proud individuality" which he inherited from his mother and father respectively (351). Aware of the ambiguity in his protest sonnets, Arthur D. Drayton interprets it as the sublimation of the poet's pride of race. He finds its source in the poet's "tender, gentle spirit" that is saving him from "racial extremism" (41). He thinks McKay's poetry emanates not from a sense of race but rather from his shocked sense of fair play:

> It is not that McKay is not reacting to Negro suffering. It is
> rather that he is meeting America's challenge as man and
> poet. He meets the challenge which America's hate sets for
> his humanity, and in his resistance he flings back his chal-
> lenge to the forces of hate in America. As poet and man he
> must discipline himself, and this gives to his pain a dignity
> through which his verse sometimes transcends racial protest
> and becomes human protest [47].

This, Drayton concludes, affected his poetry, and explains the apparent ambivalence in his love-hate relationship with America (45). McKay's ambiguous pronouncements have necessitated a full-length inquiry by Robert A. Lee. He examined if a poem should be read as specifically (narrowly) as possible or whether it should be read generally, finding a universal truth from the specific illustrations. Making both a technical and thematic study of the poem he concludes that "from both a sociological and a literary point of view, it is crucial to see what is solely, uniquely, and fundamentally racial in 'If We Must

Die'" (221). Contesting McKay's assertion that the poem is universal in scope, Lee argues that reading "the poem as a generalized statement of human conflict, applicable to any similar context, is to allow sports contests to be a legitimate subject matter of this poem, or, somewhat more seriously, is to say the poem is about the conflict between generations" (221).

It is true that McKay did react to the violent and vituperative racial hatred which he witnessed on the streets of many American cities during his railroad days. For a person brought up in a country where racial animosities were complex and subtle, but rarely violent, the American experience was a rude shock. McKay did respond as a Negro, spitting fire and anger, when his race was being crushed in the primordial violence of American racism. He lashes out at white American oppressors, employing direct images of "hungry dogs" and "monsters," and indirect images of "pack" and "foe" to suggest the brutality of racial oppression. He uses the "hog" image to indicate the oppressed condition of the black man and it becomes a regular trope even in his fictional writings. Though McKay appears to be attacking the unreflecting complacency of the American black in using the trope of "hog," its unpleasant use in *Home to Harlem* betrays his outsider status.

At the same time, words indicating race like *black, colored, Negro*, do not find a place in the poem. Trained to believe that art is universal and above mundane things, McKay was held back from an unqualified identification with his race. The label that he is a race poet shatters his sole ambition of becoming a universal poet — the resolution he made when the Browning Clubs in Jamaica looked him down. After all, the one reason for his leaving Jamaica and coming to America was the quest for recognition as a creative writer. Speaking about McKay's fears of being judged only as a race poet in the context of this poem, Tyrone Tillery says:

> What he desired most in 1919 was to be the "individual soul" who sought what was noblest and best in the life of the individual. He put his faith in the maxim "each soul must save itself," which had expressed his approach to life and literature since his boyhood days in Jamaica [37].

In a strongly worded letter dated 18th June 1928, to Du Bois, for print-
ing his poems in *Crisis* magazine against his wishes, McKay castigates
Du Bois for mixing propaganda with art. There he spells out his objective for writing, which underscores universalism in art:

> My motive for writing was simply that I began in my boy-
> hood to be an artist in words and I have stuck to that in
> spite of the contrary forces and colors of life that I have had
> to contend against through various adventures, mistakes,
> successes, strength and weakness of body that the artist-soul,
> more or less, has to pass through.... Therefore, I should not
> be surprised when you mistake the art of life for nonsense
> and try to pass off propaganda as life in art! [qtd. in Cooper,
> *Passion* 150].

The demanding racial situation in America and his objective of becoming a universal writer created enough friction to affect his writings.
Pulled by these opposing forces of race and universality in art, McKay
was condemned to dwell in ambiguity. It took its toll, affecting both
the content and form of his poetry. McKay's first publication after leaving Jamaica was *Spring in New Hampshire* (1920), a collection of poems
published in England. *Harlem Shadows* (1922), his second collection,
was published later in America, and contained many poems that
appeared in various magazines in the years 1917, 1918 and 1919 in the
United States. The posthumous collection *Selected Poems of Claude
McKay* brings together these two volumes along with his later poems.
The collection is divided into five sections. "Songs for Jamaica" are
chiefly poems of nostalgia for his distant island while "Baptism" and
"Americana" are poems that contain strong racial protest tinged with
his characteristic ambiguity. "Different Places," as the title indicates,
is a celebration of his stay in Russia, Barcelona and north Africa during his long exile. "Amoroso" is a collection of sensual poems that fulfill
McKay's dream of becoming a universal poet. However, of all the sections only "Baptism" and "Americana" received much critical attention
in the African American literary tradition for their supposedly racial
content. The rest were considered either nostalgic poetry about Jamaica,
or irrelevant, because they do not deal with the issues of race.

If "If We Must Die" brought McKay fame and recognition, "Harlem Dancer" and "Invocation" were his earliest publications under his *nom de plume*, "Eli Edwards," in the United States. The poem is the description of a Harlem dancer in a cabaret: "Applauding youths laughed with young prostitutes / And watched her perfect, half-clothed body sway; / Her voice was like the sound of blended flutes / Blown by black players upon a picnic day" (*SP* 61). While giving a graphic description of the dancing woman where "even the girls / Devoured her shape with eager, passionate gaze," McKay subtly highlights the tragedy of that dancer: "But looking at her falsely-smiling face, / I knew her self was not in that strange place" (*SP* 61). Evoking images of sensuous and gay Harlem nightlife, especially cabarets, McKay subtly focuses on the sorrow, the forced circumstances and harsh living conditions of the black women. Those who come to watch and enjoy the "half-clothed bodies" cannot perceive the sad plight of the Harlem dancer. Through these poems, McKay reveals the other, darker side of the Harlem nightlife. "Harlem Dancer" and "Harlem Shadows" both dealing with Harlem prostitution ("the dusky, half-clad girls of tired feet.... The sacred brown feet of my fallen race!") are a continuation of the theme of exploitation of women in cities from his dialect poetry days, as in a "Country Girl." His comparison of the Harlem dancer as "a proudly swaying palm / Grown lovelier for passing through a storm" reveals his longing for the images of the tropical West Indies.

Though "Harlem Dancer" brought McKay immediate recognition as a poet with a "sincere gift," there were dissenters too among his contemporaries, who complained that the poem stimulated an unhealthy obsession with cabarets. His poetical sensibilities and ideas were always radically at odds with the African American intellectuals. McKay's affirmation that it was waste of time to cry "No Segregation!," in his poem "The Negro's Friend," was a slap in the face for organizations like the NAACP, who were fighting against segregation (*SP* 51). He questioned if millions of blacks were gratified if one of them can enter as a guest into a fine "white house" (*SP* 51). Instead, McKay advocated group solidarity and declared that segregation is not the whole sin but that the Negroes need salvation from within (*SP* 51). The poem reveals that McKay was quite constructive regarding segregation. He opposed legal separation of the races but recognized the futility of protesting against it. Instead, he wanted to focus more on a natural racial aggregation based upon common cultural interests and concerns. His ideas were quite advanced for that age.

The two poems "The Lynching" and "The White Fiends" unambiguously reflect McKay's deep anger against the brutal American racism. Employing the crucifixion imagery he depicts America's horrible practice of lynching blacks: "His spirit in smoke ascended to high heaven / His father, by the cruelest way of pain, / Had bidden him to his bosom once again" (SP 37). By making lynching crucifixion, he is reminding America of its perverted Christian ideals. The star that shone on the birth of the Christ is now hovering over the crucifixion scene: "All night a bright and solitary star / (Perchance the one that ever guided him, / Yet gave him up at last to Fate's wild whim) / Hung pitifully o'er the swinging char" (SP 37). "Day dawned," only to reveal "the ghastly body swaying in the sun" (SP 37). Women too "thronged to look, but never a one / Showed sorrow in her eyes of steely blue"(SP 37). Blue eyes, supposedly the symbols of beauty and grace among white women, were consummately reversed by McKay to portray their sadistic pleasure in lynching black men. He even reverses the image of childhood innocence: "And little lads, lynchers that were to be, / Danced around the dreadful thing in fiendish glee" (SP 37).

"The White Fiends" is an obvious reply to this "fiendish glee" (SP 70). Unlike many of his poems, where his universalism forces him to play hide and seek from identifying with race, McKay in these two poems openly denounces white racism, embracing his race. Hence, with a welcome relief, Blyden Jackson thinks that the poem "The White Fiends" is not like the sonnet "If We Must Die" as it "cannot be separated from its racial connotations" (45). He takes up, one after the other, stereotypes attributed to blacks by the white civilization and reverses them:

> Think you I am not fiend and savage too?
> Think you I could not arm me with a gun

And shoot down ten of you for every one
Of my black brothers murdered, burnt by you?
Be not deceived, for every deed you do
I could match — out-match: am I not Afric's son,
Black of that black land where black deeds are done? [*SP* 38].

McKay plays on two of the most prevalent stereotypes associated with blacks in the Western culture: Blacks as savage and black as evil. He momentarily indulges the irrational fears of white America, illustrating his ability to carry out all the evil deeds that were wrongfully attributed to his race. But indicating a divinely ordained purpose he desists from using violence: "But the Almighty from the darkness drew / My soul and said: Even thou shalt be a light / Awhile to burn on the benighted earth" (*SP* 38). His "dusky face" is "set among the white" to prove himself "of higher worth." James Keller is of the opinion that this "higher worth" "involves the laboring in his poetic craft, a task whose goal is to effect positive social change through creation, not violence" (451). The creation here is a sonnet, a product of the European aristocratic tradition. By containing his anger within the designated number of lines dictated by Western literary conventions, the poet subtly reveals his own cultural superiority to those who oppress him and his race. By working within those same practices and beliefs that constituted the heart of European cultural pride, McKay could portray himself as the successor to the great European aesthetic practices and represent the dominant power structure as vulgar and violent (451). In the larger context of McKay's life and artistic achievement, this poem can also be read as an assertion that however provoked into anger, he will not fall into the racial groove, but will prove his worth, if not his superiority, as a creative artist. The "higher" worth will be shown not merely by using the sonnet form but by achieving universal values in his poetry like the best icons of the European culture: "Before the world is swallowed up in night" he says, he will "go forth, go forth" "to show" his "little lamp" (*SP* 38).

In the next poem, "In Bondage," he did try to "go forth" but much to his dismay found himself bound up with his race. McKay's ambiguous situation is very poignantly disclosed in this poem. As he attempts to soar up and up like an English Romantic poet he finds himself tied down to his race. "I would be wandering in distant fields" he begins his poem, where all the living things, man, beast and bird live leisurely (*SP* 39). He will spend life by singing songs, because life is greater than the thousand wars that men wage for it. He wants to shine like the eternal stars, after all that glitters today is reduced to ashes (*SP* 39). "But," he says very painfully, "I am bound with you in your mean graves, / O black men, simple slaves of ruthless slaves" (*SP* 39). He almost seems to be castigating his race — the simple slaves — for destroying his utopian state. Had he not been bound up with his race, perhaps he "would be singing, far away" and like his literary model Shelley in his skylark poem would have been "singing still dost soar, and soaring ever singest," in "profuse strains of unpremeditated art"(624). Unfortunately, his romantic dream of "wandering in distant fields" was shattered, as he was tied down by his race. The race and its problems, to which he cannot turn a blind eye, seem to weigh heavily on his heart, choking his artistic breath. It is nothing surprising if the colonial writer who revered English romantic poets, and was desirous of following, if not imitating them, complains so unabashedly that he was bound up by his race. It is also not surprising, if Afro-American critics complain that McKay had no consideration for race, but always strived to earn recognition for his talent as a writer by trying to place art and intellect above color.

A similar theme of chastising his race runs in his poem "The Wise Men of the East,"[11] written during the last years of his life. Ethiopia, he proudly declares, was a great black empire before Rome, and became the first Christian nation (*SP* 48). From such a "high place," the black men sunk to "gutter-low" as they grew drunk with power (*SP* 48). The poem "Africa" has a similar chastising tone: "Honor and Glory, Arrogance and Fame! / They went. The darkness swallowed thee again" (*SP* 40). This illustrates how the colonial was beguiled into thinking about his own race by his Western education. James R. Giles too finds the tone of both poems peculiarly stern and chastising. He thinks that McKay is taking the position of an Old Testament prophet proclaiming that Africa's twentieth century suffering is due to its past sins (53). Though the "chastizing" tone of the poem pricked Giles, he did not realize that the "Old Testament prophet" was only a colonial with a disguised adherence to Western values, reproaching his own race for all its misery.

Even in "Enslaved," a poem marked for its triteness, where he speaks openly of his long-suffering race and its enslavement, he seems to accept the superiority of the Western civilization. McKay's "heart grows sick with hate" when his race was not only "despised, oppressed / Enslaved and lynched," but denied a "human place / In the great life line of the Christian West" (*SP* 42). Ironically, he seems to forget that it was the same "great life line of the Christian West" which not only denied humanity to his race but "despised ... and lynched" it (*SP* 42). He goes on to say that his race was not only fleeced in the country of its birth but "disinherited" and left with "no home on earth" (*SP* 42). Here the use of "Black Land" is immediately preceded by the sentence that his race was "denied a human place / In the great life line of the Christian West," giving an impression that the author is contrasting the two civilizations (*SP* 42). This creates a doubt to the reader whether the "Black Land" is merely the land of the blacks or is it the "black land where black deeds are done?" as they are now "denied a human place in the great life line of the Christian West" (*SP* 42). Anyhow, he cries "from the dark depth" of his "soul" "To the avenging angel to consume / The white man's world of wonders" in the "earth's vast womb" (*SP* 42).

That the white man has created "wonders" and that McKay had had a great awe for them was shown in another poem, "America." Like in the earlier poem, here too McKay wants to "see" America's "might and granite wonders" sink "in the sand" by the "unerring hand" of "Time," reminding us of Shelley's poem "Ozymandias." McKay's allusion to Shelley's poem serves to undermine America's cultural pride, reminding the young and arrogant country that it too will inevitably sink but not before admitting its grandeur. Seen in the context of both these sonnets one cannot escape the conclusion that McKay had immense esteem for the "great life line of the Christian West's" achievements, both in culture and architecture.

Only in "Look Within" and "Tiger," written during the last years of his life, in a Catholic asylum, does McKay attack the dubious policies of the United States of America without any ambiguity, but within the guarded walls of the European cultural apparatus — the sonnet form. In sharp contrast to the poems written at the beginning of his poetic career, these sonnets could perform their function of subversion in an unqualified manner. By the persistent use of Biblical allusions, McKay could point out to the paradox in America's avowed ideals. In the first lines of "Look Within" McKay refers to America's war with Germany and Japan in fighting racism and fascism, while its own fifteen million Negroes are praying for salvation at home from its fascist policies. By paraphrasing the gospels, the poet chastises the American power structure, which closed its "eyes not to perceive the fact," to "...Remove the beam / (Nearly two thousand years since Jesus spoke) / From your own eyes before the mote you deem / It proper from your neighbor's to extract!" (*SP* 44).

McKay thus harnesses religion in order to demonstrate the legitimacy of his cause and to portray the oppressive American government as inconsistent with Christian tenets. Similarly, in "Tiger" McKay exposes the duplicity of the America's new diplomatic initiatives with Europe, Africa and Asia, while it is destroying the Negro, physically and spiritually at home. While portraying itself as a model democratic nation, the American power structure is covertly trying to expand its political and economic influence. He transforms the stripes of the American flag into the stripes of the predatory tiger and says, like in his poem "America," that the white man is a tiger at his throat sucking blood. Like a true colonial in rebellion, McKay hits hard on the dominant culture's inherent ideological contradictions in tropical animal imagery. McKay employs images of hunting, bestiary, violence and diabolism throughout his poetry and fiction to portray the oppression and exploitation of the black people. Tigers, packs of wolves, hungry dogs, monsters, and fiends are all symbols of white oppression drinking blood at the black man's throat.

The theme of exposing the duplicity of the American political practices continues in "The Negro's Tragedy." The poet openly identifies with his race emphasizing that only a "thorn-crowned Negro" can understand the Negro's suffering (*SP* 50). Employing a series of images, he expresses his uninhibited sympathy for the Negro cause. He feels the Negro's tragedy as it binds him like a heavy iron chain. He wants to heal the wounds of the Negro because he knows the keenness of his pain. He seems to anticipate *The Invisible Man* of Ralph Ellison when he speaks of the "shroud of night" that hides the Negro from the rest of the humanity (*SP* 50). The final couplet of the sestet iterates the theme in "Look Within" and "Tiger." He sneers at the American statesmen trying to set things right in other countries, while their own minority was crushed both physically and spiritually.

"The White City" and "The White House" are two examples of how the poet is trying to contain his rage, and retain his humanity, at the racial atrocities committed by white America: "Deep in the secret chambers of my heart / I muse my life-long hate, and without flinch / I bear it nobly as I live my part" (*SP* 74). The poem shows how his disgust against the oppressive practices of white America inspired and gave him an identity: "My being would be a skeleton, a shell, / If this dark passion that fills my every mood, / And makes my heaven in the white world's hell, / Did not forever feed me vital blood." Giles' interpretation that the "positive facts of its creation rests upon essentially negative emotions" which are very much "relevant to much black literature" is quite right (48).

"The White House"[12] also stands witness to McKay's perseverance in the face of vituperative racial discrimination in America. In bold and brilliant images of violence, he shows how the Negro masses were marginalized and excluded from the mainstream American life of capital and industry: "Your door is shut against my tightened face, / And I am sharp as steel with discontent" (*SP* 78). Evoking the familiar image of a lost, excluded and alienated black man loitering on the streets of any American city, McKay says that even if his "passion rends" his "vitals," as the "shuttered door of glass," signifying affluence "boldly shines" in his (Negro masses') excluded face, he still has the "courage and the grace / To bear ... anger proudly and unbent" (*SP* 78). Like in the poem "To the White Fiends," he takes up the word "savage," attributed to blacks by the white power structure, and reverses its connotation: "The pavement slabs burn loose beneath my feet, / A chafing savage down the decent street." Juxtaposing the words "savage" and "decent" McKay creates effective irony. McKay could thus show that true evil savagery is at the basis of the "decent" white establishment but not in the dehumanized and discriminated "savage" (*SP* 78). Keeping his anger in check, "Oh, I must search for wisdom every hour," the poet narrator underlines the rationality and control of the black man, in contrast to the irrational "potent poison of" the white man's hate (*SP* 78).

If one takes into consideration the entire collection of his poems, written in America, these sonnets seem to be more occasional explosions than showing an undeviating attention to issues of race. Indeed, he admits in his autobiography that a series of sonnets expressing his "bitterness, hate and love" for America were written when he was insulted at a play, "He who Gets Slapped," in his sub-editorship days at the *Liberator*. That they were mere isolated explosions is proved when McKay finds enough leisure to write poems about nature in the "white world's hell" like "Morning Joy," "Winter in the Country," "To Winter" and on sundry topics like "French Leave" and "On the Road." Those sonnets with supposedly revolutionary content easily fall into the larger framework of McKay's poetic consciousness, betraying a universal poet at work rather than a poet with revolutionary ardor.

No poem portrays more exquisitely the ambiguous situation that McKay was caught in than "Outcast." The division and resultant acute pain that he was undergoing as a black man, caught between two cultures, surfaces in a poem. As Lloyd Brown emphasized, "Outcast" is McKay's most effective analysis of that duality (59). His "spirit, bondaged by the body, longs for the dim regions" from where his forefathers came and where his "soul would sing forgotten jungle songs," had not "the great western world" held him "in fee" (*SP* 41). By using the words *dim, jungle* and *dark* for Africa, McKay seems to validate the dominant culture's opinion about Africa. The poet speaker "would sing forgotten jungle songs" and "would *go back to darkness*[13] and to peace" (*SP* 41). This emphasizes its obverse statement that going "forward" is "light" and light is Europe falling into the trap of the imperial discourse. Africa is only a jungle where people sing only jungle songs compared to the *great* Western world that now "holds" him "in fee." Africa may have been a "cradle of power" once, but "darkness swallowed" it again. Moreover, how can a poet writing in the standard language and traditional form of the master go back and sing jungle songs in Africa?

He can "never hope for full release / while to its alien gods" he bends his "knee" (*SP* 41). The alien gods are the icons of the dominant culture he now follows. He has already pledged his soul to them, and so like Faustus he laments: "Something in me is lost, forever lost, / Some vital thing has gone out of my heart" (*SP* 41). As he lost his soul, he is now "a thing." "Thingification" of the colonial, as Aime Cesaire would say in *Discourse on Colonialism*, is now complete as he "was born, far from" his "native clime," "Under the white man's menace, out of time" (*SP* 41).

McKay's literary consciousness, disposed always around two poles, manifested in a variety of binary units in this collection. The most notable one is city versus country, which can be traced back to his dialect poetry. Before McKay left Jamaica, the remote Clarendon Hills symbolized the pastoral image in contrast to Kingston, the corrupt city. After he left Jamaica, the entire island became the distant countryside in contrast to Western cities like New York and London. "When Dawn Comes to the City" is a fine example of this pattern. The city, here New York, is immediately contrasted with Jamaica, symbolized as the Country in the next stanza. If the first stanza describes the city street early in the morning: "The tired cars go grumbling by, / The moaning, groaning cars, / ... Tis dawn, dawn in New York," the second leaps to "...the heart of island of the sea / Where the cocks are crowing, crowing, crowing, / And the hens are cackling in the rose-apple tree" (*SP* 62). "There," says the poet speaker "oh there! on the island of the sea, / There would I be at dawn" (*SP* 62).

The distant Jamaica remained McKay's imaginative safe retreat. The poems in, "Songs for Jamaica" were indeed songs of and for Jamaica penned by an exile Jamaican. For the typical exiled, the absent landscape of Jamaica remained a permanent backdrop in his consciousness, against which everything would be compared and evaluated. The Jamaican landscape was not only vividly remembered in the "Flame Heart," which was written in England, but the poet seems to have become sentimental when he scolds himself for forgetting it:

So much I have forgotten in ten years,
So much in ten brief years! I have forgot
What time the purple apples come to juice,
And what month brings the shy forget-me-not [*SP* 13].

The poem acquires its significance from the fact that it was written in the mother country. It appears that time, distance and bitter experiences in England had had their influence in making Jamaica an idyllic countryside. Hence, when the poet speaker in "Flame Heart" concludes, emphasizing "we were so happy, happy, I remember, / Beneath the poinsettia's red in warm December," he seems to set off the unhappy present. However, one can easily trace the influence of English romantics in these poems. The triteness of language, and the use of worn out clichés, remind the reader of Wordsworth not at his best.

"Tropics in New York" also has the same urgency and immediacy as almost to displace the New York scene, the immediate locale and the subject of the poem. The poem portrays powerfully McKay's longing for the absent landscape of Jamaica. Quite movingly, he brings out the pain of the exile when he longs "for the old and familiar ways": "My eyes grew dim, and I could no more gaze; / A wave of longing through my body swept" (*SP* 13). "Home" and "mother" have significant associations for the exile. They are generally synonymous and signify the exile's nostalgic longing. They are important landmarks around which revolves the exiled writer's imagination. Finding a home, or returning to home, remained an important motif of McKay's fiction as well as poetry, like many third world exiles. The section concludes with the poem "I Shall Return," promising himself that he will return: "I shall return again, I shall return / ... To ease my mind of long, long years of pain" (*SP* 32). As is evident from his life, McKay neither returned, nor eased his pain. The poem heightens the predicament of the poet, who dreams to return, but never endeavors to return. He can return only in flights of imagination, which he did continuously throughout his literary career, much to the amazement of his admirers and critics. His literary writings became the battleground for reconciling these warring identities. Unfortunately, without considering this background, many Afro-American critics, both McKay's contemporaries and later scholars, expected him to immerse himself in the Afro-American milieu. When he was found incompatible, his fellow Harlem writers, who were not seized of this unique dilemma, taxed him.

McKay's dream of becoming a universal poet seems to have been fulfilled in the "Amoroso" section. Highly erotic in imagery, McKay has almost outdone Donne, the English metaphysical poet. The metaphysical imagery as Giles has pointed out is "not inherently black" but was "masterfully handled" (63). These poems make clear that McKay has not gone to his folk roots in celebrating the theme of erotic love. His models were undisputedly English writers. The poem "Flower of Love" builds upon the imagery of sexual intercourse: "Uncovered on your couch of figured green, / Here let us linger indivisible. / The portals of your sanctuary unseen / Receive my offering, yielding unto me" (*SP* 97). Even the fall of snow acquires a symbolic significance when combined with eroticism. The snowfall has a special association for the tropical colonial. It reveals the ideological influence of the imperial education on the colonial subjects. In his autobiography, *My Green Hills of Jamaica*, he remembers seeing pictures of snow falling in the elementary text books, and English, German and Dutch children playing in it. Naturally, he celebrates it in one of his most romantic poems.

Another important section often neglected is "Different Places," a small collection of poems that McKay wrote about the different places he visited in Europe and Africa during his wandering career. Though the poem "Moscow" reflects McKay's admiration for that city, it also reveals his complex relationship with the Soviet Union. The opening line has a sad and sympathetic note for the death of the old pompous Moscow, revealing McKay's romantic sensibility. Even if its pompous days ended, McKay could see "a bright Byzantine fair, / Of jewelled buildings, pillars, domes and spires" (*SP* 83). As he remembers that he was the guest of Communist Russia, he starts praising that "the color red" was reigning all over, making it orthodox Marxist verse. Dichotomy, the typical feature of his poetry, affects even in this poem. McKay the poet seems to have dominated initially, but his political affiliations, at that moment, have certainly deflected him from indulging in the purely picturesque. The entire collection, with a few exceptions, is undermined by divided loyalties, which he could not resolve as a poet: between racial affiliation and universalism of art, between political affiliations and the purely romantic.

Form is another aspect of his writing, where McKay betrayed his colonial background. The choice of the sonnet, a product of the aristocratic European tradition, to pour out his invective surprised many of his contemporaries. Those were the times when the young literary radicals challenged older schools of writing. James Oppenheim, the editor of *Seven Arts* magazine, who advocated a new course in style and content, rejected McKay's poems for their sonnet form, though he liked their spirit. McKay expressed his frustration in a letter to Spingarn about Oppenheim's stand, saying, that in the context of his training the form was correct. After futile attempts to use free form, McKay admitted sonnet suited him for a moment's thought. He felt that the tight rhythmic and metric forms checked his diffusive and repetitive tendency.[14]

Even the latter day critics like James R. Giles think that McKay's use of traditional poetic conventions has imposed avoidable limitations on his outcry. He thinks that the "conflict between McKay's passionate resentment of racist oppression and his victorianism in form and diction creates a unique kind of tension in many of his poems, which weakens their ultimate success" (42). Hence, Giles believed that McKay's fiction, not his poetry, represents the major achievement of his career (Preface 9). Although as a poet, he was more influenced by English literary masters like Shakespeare, Milton and Wordsworth, McKay as a novelist was more receptive to the influences of contemporary white prose innovators and was willing to experiment with inherently black form and language.

The poem "If We Must Die" had an impeccable English form with the structure of three quatrains and a final couplet giving the conventional effect of sequential argument and concluding moral apothegm. McKay used the elements of prosody to perfection, constructing a finely wrought sonnet making true the quote "more English than English." Critics like Robert Felgar, who think that form and content mutually accommodate each other, making it a "symbiotic relationship," consider the use of European art forms by black writers as "apparently unconscious testimony to the power of white culture" (28). For him the uniquely Black experience is threatened and bleached when poured into Occidental molds" (29). Much of the structural strength of black culture, he says, is in the oral tradition, in spirituals, the blues, jazz, and the black church from which he suggests that black writers should draw "organizational techniques to shape Afro-American experiences in literature" (29). It was only Jean Toomer and Langston Hughes who experimented with configurations which are not dissonant to content.

The use of traditional literary forms by McKay, critics like James R. Keller think, is not merely the result of the accident of his education but has a purpose. The purpose is to subvert the dominant culture from within, exploiting its cultural apparatuses. By choosing a verse form that signifies the aristocratic European literary tradition to carry his politically volatile subject matter, McKay seems to be leading the battle with the dominant culture on its own turf. Houston A. Baker, Jr., too has a similar opinion when he says that McKay's "sonnets," like Countee Cullen's "ballads," are just as much mastered *masks* as the minstrel manipulations of Booker T. Washington and Charles Chestnutt are:

> The trick of McKay and Cullen was what one of my colleagues calls the denigration of form — a necessary ("forced," as it were) adoption of the standard that results in an effective *blackening*.... Hence, one would have to present *recognizably* standard forms and get what black mileage one could out of subtle, or, by contrast, straining (like McKay's rebellious cries) variations and deepenings of these forms. If the younger generation was to proffer "artistic" gifts, such gifts had to be recognizable as "artistic" by Western, formal standards and not simply as unadorned or primitive *folk* creations [85–86].

He thus gains a voice among those whose project of subjugation has been to efface the native cultural heritage of African Americans and to silence the discourse of dissent (Keller 448). Perhaps that is the reason he chose white magazines and journals to launch his tirade. What can be the best form but the sonnet to gain access into the group? This is akin to the stand taken by Althusser and Pecheux when they speak about the subject exploiting the "contradiction-unevenness-subordination between those regions that constitute what is at stake in the *ideological class struggle*" (Pecheux 99).[15]

While the application of conservative European form can be subversive, Keller's contention that the choice is "not merely an accident of McKay's education" but is "specifically selected," is doubtful (448). As a colonial who came to consciousness within the traditional English literary canon, he felt the sonnet more comfortable to work with. McKay himself admitted in his letter to W.S. Braithwaite that he found the sonnet form admirable for a moment's thought after trying free form without success (qtd. in Tillery 29). Gary Smith wonders how these New Negro writers like McKay and Countee Cullen were drawn to the four hundred year old European sonnet "as opposed to folk forms more native to the black American experience, such as the antebellum sermon, folk songs, blues, and spirituals" (2). To answer this paradox Smith goes back to their respective backgrounds and rightly points out McKay's colonial education, which stressed traditional English verse and persuaded students that the English Romantics were the only *real*[16] poets (3). Chauhan rightly concludes that if McKay's bitterness was the result of his experience as a subaltern in a British colony, the sonnet form was the result of his formal education in the master's classics (74). This rare amalgam of expressing anger against white racism in European forms affirms McKay's ambiguous condition as a black man brought up in a European tradition.

Though stifled by his colonial sensibility, McKay's American poetry brought to the American Negro literature a new vigor, liberating it from the plantation school. Some of his poems did give a clarion call to the new Negro movement and inaugurated the Harlem Renaissance. To say that his poetry is beset by his colonial sensibility is not to deprecate his contribution to the movement. He did carve out a path, which black writers all over the world and not only the African American could follow. McKay undoubtedly looked forward to, if not anticipated, the angry black poetry of Baraka and Lee. From poetry of rebellion, McKay moved to a more positive affirmation of black life in fiction. After his visit to England and his later exile to Europe and Africa, McKay turned to the black common folk and to a rural Jamaica idyll in his later writings. The painful evolution of the colonial to reconcile his warring identities had already started.

— 4 —

The Exile: Is Harlem Home?

McKay arrived in France in the fall of 1923 after his "magic pilgrimage" to Russia. He reached Paris, the mecca of America expatriates in the post war years. He arrived with immense physical pain due to syphilis, compounded by the difficulty in procuring enough money for his treatment. His attempts to raise money by selling poetry to the magazines were not encouraging, as living solely by writing poetry was seldom an attractive option for writers. Hard pressed, but resolute that his creative work should pay, McKay eventually turned to prose. Misery appears to have diluted his opinion that a writer should write merely for the love of writing. An artist who believed throughout his life that poetry was his forte found it difficult to switch over to prose. McKay from his early literary career was encouraged by his patrons, Jekyll and later Eastman, that he was a gifted poet. Even though he read prose for his pleasure, he was ignorant of modern prose techniques.

Forced by the circumstances, McKay finally turned to prose and planned a novel on Harlem society along with other short stories. Initially he wrote some short stories but found it difficult to sell them. Even after the best efforts of his friends like Walter White, no publisher took them. As his friends in the United States kept on informing him that the Negro artist was very much in vogue, McKay went ahead with the novel he planned. That was the time when Harlem Renaissance was picking up momentum. However, McKay never sought any advice from his black artist friends regarding style or content, except for some practical matters regarding publishing. In his characteristic way, he turned to established white writers like H.L. Mencken and Sinclair Lewis for technical assistance, and for inspiration to D.H. Lawrence, Ernest Hemingway and James Joyce.

McKay was one of the earliest black writers after the First World War to take temporary residence in Paris. Countee Cullen, Walter White, Langston Hughes, and Gwendolyn Bennett were among the other prominent African American exiles between the two World Wars. For different reasons, France, particularly Paris, held much attraction for both black and white expatriates from America, including the West Indies, and other parts of Europe. The white expatriates from America sought Paris as an antidote to the mechanized life that was hostile to the arts in their own country. Gertrude Stein observes: "The reason why all of us naturally began to live in France is because France has scientific methods, machines and electricity, but does not really believe that these things have anything to do with the real business of living. Life is tradition and human nature" (Stein 2). The Lost Generation — Ernest Hemmingway, Ezra Pound, Stein, and Fitzgerald from the United States, James Joyce, and other writers from the continent — drifted to France in search of their existential selves. If exile was a fashionable theme of search for the lost soul to the metropolitan writers, it was also an escape from the oppression of color for the black writers from the United States and other European colonies. It was the general impression that France was colorblind that attracted many black writers.[1] McKay too grasped the different reasons for migrating to France when he says that he never considered himself identical with the white expatriates:

> It was the problem of color. Color-consciousness was the
> fundamental of my restlessness. And it was something with
> which my white fellow-expatriates could sympathize but
> which they could not altogether understand. For they were
> not black like me. Not being black and unable to see deep
> into the profundity of blackness, some even thought that I
> might have preferred to be white like them. They couldn't
> imagine that I had no desire merely to exchange my black
> problem for their white problem [LW 245].

Though he kept himself distant from cults like those that the one Gertrude Stein enjoyed among the literary circles, McKay took interest in the new works published by expatriate writers like Hemmingway and James Joyce. Joyce's *Ulysses* was published when he arrived in Paris. Though he had great respect for Joyce as a "seer and Olympian" he preferred D.H. Lawrence, who was, however, not part of the Paris expatriate scene (*LW* 247). Indeed, McKay felt that Lawrence was not only more modern than James Joyce, but closer to his own outlook of life. He says:

> In D.H. Lawrence I found confusion — all of the ferment
> and torment and turmoil, the hesitation and hate and alarm,
> the sexual inquietude and the incertitude of this age, and the
> psychic and romantic groping for a way out [*LW* 247].

McKay's friends in Paris believed that he preferred Lawrence because of his dissident views. But Lawrence's appeal for McKay, Wayne Cooper says, lies in his "compulsive and impassioned struggle to overcome the psychological traps that threatened to imprison and destroy man's direct appreciation of life and its mysteries in the modern age" (*Sojourner* 208). McKay, Hamalian asserts, believed that Lawrence's distinguishing trait, mirroring his own, was a "psychological restlessness that drove him steadily towards artistic achievement and away from the marginal existence of his natal community [i]n his own life" (583). Though Lawrence came from a very different culture, he resembled McKay as a writer in fundamental parental loyalties, social status, and young manhood. Cooper, perhaps for this reason, calls this a "psychic kinship" (*Sojourner* 208). Just as Lawrence hated the idea of returning to class-conscious England to live, McKay dreaded the prospect of facing the pervasive racial oppression of America, especially after he had been virtually lionized during his stay in the Soviet Union.[2]

McKay's first two attempts in publishing novels on Harlem society and blacks on the railroad had failed. Having failed to live on his writings, McKay did many odd jobs from posing nude as a model to working as a servant from 1925 to 1926. Finally, in 1928, *Harper* published his first novel, *Home to Harlem*, which was an instant success. The lower-class black American life, which he thought of using for short stories, was the principal focus of this novel. Carl Van Vechten, before McKay, prepared the ground by portraying lower-class Harlem life in his novel *Nigger Heaven,* published in 1925. Though Vechten's book has roused loud uproar and protest from the conservative sections of both black and white societies, it was generally hailed as a realistic portrayal of black life. It paved the way for McKay's candid portrayal of lower-class life in Harlem. However, McKay takes pains to explain that he did not write this novel just "because Carl Van Vechten wrote *Nigger Heaven" (LW* 283). The pattern tale of the book, he asserts, was written for his collection of short stories in 1925 under the same title. It was on the advice of his literary agent that McKay expanded a short story "Home to Harlem" into the present novel.

The novel has a simple plot to which are stitched various episodes depicting lower-class Harlem life. It opens with Jake, a purely "instinctual" man, eagerly stoking back home to Harlem after desertion from a black work crew in wartime Brest. Jake readily finds a prostitute who returns his payment as a gift. Unable to forget the first night rendezvous, Jake starts searching for her, leading the readers into cabarets, dives and house parties. He later joins the railroad, like his author, as a waiter. On the railroad, he meets a Haitian emigrant, Ray, who is bent on writing. They soon become friends; tutoring each other in the particular aspects of life, they are interested. Jake takes the reluctant Ray to brothels, while Ray lectures Jake about black civilization. After many episodes, Ray feels frustrated by life in the black belt and leaves Harlem for Europe. Jake finally finds his sweetheart, but finds himself involved in a fight over the girl with Zeddy, his friend. So both Jake and his sweetheart have to leave Harlem, in search of a home in Chicago.

The novel marks a paradigm shift in McKay's literary career as he started to take on the duality that structured his literary consciousness. He became fully aware of his ambivalent state that marked his poetry and life and tried to come to grips with it by fictionalizing and debating through his protagonists: Jake and Ray in *Home to Harlem*, Ray and Banjo in *Banjo* and Bita Plant in *Banana Bottom*. The first two novels are a platform for McKay's philosophical and artistic struggle to find a viable identity for the black man in the Western world. The use of double protagonists, one representing instinct and the other intellect, and the long debates concerning blackness and whiteness in the first two novels, reveal McKay's struggle and painful evolution. The debate runs its full course, resolving finally in the last novel *Banana Bottom* through his female character Bita Plant. Giles recognizes this struggle and evolution in McKay, when he says that between *Banjo* and *Banana Bottom*, McKay arrived at a racial position with which he was at ease. This newly found ideological maturity enabled him to write a novel aesthetically much superior to the first two (72–73).

Initially, McKay tried to project what George E. Kent. calls, "positive *niggerhood*," which stems from his evolving belief that the black community possesses the inherent strength requisite for spiritual progress (*Soul* 36). He turned to the Negro masses in the United States that he knew very closely when he worked along with them as janitor, porter etc. McKay was firmly convinced that it was the lower classes, represented by such characters as Jake and Banjo, that refused to "go down and disappear under the serried crush of trampling white feet" (*BJ* 314). The negation of identity of the black man in the West had made it imperative for him to stress racial consciousness among his people. Hence, in the first two novels he reached a state which Pecheux calls counter-identification, where he advocated black pride, which projected a thesis of positive black and negative white values.

However, this mode was fraught with dangers. As Pecheux points out, counter-identification implies the danger of counter-determination; that is, it may inadvertently support what it seeks to oppose by confirming a symmetry between the two. McKay's projection of the ordinary black as warm, with an assertion of spirit in the face of pain, a bounce and spontaneity of feelings and emotions, and possessed of an instinctive healthiness and innocence, implies the assertion of its obverse for the white man. In his attempt to carve out an identity for the black man he attributed certain essential characteristics to whites — materialism, sexual inhibition, greed — and then claimed their opposites — affinity with nature, sexual naturalness, and generosity — as aspects of the black soul. Portraying Jake in the Harlem backdrop with these attributes, he unconsciously reinscribed certain Western values by portraying women as a threat to black masculinity.

To define black consciousness, McKay turned completely to urban lower-class Negro folk in Harlem for his material, while his contemporary African American writers like Langston Hughes, Jean Toomer, Zora Neale Hurston, and Rudolph Fisher turned conspicuously to the rural, especially Southern, African American folk roots. The Dixie, the land of spirituals, sermons, work songs, blues and children's games was the chief resource for their writings. Though McKay celebrated African American music while portraying the urban lower-class folk life, his approach is that of an outsider and of a colonial. Many psychological slips in the novel reveal his superior West Indian attitude, when he describes the underground life of Harlem. It is impossible to expect McKay, a writer with a colonial mindset, drawing literary inspiration from Anglo-Saxon masters, to adopt the literary genealogy of his African American peers. Yuan Wen Chi too asserts: "Throughout his career, McKay remained an outsider. His experiences of doing various odd jobs enabled him to have a better understanding of the thought, emotion, and sense of solidarity and brotherhood among black people around the world. But he still had some difficulty in identifying himself whole-heartedly with the life of the drinking bout and cabaret of the working class" (105). He portrays the lower-class life with all the sympathy and pride of a black writer, but turns and mocks at them with his master's voice.

Wayne Cooper and other African American scholars, while trying to locate McKay as a New Negro writer, have erroneously equated McKay's "discovery of the folk" with that of Jean Toomer and his peers (Cooper, *Phylon* 303). Wayne Cooper arrived at this opinion by equating McKay's migration from Jamaica to New York with the Negro peoples' migration in the twenties from the rural South to the urban North. Although Cooper recognized in his essay that McKay's "career differed from that of the typical Negro writer of the twenties," he felt that McKay "represented much that was characteristic of the New Negro." He thought that McKay's movement from rural Jamaica to the big city and the literary world of the twenties was itself symbolic of the larger movement by Negro people from the rural South to the broader horizons of the urban North (Cooper 305–306). This movement may appear similar on the surface but at a deeper level, it is as much different as the topography of Jamaica is from the American mainland.

McKay's portrayal of the Harlem lower-class life has generated great controversy, with much of the African American old guard denouncing it as exotic and sensuous. W.E.B. Du Bois, the proponent of the "Talented Tenth," was truly appalled by it. In his review of *Home to Harlem,* he dismissed the book, saying that it "nauseates" him, and "after the dirtier parts of its filth" he felt "distinctly like taking a bath" (*Crisis* 202). The book's popularity too has added fuel to the fire.[3] For the conservative black intellectuals it was mere Van Vechtenism. Echoing them, Du Bois concluded that McKay had set out to cater to the prurient demands of the white folk. Even later literary historians like Huggins held a similar opinion: "Ironically, despite its disparagement of white values and commerce, the novel became a best seller precisely because it pandered to commercial tastes by conforming to the sensationalism demanded by the white vogue in black primitivism" (126). Indeed, for many critics, Jake was a carefree hedonist with a tremendous sexual appetite, fitting the white man's racially and socially stereotyped view of the black male. Hence, many of McKay's contemporaries, including his fellow West Indian and nationalist Marcus Garvey, charged that he was confirming the white man's fantasies that a black man was a slothful, sexual animal. He made a full-page scathing attack on McKay's novel:

> Our race, within recent years, has developed a new group of writers who have been prostituting their intelligence under the directions of the White man, to bring out and show up the worst traits of our people. Several of these writers are American and West Indian Negroes. They have been writing books, novels and poems, under the advice of White publishers to portray to the world the looseness, laxity and immorality that are peculiar to our group [1].

No doubt Garvey's criticism is vituperative and exaggerated, but if one considers the ideological climate that McKay and his fellow writers aspiring for literary success were operating in, one may find it difficult to refute the charge entirely. Black writers had to contend with many of the constraints that the ruling literary practices of the 1920s and 1930s had imposed on them. A popular but new and repressive image of the African American had developed as white intellectuals began to respond to the human consequences of mass, modern, industrial society culminating in the disorder and chaos brought by World War I. These intellectuals started using Freudian psychology to interpret their predicament and found that mechanization was stifling them from attaining happiness. They came to believe that if they could strip away these "civilizing" and mechanizing influences, they too could enjoy life uninhibited like the "primitive" African. The black man, who retained the primitive, natural and uncorrupted values as against the white man who, like Alfred Prufrock,[4] counted his life with "coffee spoons," became their salvation (*Norton Anthology* 994). They saw the Afro-American life as immediate, instinctive, and honest, and believed that all aspects of the Afro-American life — music, dance, art — uncoiled deep inner tensions. Indeed Carl Van Vechten was one such white writer who consciously promoted this cult in his writings.[5]

As an expatriate in Paris, McKay was well aware that his fellow white expatriate writers were alienated individuals trying to flee from the dehumanizing grasp of Western civilization. He was also well aware that these writers were cultivating primitivism as a therapeutic alternative to the insidious disease of Western culture, which before the war was hailed as the only recourse to world's salvation (3). As revealed in his poems, McKay is conscious of the evil affects of modern Western civilization — materialism, mechanization, and colonialism. Like his white counterparts, he too believed that the black man retained certain positive primitive values, which he set out to delineate through his protagonists. Moreover, if Afro-American writers were to publish and sell, they had to reproduce this particular image of the black man or derivatives of it. Like many Harlem writers, he was dependent on a direct and indirect patronage system, which only reinforced the reproductions of "primitive" and exotic themes, images and subjects.[6] Any genuine interests, other than those defined by the ideological cultural apparatus that McKay and other Harlem Renaissance writers had, were excluded or ignored. So if the white reading public admired and appropriated the text for "primitive and exotic" reasons, the black intellectual establishment denounced it exactly for the same reasons.

Home to Harlem was published at a time when the cultural New

Negroes like Alain Locke, Du Bois and James Weldon Johnson sincerely hoped that recognition of the black man's artistic ability would bring racial equality. The principal aspiration for most blacks in the twenties was the desire for first-class citizenship. They felt that the deep-rooted white man's notions of black intellectual inferiority was the cause of black oppression. A destruction of these false notion of intellectual inferiority, they believed, would bring about social equality. Therefore, the black culturalists hoped that the sprouting literary movement in Harlem would help blacks to redefine themselves and reshape the American social fabric. The Renaissance, which did not completely repudiate American values and ethics, represented a hope for the integration into the mainstream of American society. This explains Du Bois' theory of the "talented tenth" that would project positive and progressive images of the black man fostering the transformation of the society. For Du Bois and his compatriots, literature constituted a weapon to counter the Darwinian belief that African Americans were congenitally incapable of creating and expressing their own culture. The perception that literature could advance race relations was supported by a broad spectrum of blacks and repeatedly found its way into discussions of the cultural Renaissance. Hence, the movement was institutionally encouraged and directed by leaders of the national civil rights establishment for the supreme purpose of improving race relations.

It was within this context that McKay's novel fell like a hard stone in the Renaissance nest, which was covetously nurtured and guarded by militant culturalists like Du Bois. The reason for McKay's failure in grasping the full significance of the Renaissance lies in his colonial background. His colonial English education had taught him that art should have a universal appeal and should not be limited by race or propaganda. Coming from a society where blacks are a majority, though impoverished and socially and racially deprived, McKay could not empathize with the peculiar minority blacks' aspiration and struggle in the United States for first-class citizenship and the use of art to that end. Though he too was for some sort of black Renaissance, he wanted it to be expressed in pure artistic terms. Moreover, the blossoming of the Renaissance coincided with McKay's exile to Europe and Africa making it even more difficult for him to understand the complexity of the movement. Tillery rightly estimated the reasons for McKay's inability to grasp the full significance of the Renaissance:

> In his view, the Negro Renaissance was simply a social uplift movement, a vehicle to accelerate the pace and progress of "smart Negro society" [94].

The black artist's choice of subject matter provoked a controversial but stimulating debate. It culminated in an open discussion when a symposium was conducted by *Crisis* magazine in 1926 under the title "The Negro in Art: How Shall He Be Portrayed."[7] To the question of whether any artist was under obligation or limitation as to the sort of character s/he portrayed, the overwhelming majority, as expected, said no. However, there is a qualitative distinction in the wording of the replies between black and white respondents. Almost all the white writers expressed an unequivocal no. The black writers too agreed that the artist's freedom could not be impinged but with certain caveats, keeping in mind the peculiar history of the black race in the New World. Walter White, Jessie Fauset, Countee Cullen, and other intellectuals thought that since black literature was still in its nascent stages, and given the continuing problem of race relations, they could not afford the luxury of such impartiality and detachment. They all expressed the fear that inordinate and obsessive attention to lower-class black life would only reinforce the racist attitudes held by many whites. It was just this sort of promotional aspect of art, projecting positive and optimistic images of the black bourgeois, that the English educated black colonial rejected. Defending his choice of portraying lower-class black existence, McKay attacked his critics for their "idea that Negroes in literature and art should be decorous and decorative." He found fault with their inability to "distinguish between the task of propaganda and the work of art"[8] (*Passion* 133–136). Though a few writers like Langston Hughes defended McKay's stand, a majority of his contemporaries felt that he was pandering to the prurient demands of the white readers.

Striving within the upliftment ideology, little did his peers realize that for the black colonial exile, the United States was only another citadel, a more brutal one perhaps, of the perverted Western values. His project was to portray an ideal black man against the inhibiting Western civilization rather than projecting an ideal African American struggling against his peculiar American problems. The whole novel is designed to represent McKay's ideal black manhood. Instinct, innocence, and spontaneity are the hallmarks of his protagonists' life. Jake, a powerfully built, uneducated, and unaspiring black male, who is largely governed by his sexual desires, is the embodiment of that purity which the all-powerful white world is attempting to destroy. Characters like Jake are an antidote to the rotten Western civilization.

To argue that McKay has merely cashed in on the primitive and exotic, reinforcing the racial stereotypes, is to misjudge McKay's artistic ability. He is quite aware of the black stereotypes that the white civilization has imposed as he attempted to reverse them in his poetry. Acknowledging the influence of French expressionists and the "vitalism of D.H. Lawrence and Sherwood Anderson" on McKay, Adam Lively rightly felt that "McKay's primitivism is not merely an aesthetic celebration, but a protest against, and well-defined critique of, the dominant white culture. This quality distinguishes it from the Negrophile exoticism of the 1920s, especially Carl Van Vechten's *Nigger Heaven*"[9] (231). Only the passage of time has helped to erode or modify the hostile critical judgements of the novel.[10] Quoting George Kent, Barksdale says that "critics have come to believe that the racial settings of *Home to Harlem* are positive and racially affirming rather than negative and racially demeaning," capturing the "*elan* of the Black experience in all of its color and rich emotional variety" (339). Calling Jake a good hearted and virile black Tom Jones, Barksdale shows that he is not simply an instinctual and easygoing profligate, but a character symbolizing order. He argues that Jake is a wise primitive who has been blessed with an intuitive sense of order and rarely feels insecure or incapacitated by uncertainty, fear or doubt:

> In this sense he is different from Zeddy, Congo Rose, Billy Biasse, and Ray who either become disconcerted by the disorder surrounding them or deeply involved in that disorder. This is not to say that Jake is an outsider or a neutralist or

an observer who stands apart. Like Ellison's much more intellectualized hero of a later date, Jake participates in the seething disorders that swirl around him, but unlike Ellison's hero he always carefully extricates himself in time to remain his own man. He does not have to suffer the happy accident of falling out of the world of time and space into a hole of self-discovery [340].

Yet, the character of Jake doesn't reach McKay's ideal black manhood. He knew the limitations of mere instinct and primitive values. As a product of Western civilization, he found it difficult to deny some of its positive values. It necessitated the depiction of a contrasting but complimentary character — Ray, the educated expatriate from the colonial West Indies. Ray was not only McKay's spokesperson but also an autobiographical representation. Like McKay, Ray too became a helpless intellectual searching for a viable identity in the Western world, drifting from one country to another, dwelling in a limbo. Jake and Ray stand as representations of McKay's dual personality. Tillery sums up the significance of Jake and Ray to McKay's own predicament and concludes that though McKay lived a Jake-like life and a Ray-like life he was never comfortable with either (85). *Home to Harlem* for him is a biographical statement about McKay's own inner conflicts.

No doubt, the novel bears the imprint of this conflict. It opens with Jake stoking back home on a freighter to Harlem. He is happy that the ship is taking him back to Harlem and to "the brown-skin chippies 'long Lenox Avenue" (*HH* 3). He voluptuously looks forward to his arrival in Harlem and the sexual promises Harlem holds in store for him. He was ecstatic about the tantalizing brown girls rouged and painted like dark pansies:

> Brown flesh draped in soft colorful clothes. Brown lips full and pouted for sweet kissing. Brown breasts throbbing with love. "Harlem for mine!" cried Jake [*HH* 8].

Jake lands in New York and heads straight to Harlem. From here, McKay gives what many of his contemporary critics alleged was a guided tour of the black belt. Jake with his boundless animalistic sexual appetite starts sniffing around the cabarets in Harlem. Like a hound, his eyes are alert as his blood gets hot (*HH* 10). The first night of his arrival finds him with a "tantalizing brown prostitute" who returns his money the next morning. Their encounter in the cabaret, with each shooting shafts at the other with their eyes, reminds one of the many inn scenes in Tom Jones[11] (*HH* 11). The candid portrayal of their rendezvous offended the sensitivities of the black bourgeoisie, provoking their wrath.

An avowed admirer of D.H. Lawrence, McKay certainly had firm convictions regarding matters of sex and love. He appears to have been in complete agreement with Lawrence's central thesis that sex must be more creative than procreative. He illustrates this when Jake after spending the night with Felice wakes up the next morning feeling immensely gratified and happy, even though he didn't have a cent to his name (*HH* 15). Moreover, the fact that Felice, the brown prostitute, returns Jake's $50 bill with a warm note, proves that Jake's sexual encounter on the first night of his arrival in Harlem is healthy and creative, and not based exclusively on commerce. This gesture convinces Jake that he must find Felice, giving a purpose to his otherwise free and aimless life. Just as Felice gave direction to Jake's life, the search for her gave unity to the novel, which would have otherwise been a loose and unconnected variety of episodes. On the journey back toward this "true" woman, Jake has to negotiate the vice and temptations of the city, which are embodied in a series of other women that he meets (Carby 749).

Jake's search for Felice gives McKay opportunity not only to give a peep into the cabarets, the sensual and violent nightlife of Harlem, but also into the social conditions behind them. The Congo was not only "a real throbbing little Africa in New York" and "an amusement place entirely for the unwashed of the Black Belt" but also the place where the "girls coming from the south to try their future in New York always reached" (*HH* 29–30). McKay faithfully represents these marginal sections and captures the black urban society of the 1920's in its formative stages. Those were the times when many black women from the South came to urban centers like New York to escape poverty and persecution. This migration created a moral panic in the conservative sections of both the white and black society, which felt that these female migrants were "sexually degenerate" and posed a danger and threat to the progress of the black race and establishment of respectable urban black middle-class society.

Many texts of that period deal with black female sexuality, but Vechten's *Nigger Heaven* and McKay's *Home to Harlem* are prominent among them, because neither of the authors, says Carby, "overtly prescribe a program of social engineering." Nevertheless, she continues, "in each text representations of urban black women are used as both the means by which male protagonists will achieve or will fail to achieve social mobility and as possible threats to the emergence of the wholesome black masculinity necessary for the establishment of an acceptable black male citizenship in the American social order" (747). She further asserts that central to the success of the emergent black middle class in these two novels is the evolution of urban codes of masculinity (747). McKay, who had a deeper, richer and more complex understanding of the cultural forms of black landscape as revealed in his poetry, still situates his female figures in a very simplistic manner in various degrees of approximation to uncontrolled and, therefore, problematic sexual behavior.

As a poet in *Harlem Shadows* he bemoaned the corruption of "little dark girls who in slippered feet / Go prowling through the night from street to street" (*SP* 62). But as a novelist he portrayed the destitute girls of his race as brown "Chippies" who like shameless wild animals hungry for raw meat savagely searched the eyes of the males (*HH* 68). McKay, who, as an insider, felt the shame of "the sacred brown feet of [his] fallen race," mocked, as an outsider, the promiscuity of Harlem, exercising a freedom available only to the colonial, who at once lives in two worlds — one of his own people, the other of his master. Hence, it is difficult to deny Carby's conclusion that Jake's journey is not just a journey to find the right woman but is "a journey of black masculinity in formation, a sort of *Pilgrim's Progress* in which a number of threatening embodiments of the female and the feminine have to be negotiated" (749). The importance of women is brought out very early when Jake expresses his helplessness:

Sometimes they turn mah stomach, the womens. The same in France, the same in England, the same in Harlem. White against white and black against white and yellow against black and brown. We's all just crazy-dog mad. Ain't no peace on earth with the womens and there ain't no life anywhere with-out them [HH 34].

For the delineator of black masculinity women are alike irrespective of race and place. Almost all the women in this novel, restaurant entrepreneurs like Aunt Hattie, prostitutes like Madam Laura, cabarets singers like Congo Rose, society women like "Gin-head" Susy and Miss Curdy, enjoy economic autonomy and geographic mobility, the freedom only men can afford. However, Kimberley Roberts argues that this form of female freedom results in a curious tension in the novel. Though McKay's women enjoy sexual freedom, participating in the society at large, they are mostly "configured as obstacles in the way of black male freedom" (120–121). While sexual promiscuity in the life of his women was not an objection for Jake, which is clearly a dig at middle-class ideology, their "attempts to rein him in and their relationship to money and financial transactions certainly do" (Roberts 121).

The Congo Rose episode is a good example. When she offers an incentive to Jake that he need not have to work for being her "man," Jake rejects it, saying that he never lived on women (HH 40). Jake shows as little interest in her earnings as in her laxity. Rose gets disappointed, as he did not live in the usual sweet way, beating her up and snatching her money: "she felt no thrill about the business when her lover was not interested in her earnings" (HH 114). As her demands pose a threat to Jake's masculinity, he leaves her. McKay in portraying the departure of Jake convinces the reader that the masochistic demands made by Rose are clearly unacceptable and unhealthy. Roberts rightly argues that the real "enmity stems from Rose's relationship to money and from her ability to use her buying power to control the men in her life" and hence concludes that "a relationship tinged with financial inequality is disempowering to the male ego and, in effect, turns him into a commodity" (122).

In McKay's scheme of black masculinity, this is unacceptable. Though Felice and Jake's romance is also intertwined with money, it stands as a contrast to Rose and Jake's relationship. Jake's exalted opinion of Felice is cemented when she returns the fifty dollars he paid for her services. According to Roberts not only does this move displace the definition of prostitute onto Jake — as, in a sense, she is paying him for his services — but it simultaneously evens the score between them (121). This dynamic of "no strings attached" makes Jake feel comfortable. Though one cannot understate the healthy, invigorating sexual encounter between them, one cannot but agree with Roberts that the financial aspect also has a role to play in this affair.

McKay plays out similar dynamics in the relationship of Zeddy and Susy. Zeddy has neither the charm nor the cash to hold women for a long time (*HH* 55–56). The best and the only way for him is to be a sweetman to a "Negro lady of means" (*HH* 82). Though not good looking like Jake's "fair brown queen," Susy was that woman. Zeddy admits it: "You know when a ma-ma ain't the goods in looks and figure, she's got to make up foh it some. And that Susy does. And she treats me right. Gimme all I wants to drink and brings home the goodest poke chops and fried chicken foh me to put away under mah shirt" (*HH* 77). In spite of all this Zeddy gets evicted when he painfully realizes that there are "strings to Susy's largesse" (*HH* 82). Susy, who had "paid and paid fully," not only successfully bossed over him but also curtailed and rationed his freedom in the "proprietary sense" (*HH* 82). Zeddy discovers that he has become a laughing stock in his "Harlem circles: 'He was kept, all right,' they said, 'kept under "Gin-head" Susy's skirt'" (*HH* 87). He even had to fight a fellow for calling him a "skirt-man." These disparaging remarks against sweetmen indicate the emerging resentment in the black bourgeois ideology that was committed in 1920s to propping up a positive black manhood. Unlike Jake, who worked longshore, and thus was financially not dependent on Rose, Zeddy did not work and was completely at the disposal of Susy (*HH* 84). Harlem black women are not only capable of commodifying black men but are a threat to the formation of black manhood. Hence, McKay tried to construct black masculinity by targeting them:

women... They were the real controlling force of life. Jake remembered the bal-musette fights between colored and white soldiers in France. Blacks, browns, yellows, whites... He remembered the interracial sex skirmishes in England. Men fought, hurt, wounded, killed each other. Women, like blazing torches, egged them on or denounced them. Victims of sex, the men seemed foolish, ape-like blunderers in their pools of blood. Didn't know what they were fighting for, except that it was to gratify some vague feeling about women [*HH* 70].

For Jake, women, whether in "America, France or in England could always go farther than a man in coarseness, depravity and sheer cupidity" (*HH* 69). Irrespective of race and nation, women are hypersexualized, overly controlling, and instigating man against man. Therefore, Roberts concludes that when it comes to promoting social stability, racial solidarity is a secondary consideration to male bonding for McKay. Hence, even if the Harlem women are sexually liberated, their movement is restricted to certain geographical spaces like whorehouses. To liberate the black male, McKay has ossified the black female within the patriarchal values of the West.

Two things appear to have guided McKay in constructing an ideal black masculinity at the expense of women. It was to refute the white man's stereotypical conception of blacks and to show that the negative attributes like uninhibited sexual strength of the black male were actually positive features, which the white man lost in the sea of materialism. This was strengthened by his participation in the discourse of primitivism that prevailed in both Harlem and Parisian literary circles of both races. However, it encouraged him to replicate certain essentialist notions about blackness and black sexuality. In his attempt to reject the repressing Western values and the taboo that surrounded the representation of black sexuality, McKay implicitly articulated the very terms that have historically been used to devalue black cultures. Even though he refused to take part in the emerging black bourgeoisie ideology of resuscitating the black male, emasculated under slavery and legal oppression in the United States, he did participate in it unconsciously. In trying to project a positive black manhood, he has actually reinscribed the patriarchal codes of the white man.

It is not women alone but "unnatural" sexual beings like gays and lesbians that were also targeted to bolster McKay's hypermasculine protagonists. McKay's biographers are of the opinion that he was bisexual though there isn't much evidence in his correspondence or writings.[12] Though he was an iconoclast in many respects, McKay did not challenge the tradition that such subjects were not to be discussed openly in creative literature. Therefore, the forms of masculinity that his narratives inscribe, which were certainly not departures from the traditional codes of maleness and masculine behavior, cannot but target sexual deviations. Chin rightly concludes: "McKay's folk heroes reflect and even reinforce dominant sexual ideologies by asserting a masculinity that is predicated on both sexism and homophobia" (3). On the railroad Jake meets Ray, the waiter "bookman" reading a "French" (a code for homosexual) novel. When Ray informs Jake the story he is reading is Alphonse Daudet's *Sappho* and mentions the two words contributed by it, "Sapphic and Lesbian," Jake does not hide his revulsion to the word "Lesbian." The epitome of masculinity expresses his disgust: "Tha's what we calls bulldyker in Harlem" drawled Jake. "Them's all ugly womens" (*HH* 129). Jake displays his aversion by humming a tune that makes explicit the link between the novel's particular figuration of masculine identity and the sexist and homophobic values on which it depends.

It can only be concluded that in his enthusiasm to exalt black manhood, McKay reinscribed a racial binary associating black with instinct, emotion, passion, and sexuality that was considered only "natural." If Jake is the prototype of masculinity and the likely answer to the dehumanizing Western civilization, then Ray the intellectual stands as a contrast articulating the colonial McKay's dilemma regarding Western civilization and his unique position in it. The very presence of Ray shows that McKay is not comfortable with his projection of Jake as the ideal of black masculinity. Ray personifies the dilemma of the inhibited, over-civilized intellectual unable to accept the hedonistic life-style of the black world's Jakes. In many respects Ray resembles McKay. Both hailed from the Caribbean and were forced to make a living in the United States. They came to America as adults after spending their formative years in the Caribbean and have a strong nostalgia for their respective countries. Both were college dropouts working on the American railroad. Though they shared antipathy towards Western imperialism and capitalism, they admired its literary masters. Their literary education taught them higher values of life, but the ivory towers they tried to reside in were shattered by the violent reality of the racist and materialistic life. And neither of them had the courage and determination to challenge the status quo nor the resignation to accept what it is in real life per se. Caught in this limbo they were always in search of a spiritual home and hence always in exile.

Like McKay, Ray takes pride in black history and heritage. He corrects Jake, for whom "Africa was jungle, and Africans bush niggers and cannibals and West Indians monkey chasers," and denies that slavery was the peculiar role of black folk (*HH* 134). He tells him about the "old destroyed cultures of West Africa and of their vestiges, of black kings who struggled stoutly for the independence of their kingdoms[13] (*HH* 135). By teaching Jake about the African heritage, Ray is actually rewriting the distorted version of African history instilled by white civilization in the minds of black people. In correcting this distortion Ray/McKay is showing signs of Negritude, which he articulates with vigor and clarity in the next novel, *Banjo*. Nevertheless, this pride in race and its grand heritage did not help him identify like his author with the masses of Negroes in America. He is forced to find "kinship" with men whom he cannot but despise. As a Haitian, he used to feel "condescendingly sorry for those poor African natives; superior to ten millions of suppressed Yankee coons" (*HH* 153). Now he was just one of them and he hated them for being one of them:

> Ray fixed his eyes on the offensive bug-bitten bulk of the chef. These men claimed kinship with him. They were black like him. Man and nature had put them in the same race. He ought to love them and feel them (if they felt any thing). He ought to if he had a shred of social morality in him. They were all chain ganged together and he was counted as one link. Yet he loathed every soul in that great barrackroom, except Jake. Race... Why should he have and love a race? [*HH* 153].

This remained a persistent question for McKay, the English colonial aspiring to become a universal poet. His poem "Bondage" also raises a similar question. Races and nations were things like skunks for Ray, whose smells poisoned the air of life (*HH* 153–154). Despite his friendship with Jake, Ray like his author could never identify with the African Americans and remained always an outsider. Yuan Wen Chi rightly says that "due to the uncertainty of his own identity, he is constantly in an epistemological predicament which, on the one hand, makes him meditate on the meaning of life in abstract terms rather than participate in it, and deprives him of his pride in his own race, on the other" (114). Hence only "a shred of social morality" but not any emotional bonding identifies him with the Negro masses who "sweated and snored, like the cooks" without "aspirations toward national unity and racial arrogance" in the "pits" of the occidental civilization (*HH* 154).

At the same time, Ray could not identify with Western civilization. Like his author, he detested the colonialism, imperialism, and materialism brought by it. Modern civilization is "rotten" for him. Who ever is touched by it is also rotten. He is particularly critical of modern education and the narrow limits imposed by it. Hence, he criticizes educated Negroes for cultivating "old false-fine feelings that used to be monopolized by educated and cultivated people" (*HH* 242). He knew that what were called "fine human traits don't belong to any special class or nation or race of people" (*HH* 242). Through his protagonist, McKay is rebelling against the modern education that pushed him into a spiritual impasse:

> No, modern education is planned to make you a sharp,
> snouty, rooting hog. We ought to get something new, we
> Negroes. But we get our education like — like our houses.
> When the whites move out, we move in and take possession
> of the old dead stuff. Dead stuff that this age has no use for
> [*HH* 243].

Ray like his author was "dominated" by the "great books *Les Misérables, Nanna, Uncle Tom's Cabin, David Copperfield, Nicholas Nickleby, Oliver Twist* in his bright dreaming and dark brooding days when he was a boy" (*HH* 225). However, with "the great mass carnage in Europe and the great mass revolution in Russia" he understood that he had "lived over the end of an era" and that "his spiritual masters had not crossed with him into the new" (*HH* 226). Ray perfectly articulates McKay's position as an aspiring black colonial writer deeply influenced by the colonial master's writings but found them wanting in the new era as "he felt alone, hurt, neglected, cheated, almost naked" (*HH* 226). As the old dreams are shattered, he is forced to turn to his own race, the fertile reality around him (*HH* 227). As he realized the irrelevance of his spiritual masters and the necessary acceptance of his own people, it appears that the colonial is trying to break free from the ideological hold of Western civilization. Yet, like his author, he has to travel a long way before he can resolve the dilemma.

So Ray decides to leave Harlem and, along with his friend Grant, finds a job on a freighter to Australia and then to Europe. The immediate reason for leaving is that Agatha "was acting wistfully" (*HH* 263). He could see "destiny working in her large, dream eyes, filling them with the passive softness of resignation to life, and seeking to encompass and yoke him down as just one of the thousand niggers of Harlem" (*HH* 264). If he met the "subtle wistful yearning halfway" he would soon "become one of the contended hogs in the pigpen of Harlem, getting ready to litter little black piggies" (*HH* 263). Even if the aspiring writer had reasons to leave Harlem (the pattern of respectable comfort might chase his high dreams out of him and deflate him to the contented animal), the way he expresses it, Harlem infants as "little black piggies" or their delivery as a littering, reflects his contempt for the community he is living in. The spokesperson, P.S. Chauhan rightly says, clearly possesses the scorn of an outsider to the community and, possibly, of a superior (76).

Similarly, the pervasive use of animal imagery when describing black characters in the novel raises doubts about McKay's intentions. The persistent use of "hog" image for the black man's unreflecting acceptance of the status quo and the image of Harlem as "pigpen" only betrays McKay's supercilious attitude toward the black community in America. Jake is a hound prowling on the streets of Harlem searching for prey (*HH* 10). When the Baltimore cabaret is closed after a bitter fight, all the jazzers stood and talked resentfully in the street like dogs flicked apart by a whipcord (*HH* 34). If Billy Biasse is "the Wolf" because of his avid rapacity as a pimp and gambler, the chef on the railroad is a "dirty rhinoceros the ugliest animal in all Africa" (*HH* 150). The enticing Congo Rose is a "lean lazy leopard" and a "wild rearing animal" whereas the repulsive Susy and Miss Curdy are "Skunks, tame Skunks" (*HH* 71). The fight between two boys in Susie's parlour is described thus: "The chocolate leaped up like a tiger-cat at his assailant.... Like an enraged ram goat, he held and butted the light-brown boy twice, straight on the forehead" (*HH* 72). Jerco's suicide by razor reads: "Jerco had cut his throat and was lying against the bowl of the water-closet.... And he sprawled there like a great black boar in a mess of blood" (*HH* 309). This imagery has been reserved, probably unconsciously, for black characters alone. It not only undercut the stature of the black characters but the author's effort to win respect for the community is lost due to his contempt for the representatives of that community.

Speaking about the dehumanization of the native, Fanon says the "terms the settler uses when he mentions the native are Zoological terms. He speaks of the yellow man's reptilian motions, of the stink of the native quarters, of breeding swarms, of foulness, of spawn, of gesticulations. When the settler seeks to describe the native fully in exact terms he constantly refers to the bestiary" (*Earth* 33). McKay the colonial seems to have picked up bits and pieces of the white colonizer's contempt for the native black community. It is the master's stance that comes through in the colonial author's unguarded moments. The reason for McKay's less than respectful attitude towards the black characters is that unlike the African American writers such as Jean Toomer, Zora Neale Hurston, and Rudolph Fisher, who went to their folk roots, McKay sought literary inspiration from Anglo-Saxon masters — Dickens, Shaw, Whitman and Lawrence. Hence, as a person brought up in a colony, it was impossible for him totally to rid his mind of the literature and the attitudes of the colonizer and to adopt the literary pedigree of the African American peers of his generation.

It is not Agatha that Ray hated but the power in her to "yoke him down as just one of the thousand niggers of Harlem" (*HH* 264). Moreover, it is to escape from becoming one of the "contented hogs in

Harlem" that Ray prepares to abandon Agatha and the "respectable comfort" she promises. It is not Ray alone but also Jake that prepares to leave Harlem. It appears that both his protagonists have to leave Harlem if they are to preserve their personal integrity and sanity. If Jake is to remain his original self he has to leave the "stinking mess"—Harlem, before it drags him in. Already his fight with Zeddy over Felice has vitiated the atmosphere and there is every danger of his getting involved further. The narrator says that Jake "had always managed to delight in love and yet steer clear of the hate and violence that govern it in his world.... Yet here he was caught in the thing that he despised so thoroughly" (*HH* 328).

The leaving of Harlem by his protagonists raises doubt if McKay was completely comfortable with its life. Harlem has a rich, warm and colorful life but it is also replete with gang rowdyism, brutality and promiscuity. The lower-class Harlem community that made possible Jake's easy going life is very much governed by brutality and all the ills of the underworld — pimps, prostitutes, drugs, and guns. Behind the easy life of Harlem streets, cabarets and parlors always lurks the danger of raids, rivalries, and the sudden eruption of gang wars. It is not possible for Jake or Ray who are alien to Harlem's spirit to remain aloof without being touched by its organizing principles. Therefore, Jake, who was so ecstatic about Harlem in the opening pages, could not find a home in Harlem. With Felice he has to leave it in search of a home in Chicago. The very title *Home to Harlem* is finally defeated as both the protagonists leave Harlem. Tillery rightly concludes that McKay ends *Home to Harlem* on a note consistent with his own life: full of unresolved dilemmas (86). The novel closes with Jake and Felice walking away from "dear" Harlem to the subway station along Lennox Avenue. This is the inevitable outcome for most of the colonial writers: continuously searching for a spiritual home while perpetually moving into exile. Home always eludes them as their imagination is always vacillating between the land of origin and the adopted country.

Roy S. Bryce-Laporte in his discussion of the Black Diaspora captures McKay's condition. He says that the "minoritization" and "homelessness" shared by so many of them have found it necessary to be in "continual movement, thus experiencing repeated threats and periods of uprootedness, instability, and re-adaptation in having to 'be gin it all over, again and again.'" (Bonnett and Watson, Foreword xvi). Hence, for the vast majority of the descendents of the Africans who were transplanted to the Americas since the 16th century and those who have since experienced subsequent massive movements and redistibutions, the one common ancestral homeland they claim must necessarily be an amorphorous and unspecified "Africa" — an "inheritance of the epoch of slavery in Black history" (Foreword xvii). Indeed, the "unspecified Africa" became the unifying principle in the next novel, *Banjo*. Ray, Banjo and even Jake leave Harlem and come together at the port of Marseilles celebrating a Pan-African identity.

− 5 −

Negroism: The Banjo in Marseilles

From the streets of Harlem in his first novel to Marseilles, an important international seaport in southern France in his second novel, *Banjo: A Story Without a Plot* (*BJ*), McKay traveled a considerable distance ideologically. The ambiguity that marked his affinity with his race in the earlier writings has in this novel resolved into lucid race solidarity. Published in 1929 the novel marks an important milestone in the literary as well as ideological evolution of McKay. Though never recognized by the African American literary establishment, until the Black Power movement, it became one of the inspiring texts of Negritude. Aime Cesaire, in his interview in *Discourse on Colonialism*, acknowledged that he was inspired by McKay's novel *Banjo*, which for him was "really one of the first works in which an author spoke of the Negro and gave him a certain literary dignity" (71). Léopold Sédar Senghor, another father figure of the Negritude movement, in his lecture "La Poesie Negroamericaine," admitted the indebtedness of his generation to McKay: "Claude McKay can be considered rightfully as the true inventor of *Negritude*. I do not mean the word, but the values of Negritude.... So McKay calls himself 'Black' with the confidence of a rock" (Senghor, qtd. in Makward, *Centennial* 94–95). The significance of *Banjo* to the evolution of Negritude concept was highlighted when Lylian Kesteloot interviewed the Negritude triumvirate — Senghor, Aime Cesaire, and Leon Damas. While working on her landmark thesis *Les Ecrivains noirs de langue française: Naissance d'une littérature*, she noted how they could still remember entire passages of *Banjo* in French translation[1] (Damas, qtd. in Robert P. Smith, Jr., 95).

However, *Banjo* was not a commercial success like *Home to*

Harlem. Some attributed this to its unfamiliar locale and others to its technical faults as a novel. A close study of its genesis reveals that McKay's literary choices were dictated by his own ideological evolution. It also influenced the structure of the novel as well as the views propounded by the characters. Such a study helps to answer the problems of aesthetics posed in general terms and helps in reconsidering the evolution of McKay's thinking at the end of the 1920s. Further, it also underlines how distant McKay was from the major concerns of the Harlem Renaissance group, more original in his outlook, and definitely more cosmopolitan and internationally-minded, than has been hitherto admitted (Fabre, *Aesthetics* 197). Perplexed by McKay's choice of the French locale, Tillery quoting McKay's correspondence surmises that McKay had gathered all he could from his Harlem experiences and exhausted it in his first novel[2] (112). The reason, Tillery thinks, for McKay's abandoning the American scene to write a novel set in France lies in his superficial knowledge about African-American life which is little more than that of some bohemian and radical whites (111–112). As his poetry and his first novel reveal, McKay, in spite of his assertions, has never comfortably identified with the masses of his race. In fact, he expressed this dilemma in *Home to Harlem* through his spokesperson Ray. The African American minority life and its problems were never the focus of the questing colonial. The United States was only a stopover in his life long quest for a spiritual home.

After his sojourn in various cities and towns of France, McKay reached Marseilles in 1926, the place that "stirred" him to "creative expression" (*LW* 283). Situated squarely between Europe and Africa, Marseilles was a geographically symbolic locale, as it became an important transit point for the black colonial writer's spiritual journey in search of an identity. Like his protagonist Ray, McKay "had fallen for its strange enticement" as it "offered him a haven in its frowsy, thickly-peopled heart where he could exist *en pension* proletarian of a sort," giving him the "necessary solitude to work with pencil and scraps of paper" (*BJ* 66). He met a picturesque congregation of black beach boys of "doubtful" nationalities at "Europe's best back door" leading a picaresque life on the margins of the white civilization with whom he enjoyed not only the harbor life but also the warm solidarity of a group[3]

(*BJ* 69). With the intention of recreating their life in fiction, McKay took lodgings at Hotel Nautique, Quai des Belges in April 1927. The group, representing Negro boys from the continental triangle of Africa, America and Europe, had already disbanded. Two of them died in a hospital. The banjo players had left the town touring with a band, and those who remained were longing to leave Marseilles. McKay set out to capture their life where the port town played more than a background role. Within eighteen months, he completed the novel, with the group of black beach boys and dockers being the collective hero.

The novel as the subtitle indicates is only a simple "story without a plot." It opens with Banjo, a Negro from the American South, meeting the black beach boys. He is already broke, losing his money on a white prostitute. The beach boys take him as their pal. Banjo soon plans an orchestra group to play in bistros and clubs in the ditch. In one of the restaurants, he is injured over his white girl and is taken in by Latnah. Then follows a series of adventures of the black boys on the beachfront — bumming, quarreling, singing, and swimming. In the second part, Banjo meets Ray. Taken into the group, Ray finds himself more at home with the boys. After many episodes of telling stories and jokes, the group breaks up with Banjo joining the "blue cinema" group. Later, Ray finds Banjo in a bad condition working in coal yards. After a bout of ill health, the boys come together again into a group. Even Jake from the earlier novel joins them. However, the beach boys sign onto ships to various destinations, while Ray and Banjo decide on another bout of vagabondage at some unknown destination.

So McKay's contemporary African American literary establishment felt that he was trying to repeat the commercial success he had achieved with his novel of low life in the black metropolis. Friendship and group solidarity, pan-handling, casual love making, drinking, dancing, stealing, fighting among themselves and with police, deceiving immigration authorities; these are the recurring events in the lives of McKay's characters which many a Harlem critic saw as too close to the happy-go-lucky Jakes and Felices of *Home to Harlem*. Hence, the main objection for Du Bois in this novel as in *Home to Harlem* is the portrayal of blacks: "Here [are] a lot of people whose chief business in life seems to be sexual experience, getting drunk, and fighting" (*Crisis*

234). Even Walter White, usually a strong supporter of McKay, felt indignant at the belittling references made to African Americans in the novel. They felt that McKay due to his West Indian background was unable to understand them, and hence the novel reflected his own personal prejudices and biases against them.

It is difficult to deny the criticism that McKay has too apparently used this novel as a platform to settle his scores with the critics of his first novel. He articulated his antagonism through Ray, his double, continued from *Home to Harlem*. Rather than weaving his reaction into the fabric of the novel artfully, McKay made Ray lecture his opinions, weakening the narrative flow of the novel. Structurally, too, many reviewers and critics felt the novel was faulty, because loose and unconnected. The novel is a stitching together of episodes linked more by shifting group of characters than by any cohesive developing plot. Du Bois' remarks are not unfounded: "It is described as a story without a plot, but it is hardly even that. It is in no sense a novel, either in the nature of its story or in the development of character" (*Crisis* 234). That McKay is trying to repeat his success by depicting black low life can be contested from his correspondence with his literary agent William Aspenwell Bradley during 1927–29. McKay started writing this novel months before *Home to Harlem* (1928) was published. In a June 1927 letter to his publisher, McKay wrote:

> I spent the better part of 1926 here in Marseille, existing in any way I could, doing a day's work on the docks or sometimes touching a small cheque for a poem. I lived most of the time in the Quartier Reserve with Negroes from America, British, French and Portuguese Africa, the West Indies. It was then that I got the idea of doing a novel around them with the Vieux Port as a background [qtd. in Fabre 198].

This letter stresses not only the date of its inception, but McKay's intention that Marseilles was meant to remain the backdrop, with the group of black beach boys and dockers as the collective hero of the story. He wanted to celebrate the pan–African gathering at the Marseilles port in fiction and capture their healthy lower-class black reactions to life and their environment. By doing so, he wished to portray the common attributes of the race — humor, a gift for ripe laughter, uninhibited sexual enjoyment and a particular rhythm of life — a definite set of values that can be categorized as non–Occidental. This fits into McKay's favorite turf of drawing on the post–world war discourse of black spontaneity and primitive but healthy response to life, in contrast to the dehumanizing rotten white materialistic values. He did not aim, as his literary agent has suggested, at creating triangular love stories involving black and white characters. Even within the novel, he did not stress and complicate Banjo's relation with the white girl. Even though Latnah did not approve of Banjo's renewed relation with the white girl it is not because of feminine jealousy but because Banjo is spending his money recklessly on an ungrateful woman:

> She had never been jealous of his change of pillow. That she understood, Orientwise. But for him to lose good money to those things in the Ditch, and for what? For the benefit of their two-legged white rats [*BJ* 169].

Banjo was "color blind" regarding women and "he took all women as one — as they came — roughly, carelessly, easily" (*BJ* 170). It is the spontaneity and naturalness of their relations that McKay wanted to stress in this novel. Any amount of sentimentality of bourgeois standards would have spoiled McKay's scheme of portraying amoral black characters in the rough, treacherous life of the ditch. There are also other reasons for McKay's choice of not problematizing black-white relations. As a fierce individualist, he could not compromise on his perception of social and racial issues that had developed with his cosmopolitan experience. A staunch advocate of race pride, McKay was never in favor of the themes of integration and segregation that the African American intellectuals were after. He consistently found fault with them for their obsession with the issue of segregation and for lacking a group soul.

Another aspect that critics object to was the lack of structure, the absence of a plot as a well-defined story element. Dealing with vagrant black characters with unsophisticated relations between them, that too in an unfamiliar locale, and with lack of movement in the story and with the episodic character of its narration, Saxton, McKay's editor at

Harper, feared the reader might lose interest. The reply that McKay gave to his suggestions underlines his priorities, especially his conception of the novel as a genre and the purpose of creating characters like Banjo. Being well aware that this was not a novel in the conventional form he defended his position that the events around Banjo form the connecting thread of the story. He wrote:

> Banjo coming to Marseille, finding Latnah after losing the other girl; his neglect of Latnah; ... Banjo being ill in the hospital, getting better and obtaining by ruse a sum of money to leave Marseille. It is a plot alright, but not a complicated one that thickens as the story progresses, but a slight one carried along by the episodes [qtd. in Fabre 201].

McKay's sole purpose of recreating Marseilles' Ditch atmosphere that held the Negroes in a sort of Pan-African conference during the summer of 1926, and his project of portraying common racial attributes of that international group, dictated the episodic character of the novel. It is not the story line, but the rough, instinctual, and humane group life of the Negroes, gathered at the margins of the white man's civilization, that went into the episodic construction of the novel. This was at odds with the aesthetic expectations — European middle-class standards of fiction — of the times. However, by taking a new path in writing fiction suitable to his objective, McKay for the first time was showing signs of breaking free from his colonial training and the conventionalities of Western literature. It appears that during this Negritude period McKay was more receptive to changes and experiments in fiction writing than he was in writing poetry. Hence, Usha Shourie rightly concludes that McKay was evolving a theory of black literature that would jump across at least three decades to inspire and influence his successors (*Centennial* 144). Little did the Harlem intellectuals and even later scholars like Tillery realize that the locale, setting and the construction suited the colonial's evolving pan-African identity:

> It was a relief to get to Marseilles, to live in among a great gang of black and brown humanity. Negroids from the United States, the West Indies, North Africa and West

Africa, all herded together in a warm group. Negroid features
and complexions, not exotic, creating curiosity and hostility,
but unique and natural to a group. The odors of dark bodies
sweating through a day's hard work, like the odor of stabled
horses, were not unpleasant even in a crowded café. It was
good to feel the strength and distinction of a group and the
assurance of belonging to it [LW 277].

Beleaguered by a paralytic duality, and in search for a home and identity, the Marseilles port, where Negroes met who represented all the
key geographical areas inhabited by the black race, had a catalytic effect
crystallizing into a pan–African identity. Moreover, however distant
McKay remained from the Paris Negro circle during the late 1920s, he
was very much a part of the developing Pan-African consciousness
among the dozens of "Negroes of diverse origins" that gathered in Paris[4]
(Cesaire 72). To Rene Depestre's question as to whether in this circle
of Negroes in Paris there was a consciousness of the importance of
African culture, Cesaire replied: "Yes, as well as an awareness of the
solidarity among blacks. We had come from different parts of the world.
It was our first meeting. We were discovering ourselves. This was very
important" (72). McKay was very much part of this confluence and so
came to believe that under this artificially imposed divisions of shades
of color on the Negroid race by the imperial West lay "one true self,"
which people with a shared history and ancestry held in common.
Through this text, he was reconstructing the underlying unity of the
black people whom colonization and slavery distributed across the
African diaspora. Moreover, his forages into the white world — America, England, France, and other European countries — had laid bare the
hypocrisies of the metropolitan center, cleared him of the many idiosyncrasies he acquired as a colonial subject, and brought him unambiguously closer to his race.

Hence, as a writer he not only felt it his responsibility to challenge the discourse of inferiority imposed on the Negroid race, but to
show how his "primitive" earth loving race clashed with the mechanical civilization of the West. He came to believe that it was not only
the traumatic history that brought them together but despite regional
differences there were certain basic cultural similarities that one could

recognize among African people wherever one went. Hence he projected what he felt to be some of the essential qualities of a black soul — instinct, spontaneity, love for music, story-telling, sensuality, etc. — as common features of the Negro race. Their love for music and group life had no national and language barriers and showed their unity in diversity:

> They went playing from little bistro to bistro in the small
> streets between the fish market and the Bum square. They
> were joined by others — a couple of Senegalese and some
> British West Africans and soon the company was more than
> a dozen. They were picturesquely conspicuous as they loi-
> tered along, talking in a confused lingo of English, French
> and native African [BJ 24].

The languages of the West and the power implied in them could not divide these sons of Africa. Gwendolyn Bennett, who was a close friend of McKay and had lived in France during those years, recorded McKay's eagerness for the life the Negro group led on Marseilles dock: "with unsullied curiosity [he] looks about him for the little earmarks that make Negroes outstanding in a world where all men are abandoned"[5] (qtd. in Fabre, *Aesthetics* 197). Hence, Jacqueline Kaye rightly concludes that the novel *Banjo* "seeks to arrive at the common black denominator, the essential Negroness, the equivalent of the Negritude to be generated by the poetry of Francophone blacks" (165–69). The silenced Africa, the common denominator, speaks through this grouping, giving coherence to the fragmented identities of the black diaspora. Individuals without an anchor, without a horizon, colorless, stateless, rootless, were given identity with Africa, the missing link (Fanon, *Wretched* 175). As Dixon puts it:

> The spontaneity of the storytelling and music-playing
> events proves the existence of a common base for black art.
> The various types of performance the vagabonds elicit from
> each other manifest group membership and solidarity. The
> improvised storytelling Ray participates in establishes African
> folklore as a common source for many New World black lit-
> eratures. Likewise, the orchestra Banjo wants to create

becomes a symphony of disparate instruments and voices
when the men gather to play blues and jazz numbers such as
"Stay Carolina Stay" (a version of "Jelly Roll Blues" [46])
and "Shake That Thing." The art reflects the residual "international" Africanist philosophy emerging from the core
friendship between Ray and Banjo [50].

Though McKay portrayed the common attributes of the group, he did
not overlook the individuality of his protagonists and their specific
responses along national lines. West Indians are "monkey chasers" for
Banjo, while Senegalese are "savages" for all the New World colored
protagonists. While Jake recognizes Marcus Garvey as "illiquint,"
Banjo, another African American, has nothing but total contempt for
Garvey. If Goosey, the race man, strongly advised by his mother to keep
away from back-to-Africa bauble as Africa is jungle land, his partner
and friend Taloufa has purchased a hundred dollars of Black Star Line
shares (*BJ* 91). If Taloufa refuses to get a girl who cheated him arrested
as she is of his "own race," it is a white chauffeur who helps Ray to
take Banjo to a hospital. McKay, in his enthusiasm to portray racial
solidarity did not wipe out the differences that characterized their individual responses. In fact, Fabre says, his major desire was to stress these
nuances of feeling and differences in attitudes among his colored protagonists, nuances which the white reader was unlikely to notice
(blinded as he was by racism to differences within what seemed to him
the same group), nuances which the black bourgeoisie in the United
States affected not to consider (204). He quotes McKay:

> To me the most interesting thing is that people are funda-
> mentally human under the apparent differences. That will
> not prevent individuals from thinking and trying to act
> along tribal, national and racial lines. The fact is that the
> majority of the people do so quite unconsciously and the
> non-conformists are very few [qtd. in Fabre, *Aesthetics* 204].

So even if people are fundamentally human in McKay's scheme, there
were many historical and political factors that were dividing them along
racial and color lines based on false notions. Attributing stereotyped
specificities to the Negro race, the white man did not only oppress

them but also caused great damage to their psychological equilibrium, by instilling inferiority among them. Therefore, the immediate task for McKay and his compatriots was to restore equilibrium. Hence, his focus on elevating those attributes considered inferior and "uncivilized" as healthy and invigorating. Reverse racism was the necessity of the day. So McKay puts black against white while inverting the values of each: "the casual against the calculated, the simple against the sophisticated, the natural against the artificial and so on throughout the whole spectrum of those contrasts that have been ascribed to white and black absolutely" (Kaye, *Banjo* 168). In this context, he cannot simply be brushed off as a race chauvinist, or his work dismissed as reverse ethnocentrism simply reproducing existing categories, producing the same effects as the system it contests.

McKay's angry but calculated response in this text constituted the basic tenets of Negritude. So what McKay shared with the succeeding generations of francophone black intellectuals was above all their frustrations, their angry rejection of alien values, their self exploration that would lead to a better understanding and the assertion of their rightful place among the races of the world. Hence, even though he rejected the book for its incongruous aesthetics, Du Bois recognized its vision. He says:

> It is, on one hand the description of a series of episodes on
> the docks of Marseilles; and on the other hand a sort of
> international philosophy of the Negro race. The first aspect
> of the book is negligible.... The race philosophy, on the
> other hand, is of great interest. McKay has become an inter-
> national Negro. He is a direct descendent from Africa. He
> knows the West Indies; he knows Europe; and he philoso-
> phizes about the whole thing [*Crisis* 234].

Du Bois was able to recognize McKay's vision as he found articulated the ideas he was to propagate in his later years, espousing Pan-Africanism. This unqualified identification with the race in *Banjo* proves that McKay had traveled a long way from the ambiguous stand he sometimes took in *Home to Harlem* and his poetry. McKay's spokesperson and double, Ray, who in the earlier novel questioned "why should he have and love a race," is immensely happy to immerse himself in the vagabond life of the large congregation of international Negroes on the Marseilles docks. Ray "loved the piquant variety of the things of the docks as much as he loved their colorful human interest. And the highest to him was the Negroes of the port" (*BJ* 68). Repulsed in the earlier novel by the thick, promiscuous, lower-class Harlem life, Ray is now ecstatic to see Negroes of all shades collecting and leading a vagrant life at the "backdoor" of European civilization. Frustrated by Europe's incorrigible racism and imperialism, Ray joins Banjo and his group in avenging their race's rejection, by pan-handling and beach-combing. It is France, the white man's land, that turned out to be exotic for these displaced, deracinated, pillaging Negro vagabonds threatening the "respectability" and "superiority" of the white values. The instinctual and healthy lives of the black characters stand as an alternative to the decayed materialism of the West.

As in *Home to Harlem*, McKay created a pair of characters representing instinct and intellect. Even if they represented their respective ideals quite intensely, the division is not as neat and sharp as in the first novel. The intellectual Ray and the instinctual Banjo take part in all the activities of the beach boys. The divisions blur further as Ray and Banjo finally decide to lead a vagabond life together unlike in the first novel where Ray and Jake have gone their own way. This was precisely the reason why McKay rejected Saxton's suggestion of beginning the novel with chapter six, where Ray was introduced. This would have made Banjo secondary and would have spoiled McKay's project of portraying two philosophies of existence, which are complementary, rather than opposed.

Lincoln Agrippa Daily aptly called Banjo by the instrument he plays, whose main thematic function is to personify black values drifted from the American South to the "seaman's dream port" of Marseilles (*BJ* 11). His banjo is doubly instrumental, says Dixon; "[I]t is a source of identity, and it makes music" (50). Banjo asserts it is "moh than a gal, moh than a pal; it's mah-self" (*BJ* 6). A "child of the Cotton Belt," his "life was a dream of vagabondage that he was perpetually pursuing and realizing in odd ways, always incomplete but never unsatisfactory" (*BJ* 11). Though he was like Jake from the American South, who personified black values, there are marked differences in his outlook. Unlike Jake, who was very American in spirit and "looked askew at foreign niggers," Banjo from the beginning was a truly international Negro. If Jake eagerly looked forward to returning to Harlem, Banjo explored devious methods to leave the United States like convincing the immigration officials in "straight Yankee" for deportation. He assimilates easily with the international gathering of Negro boys in the Marseilles Ditch. His pals on the beach are Malty and Ginger from West Indies, Dengel from Senegal, Taloufa from the "Nigerian Bush," the English speaking Bugsy, and Goosey from the Cotton Belt.

When Banjo meets the beach boys at the beginning of the novel, an episodic account of their largely loose life is underway. The profile of each beach boy is a story of subversion and breaking of the white man's laws. The theme of international brotherhood is introduced when the black beach boys pool their money to give a meal to Banjo at their first meeting when he tells them that he is "broke already" (*BJ* 4). No sooner had Banjo alighted in Marseilles than he "naturally" found a girl and as easily lost her as he spent away his money. A colored woman of mysterious origin, Latnah, took him in when he was wounded in a skirmish over the white girl who refused to recognize him. Having lost everything, Banjo takes to the Ditch life as easily as a duck takes to water, beach combing with the other black boys. Sleeping in box cars and eating off the remains of a ship's kitchen, panhandling, raiding casks of wine, bathing on the break water, is the life of black beach boys, joined in a joyful camaraderie in Marseilles. McKay paints the picture quite romantically and in contrasting the black and white enjoyment in the Ditch, he exposes the decayed materialistic values of the white civilization:

> Most of the whites, especially the blond ones of northern
> countries, seemed to have gone down hopelessly under the
> strength of hard liquor, as if nothing mattered for them now
> but that. They were stinking-dirty, and lousy, without any
> apparent desire to clean themselves. With the black boys it
> was different. It was as if they were just taking a holiday.
> They were always in holiday spirit, and if they did not
> appear to be specially created for that circle, they did not

spoil the picture, but rather brought to it a rich and careless tone that increased its interest. They drank wine to make them lively and not sodden, washed their bodies and their clothes on the breakwater, and sometimes spent a panhandled ten-franc note to buy a second hand pair of pants [BJ 19].

However, that does not mean McKay approved entirely of the black boys' vagrant life in the Ditch. He upbraids them through his protagonist Banjo for lacking "self-respect." It is the habit of the beach boys, white and colored, to assemble down at a ship to feed on the remains of the food handed down to them. He disapproves the way they all rush and grab the food "like swine," each elbowing and snapping at the other to get his hand in first and stuffing themselves, "smacking, grunting, and blowing with the disgusting noises of brutes" (BJ 40). Banjo does not join the melee, "standing a little way off," and watches them in "contempt and anger" (BJ 40). He is particularly resentful about an officer referring to the black boys as "a dammed lot a disgusting niggers," and tells his pals:

> ... and I don't want no gitting used to that. You fellahs know what the white man think about niggers and you-all ought to do better than you done when he 'low you on his ship to eat that dawggone grub. I take life easy like you-all, but I ain't nevah gwine to lay mahself wide open to any insulting cracker of a white man [BJ 42].

With a brother lynched before his eyes, Banjo's anti-white sentiments are quite bitter and vindictive. He not only hated white racists but also believed that they constitute the majority of white people. Even though he enlisted in the army to "make the wul' safe foh democracy" he came to realize after the war that "the wul' safe foh democracy is a wul' safe for crackerism" (BJ 194). But his hatred was not consistent as he "never bore rancor for any length of time against anybody or anything" (BJ 170). In fact, he gives five francs to a hungry white boy much to the resentment of his pals like Bugsy. Banjo "would not see life in divisions of sharp primary colors and in matters of generosity and sex he was color-blind" (BJ 170). Banjo's attitude toward whites, Giles rightly says, which was a curious combination of shrewd wariness, potential hatred, and humane impulse, was "probably not a great deal different from McKay's own" (Giles 87). Unlike Ray, he rarely talks about race, but when he does, he is quite emphatic. When Goosey, the Negro elite spokesman, chides him for not being a "race man," he bursts out: "I ain't one accident made nigger like you, Goosey. Ise a true-blue traveling bohn nigger and I know life, and I knows how to take it nacheral. I fight when I got to and I works when I must and I lays off when I feel lazy, and I loves all the time becausen the honey-pot a life is mah middle name" (*BJ* 305). Though he was never "bellyaching about race" his code of behavior and life-sustaining spirit stands for McKay's ideal of a black soul with spontaneity and love of music permeating his person (*BJ* 76).

The most signifying element of this pan–African identity is music, and Banjo's attempt to organize a black orchestra comprising the black beach boys becomes the only unifying link in this otherwise loose plot. McKay not only extols black music by making it a refrain in the novel but also utilizes it as common glue to stick Negroes of all regions, shades, languages, and nationalities together. It is the black music dance floor which makes Negroes of all shades and hues drop their epidermic distinctions:

> Senegalese in blue overalls, Madagascan soldiers in khaki,
> dancing together. A Martiniquan with his mulatress flashing
> her gold teeth. A Senegalese sergeant goes round with his
> fair blonde. A Congo boxer struts it with his Marguerite.
> And Banjo, grinning, singing, white teeth, great mouth,
> leads the band.... Shake that thing [*BJ* 49].

The importance that music plays in this novel is signaled by the title *Banjo*. By promoting the banjo, the instrument of the American Negro that symbolizes an affirmation of his hardy existence, McKay proves his adroitness in reversing stereotypes, even if it is at odds with the upliftment philosophy of Harlem intellectuals. Anticipating their anger, he did challenge them through Goosey, whose sole function is to expound the "uplift" philosophy. Coming from the Dixie, he refuses to join the black orchestra because of the banjo:

No. Banjo is bondage. It's the instrument of slavery. Banjo is
Dixie. The Dixie of the land of cotton and massa and missus
and black mammy. We colored folks have got to get away
from all that in these enlightened progressive days. Let us
play piano and violin, harp and flute [*BJ* 90].

While white classicists coming from the New England heights, like T.S.
Eliot,[6] felt that these jazz tunes signaled the perversion of the age in
the modern "waste land," McKay made them one of the symbols of
black identity. Jazz music, McKay recognized very early, is more than
a sound or a name, but quite assertively a state of being. Though Banjo
thinks of gathering "panhandling fellahs" into an orchestra, he doesn't
want to play cheap, moving from café to café, handing out his "hat for
a lousy sou" like the white itinerants (*BJ* 14). Contrasting Banjo's playing for fun the narrator says that the white musicians "played in a hard,
unsmiling, funeral way and only for sous" and that is the reason why
their music was so "execrable" (*BJ* 40). It is only Latnah who made a
collection whenever she was present in any of the bistros. As Latnah
used to provide him with a ten-franc note whenever he required, Banjo
never objected to the collection except when he is playing in ecstasy
for "fellows just like himself" (*BJ* 46). Unlike Jake in *Home to Harlem,*
Banjo had no objection to taking money from women. McKay was
quite emphatic in his earlier novel that Jake never "lived off no womens and never will" like Zeddy and other sweetmen. But surprisingly
Banjo and his pals were not averse to women's money.

It appears that McKay had finally overcome the trap of the patriarchal codes of the West, to which he unconsciously subscribed in his
earlier novel, in portraying black masculinity. The beach boys treated
Latnah, the colored female character of the novel, as one of their pals.
She not only moves on equal terms with the gang but to give herself
to any of the beach boys remained her prerogative — be it Banjo, Malty
or Ray. She is not like the "tantalizing brown" of *Home to Harlem,*
merely an object of sexual desire, but a tough woman of the Ditch car-
rying a dagger in her bosom with strong opinions against white racism.
This portrayal of a female character marks a significant step in McKay's
ideological evolution. Still the novel is undoubtedly a "homosocial"

world of men celebrating and reinscribing the values and codes of masculine domain.

If many critics often see *Banjo* as a continuation of the hypersexed, care free Jake, Ray, continued from the earlier novel, is often dubbed as McKay's mouthpiece. Tillery thinks that until Ray is introduced in the second part, the novel lacks "any direction or purpose" (120). Once he is introduced, Tillery thinks, *Banjo* becomes simply "a sequel to *Home to Harlem* or, more accurately, an autobiographical medium in which McKay continues to sort out his personal view of life, race, class, and his general philosophy of the world. And hence Banjo assumes a secondary importance as a character" (120). Though it is difficult to deny that Ray, the brooding recluse of *Home to Harlem*, has become a more outspoken carefree person in *Banjo,* as commentator and spokesman of McKay, the charge that Banjo assumes secondary importance for that reason can be contested.

If Ray is taken as the autobiographical representation of McKay, the ambiguity ridden colonial exile drifting between two poles of existence, then a closer study of the text shows that it was with Banjo and his way of living only that Ray/McKay could explicate his life. It is only Banjo that ultimately gives direction to Ray's unresolved end of life. Banjo remains the ideal for which the intellectual and undecided Ray must strive. Ray arrives in Marseilles after much voyaging in Europe convinced more than ever of the perils of white materialism and the hardened racial discrimination. He becomes aware of the hollowness in the claims of white man about the superiority of the white culture and civilization. Therefore, when the novel opens, he is almost but not quite ready to accept proudly the black races of the world as they are. However, by the end of the novel, he overcomes this dilemma due to the inspiration he derives from Banjo and other beach boys (Giles 90).

Despite Ray's more candid expression of McKay's ideas and opinions, Banjo remains the keystone of the novel, structurally and thematically. Viewed on a larger scale the two are to play a complementary role, balancing the two philosophies of existence — Ray's intellectual point of view and Banjo's sensual and spontaneous stance, which McKay himself was struggling to resolve. The very fact that he introduced Ray in these two novels, to articulate his dilemma, proves McKay's pressing inner conflict and his struggle to overcome it. Ray joining Banjo in the beach life, without any of his earlier qualms, shows his ideological progression. Ray and Jake despite their friendship and admiration for each other had to choose their own separate destinations in *Home to Harlem*. It is only in *Banjo* that McKay shows signs of resolving his conflict by bringing together Ray and Banjo in a mutually sustaining union.

Yet there is no denial of the fact that McKay could not restrain his lyrical double. Ray's role became prevalent, at times detracting from action. In a letter to Bradley dated May 23, 1927, McKay wrote that the character of Ray gives him a chance to "go a little" and that he was more interested in his ideas than in his life (qtd. in Fabre 203). Still, McKay feared, and rightly, that Ray as a strong and sophisticated character might make the story too interpretative, spoiling the humor of the book and depriving the scenes of gusto. The text confirms McKay's fears. The reasons are obvious. He did let "go" Ray, not only for articulating his peculiar problems of identity as a black colonial in exile but to give vent to his anger against his African American peers, while focusing on pan–African consciousness.

When Ray meets Banjo and rescues him from the restaurant maid, he had turned his back on Harlem and done much voyaging in Europe, making a prolonged stay in ports that stirred his imagination. He had not renounced his dream of self-expression but found it difficult to get casual work in the Old World to enable him pursue his writing. Perhaps due to these difficulties and the disappointment he felt as a colonial, McKay gave the title "The Cynical Continent" to the section dealing with his life in Europe in *A Long Way from Home*. He had to go to books and museums and sacredly preserved sites to find the romance of Europe, which he felt through the splendid glamour of history he learned and wondered at as a colonial. Like Ray he too depended on occasional checks from friends and had to pose nude in Paris studios, which affected his health. Undeterred Ray, like his author, feels even more the urge to write and any means of achieving self-expression is now justifiable for him. Arriving in Marseilles Ray soon falls for its barbarous international romance.

He likes Banjo and his rich Dixie accent reminded him happily of Jake. Soon the duo share their different geographical sensibilities. The French speaking Ray takes him to the Corniche, which Banjo had never seen, and in turn Banjo introduces him to the greater depths of the Ditch. The characters reveal to each other the inner and outer geography of Marseilles, its physical and metaphorical landscape (Dixon 51). Soon Ray has a taste of beach life with the other pals of Banjo. He gets acquainted with Banjo's idea of a black orchestra. The conversation among the beach boys and with other seamen and barkeepers was the occasion for McKay to raise the issues of race — the color hierarchy, degrees of discrimination by various white nations, behavior of the French and English in the colonies, and Marcus Garvey. The argument between the Senegalese bar proprietor who made money in the United States and was all praise for it and a Senegalese seaman who defends his mother country, France, exposes the hollowness of their respective defenses.

In addition to music and dance, story-telling is also one of the entertainments for the black beach boys that establish their common folk roots. When Ray tries to elicit the Br'er Rabbit kind of African animal fables of the West Indies from the Senegalese boys they refuse to talk. They fear that Ray, who they came to know was "a writing black," might write something funny or caustic of their life that would make them appear "uncivilized" or inferior to American Negroes (*BJ* 114). This shows how deeply the imperial ideology has infused inferiority among the black people regarding their culture. Goosey, who is supposedly the spokesman of the Harlem intellectuals, echoed their concerns that the "crackers" would use what he writes to insult the race, when Ray says that he would portray the black beach boys' life in the Ditch (*BJ* 115).

Anticipating criticism on *Banjo* from the bourgeois Negro establishment in the United States, McKay replies when Goosey persists and asks what good Ray will find in the Ditch to write about except a lot of dirt. He wants Ray to exemplify the upliftment philosophy of the Harlem "talented tenth" and advises him to write about the successful black men and women in Paris. Replying that he would write about the society Negroes only when he writes a farce, Ray launches an attack against the black press and black society. Telling jokes is another activity joyfully shared by the beach boys. But Goosey, the race man who always avoided the word "Negro" and "black" and used, instead, "race men," "race women," or "race," not only chides the group for self-derogatory jokes but also objects to Ray using the word "niggah" before white persons.[7] Ray, in a rare show of anger, bursts out against Goosey and the Harlem intelligentsia that they are made up things, while Banjo and Ginger whom they consider coons are real "Negroes" (*BJ* 183).

Holding a mirror to McKay's ambiguous state, Goosey hits back, much in the same way Harlem intellectuals would react against him:

> "Get your monkey-chasing hand out of my face, black nig —
> man," cried Goosey, getting hot. "Because you're a man
> without a country, you have no race feeling, no race pride.
> You can't go back to Haiti. You feel there's no place for you
> in Africa, after you've hung around here, trying to get down
> into the guts of the life of these Senegalese. You hate Amer-
> ica and despise Europe. You're just a lost sore-head. You pre-
> tend you'd like to be a vagabond like Malty and Banjo here,
> but you know you're a liar and the truth is not in you" [*BJ*
> 183–184].

Even though Goosey's outburst is meant to challenge and ridicule the intelligentsia's opinion that McKay lacked in race feeling it is not without some truth. As the explosion in a capsule contained too bitter a truth, Ray's reaction was quite muted. When there isn't any strong reaction from Ray, Ginger accosts him: "Ray, how come you make Goosey get you' goat like thataway?" But Ray laughs, puzzled himself at his little flare-up (*BJ* 184). Ray's silence reflects the sad plight of the African diaspora condemned to exile. Confronted intensely by such questions of identity Ray could find solace only in the black brotherhood that he was enjoying with beach boys like Banjo on the Marseilles water-front. He did not achieve his pan–African identity overnight. Amidst the thick Ditch life, there were moments of intense contemplation about his cultural marginality. Through Ray, who had the unique posi-tion of looking at the civilized scene without belonging to any, McKay questions the foundational blocks of imperialism — patriotism, nation-hood, cultural superiority and the big game of civilization:

> The sentiment of patriotism was not one of Ray's possessions
> perhaps because he was a child of deracinated ancestry. To
> him it was a poisonous seed that had, of course, been planted
> in his child's mind, but happily, not having any traditional
> soil to nourish it, it had died out with other weeds of the cur-
> ricula of education in the light of mature thought [BJ 137].

In contrast to his white acquaintances Ray found it unnatural for a man to love a nation — a swarming hive of human beings bartering, com-peting, exploiting, lying, cheating, battling, suppressing, and killing among themselves while plundering weaker peoples (*BJ* 137). Com-menting on Ray's opinion that a patriot loves not his nation, but the spiritual meannesses of his life, Tyrone Tillery says that McKay must have known from his personal experience that the abandonment of an identification with one race or nation and the attainment of complete cultural universality was always easier said than done (122). Though it is quite difficult to achieve "complete cultural universality," and what-ever may be McKay's personal experience, he stuck to his vision in this text. Ray and Banjo at the end resort to another bout of vagabondage on the periphery of Western civilization, rejecting narrow imperial con-structs of nation and patriotism that have played havoc with their race.

In another serious contemplation about the "fact of blackness," Ray discusses in Fanonian terms how his race clashed with the white man's civilization, creating a massive psycho-existential complex (Fanon, *Black Skin* 109). This contemplation is what Fanon calls the desperate struggle of a Negro who is driven to discover the meaning of black iden-tity (*Black Skin* 14). The alienation, Ray realizes, is poignant and total for an educated man in the Western civilization. With liberal European education, Ray, as he traveled in the Euro-American world, grew more and more bitter about it. He understood that however advanced, clever, and cultivated, he will have the distinguishing adjective of "colored" before his name and be rejected (*BJ* 201). He despised the condition that Bhabha calls the "mimic men" that educated colonial subjects are reduced. Products of mimicry, the most elusive and effective strategies of colonial power and knowledge, these 'mimic men' are to serve as a link between the colonial masters and the multitude they rule. Colonial mimicry, Bhabha says, is the desire for a reformed, recognizable Other, *"as a subject of a difference that is almost the same, but not quite"*[8] (86). That is, a black man in blood and color, but English in tastes, opinions, in morals and in intellect, and so having only a *partial presence* (Bhabha 87). Ray recognizes this condition when he says that the black man realizes with a shock after he attains maturity that he doesn't belong to the white race and all his education and achievement cannot give him a white man's full opportunity (*BJ* 201).

Caught in this ambivalent situation, McKay comes to the central problem of his life — the duality that has structured his consciousness and writings when Ray says that he hated the society that forced him into an *equivocal position*[9] (*BJ* 164). He bursts out in existential lamentation: "Oh, it was hell to be a man of color, intellectual and naturally human in the white world" (*BJ* 164). McKay understood how the white civilization has forced an existential deviation on the Negro. Ray/McKay, who is bitterly aware of this alienating experience, says: "Only within the confines of his own world of color could he be his true self. But as soon as he enters the great white world, where of necessity he must work and roam and breathe the larger air to live, that entire world, high, low, middle, unclassed, all conspire to make him painfully conscious of color and race" (*BJ* 165). Therefore, Ray has to come to terms with his blackness. Either he has to resign himself to his color or refuse to accept the amputation (*Black Skin* 140). He turns to Banjo and realizes that it was easy enough for people like Banjo, who in all matters acted instinctively, while it was not easy for a Negro with an intellect standing guard over his native instincts to take his own way in this white man's civilization (*BJ* 164). Therefore, he debates and resolves that civilization would not take the love of color, joy, beauty, vitality, and nobility out of *his* life and make him one of the poor mass of its pale creatures. Having fought against the Occidental life instinctively, and having now grown and broadened and come to know it better, he could bring intellect to the aid of instinct (*BJ* 164). Soon as his ire turns against educated Negroes, the pale reflections of the white man, he is prepared to abandon intellect:

> He hated the hypocritical life led by educated Negroes in the large European cities: he had often met with educated Negroes out for a good time with heavy literature under their arms. They toted these books to protect themselves from being hailed everywhere as minstrel niggers, coons, funny monkeys for the European audience — because the general European idea of the black man is that he is a public performer.... He had remarked wiry students and Negroes doing clerical work wearing glasses that made them sissy-eyed. He learned, on inquiry, that wearing glasses was a mark of scholarship and respectability differentiating them from the common types[10] [*BJ* 323–324].

He decides that rather than "lose his soul, let intellect go to hell and live instinct!" (*BJ* 165). But the frequent self-assertions about negating the intellect and taking the instinct route raise doubts about his conviction. It is not only educated Negroes that Ray castigates, but also the fair-skinned Negroes who are serving the imperial system by despising their dark brothers. Ray meets a Negro student from Martinique who is proud that Empress Josephine was born there. When Ray asks him how it helps, the student responds that she is Creole and that in Martinique they were Creole rather than Negro. He further states that they were very distinguished and speak pure French, not anything like this vulgar Marseilles French. It is the desire to become white that drives the Negro of Antilles to greater mastery of the French language, affirms Fanon. In *Black Skin White Masks* he describes how the Martiniquans take pains to distinguish themselves from the Senegalese, whom they believe are savages. When Ray invites the Martiniquan student to the African bar to keep his appointment with a student from the Ivory Coast, the student refuses to accompany him and even warns Ray against mixing with the Africans: "They are not like us," he said. "The whites would treat Negroes better in this town if it were not for the Senegalese. Before the war and the coming of the Senegalese, it was splendid in France for Negroes. We were liked, we were respected but now —" (*BJ* 200).

The reply that Ray gives underlines his progression toward his final beliefs regarding the black masses and the new black art. He corrects the mulatto student, saying that he can't get away from the Senegalese and other Africans any more than he can get away from the fact that their forefathers are slaves (*BJ* 200). This reminds him of the Renaissance, and he spells out his opinion that if it were to be more than "a sporadic and scabby thing," they had to get down to the "racial roots" (*BJ* 200). His belittling attitude towards the Renaissance shows how ideologically distant he was from the mainstream Harlem intellectuals. Voicing the criticism of the Harlem elite against McKay, the student says that he believes in racial renaissance but not in going back to savagery. Ray hits back that he is like many Negro intellectuals who are "bellyaching" about race. He attributes this to the false ideological influence of the white man's education. He exhorts the youth to find himself only in the roots of his own people; as models, he asks the youth to look to many cultural and social movements:

> You would study the Irish cultural and social movement. You would turn your back on all these tiresome clever European novels and read about the Russian peasants, the story and struggle of their lowly life, patient, hard-driven life, and the great Russsian novelists who described it up to the time of the Russian Revolution. You would learn all you can about Ghandi and what he is doing for the common hordes of India [*BJ* 201].

As sources for Negro art, McKay gave a direction when Ray recounts African folk tales followed by a speech praising the African sculpture that the French modernists have turned to.[11] When the mulatto student refuses to accompany him, Ray goes alone to hear the African dialects sounding around him in the bar. Appreciating the dialects, he slowly drops the mask of education and one can trace the pan–African consciousness taking deep roots. Africa acquires a signifying role underlying the unity of the black race. Thus, McKay becomes one of the early Caribbean writers to construct Africa as a country of the mind, and as homeland of dispersed populations in search of solidarity rather than a representation of a geohistorical place (Parry 93). Africa, the name of the missing term, the great aporia, which lies at the center of the diaspora's cultural identity, is thus given a meaning.

Though Ray's lectures are overwhelming and deflect the attention of the readers, it is difficult to conclude that he is just a passive spokesman for McKay. By the end of the second part, he is participating in all the activities of the beach boys bringing together the group after Banjo's return from the coal yard. From admitting Banjo in the hospital to securing a passage to Lonesome Blue, it is Ray who takes the active role. To indicate his total submergence into the Ditch life of the beach boys, Ray is shown participating uninhibitedly in a sexual rendezvous with Latnah.

However, when it comes to interracial marriage Ray/McKay knew that it was far from natural and conditioned by essential "neurotic orientation" in the colonial context. He anticipates Fanon in his analysis of the relationship between a woman of color and a white man in the West Indian colonies: that if the woman is not constrained by race feeling she'll give herself to the white man as he stands for power and property (*BJ* 206). In the same vein, a Negro male wishes to marry a white woman, thinking that there is some superiority in the white skin that has suppressed and bossed over them all their lives (*BJ* 207). Ray also analyses the false notions of the white man regarding the sexual behavior of the Negro. He says that Negroes were freer and simpler in their sex urge, while the white man considered sex a nasty irritable thing. Naturally, they attributed over-sexed emotions to Negroes (*BJ* 252–253).

One of the most notable topics that Ray takes up in his lectures is the hypocrisy of the French towards the black people. Of all the black expatriate writers, it was McKay who resided the longest in Paris and the provinces, mixing with all sections of the people. Even before he reached France, McKay was well aware of its politics and its role in colonizing Africa.[12] He knew that France was no better than any European nation in treating its black subjects and so had undertaken to contradict the credulous belief of his African American peers. Africans Americans like Goosey were satisfied that at least they were allowed to enter white cafes in France, and hence developed a positive image of the land in contrast to United States where discrimination is an every day fact. Nevertheless, McKay knew that behind the façade of equality and liberty lay the potential hatred for the black people, which was no less complex in quality from other imperialists. When the Senegalese barkeeper reads out the list of atrocities committed by France in Senegal from *La Race Nègre*, Ray feels that it is like hearing about Texas and Georgia in French (*BJ* 77). Unlike other black intellectuals who drifted to France, McKay's observation of the country went beyond the tourist stage. McKay admitted his deeper understanding in the text through his protagonist:

> Ray looked deeper than the noise for the truth, and what he
> really found was a fundamental contempt for black people
> quite as pronounced as in the Anglo-Saxon lands. The com-
> mon idea of the Negro did not differ from that of the civi-
> lized world in general. There was, if any thing, an unveiled
> condescension in it that was gall to a Negro who wanted to
> live his life free of the demoralizing effect of being pitied and
> patronized [*BJ* 275].

He not only resented being patronized but also hated the French proclaiming themselves the most civilized people in the world, bestowing the benefits of civilization on the Negroes. When Crosby the white French friend says unabashedly that they are especially tolerant to colored people, Ray has this reply: "They think they understand Negroes, because they don't discriminate against us in their bordels. They imagine that Negroes like them but he knew that they were the most calculatingly cruel of all the Europeans in Africa" (*BJ* 267). A cruder manifestation of Crosby's opinion is shown when a middle-aged French salesman representing the general public opinion tries to butt into the black boys' party, smirking and leering, with patronizing remarks like: "It's good here.... You get good treatment here" (*BJ* 297). The French, Ray understands, are no less talented than other white nations in making Negro stereotypes, because one black villain made all blacks villains ... and one black failure made all blacks failures (*BJ* 275).

In their growing hatred for the Western civilization, Ray/McKay couldn't exempt France. With little variation in method all, the white nations treated the Negro with contempt. He knew that in the name of spreading civilization the West has not only "uprooted, enchained, transported, and transformed, the black race to labor under its laws but also lacked the spirit to tolerate them within its walls" (*BJ* 313–314).

Deriving on the ethos of suffering common to all blacks McKay is trying to constitute an anti-colonial identity forging a larger and inclusive solidarity. Like a postcolonial critic, he is worried about the invasion of the Western capitalist consumer culture that is erasing cultural diversity. Cesaire too echoes McKay's lament that everything is being reduced to "a familiar formula by the grand mechanical march of civilization: ... what else has bourgeois Europe done? It has undermined civilizations, destroyed countries, ruined nationalities, extirpated 'the root of diversity'" (Cesaire 57–59). Therefore, Ray, who found that to be educated, black and his instinctive self was "something of a big job to put over" was shown a way by Jake and Banjo:

> That this primitive child, this kinky-headed, big-laughing
> black boy of the world, did not go down and disappear
> under the serried crush of trampling white feet; that he
> managed to remain on the scene, not worldly-wise not "get-
> ting there," yet not machine-made, nor poor-in-spirit like
> the regimented creatures of civilization, was baffling to civi-
> lized understanding. Before the grim, pale rider-down of
> souls he went his careless way with a primitive hoofing and a
> grin [*BJ* 314].

This has led many a critic to accuse McKay of essentializing the black soul. Even Tillery says that *Banjo* ends with an unconvincing appeal to the reader suggesting that blacks worldwide with their primitive innocence should resist assimilation to Western civilization (122). McKay's message in this text is not as simple as Tillery has concluded. Assimilation was certainly one aspect, which like other Negritude writers he despised. He disliked the politics of assimilation that made Africa a dark barbarous continent and Europe an enlightened and advanced civilization. The ideal that McKay hated was to turn the Negro into a Frenchman or English man with black skin. This explains his anger against educated Negroes and the Negro press whose "racial dope was characterized by pungent 'bleach-out,' 'kink-no-more,' skin-whitening, hair straightening, and innumerable processes for Negro culture" (*BJ* 322). Like many intellectuals of his age, McKay was also confronted by one big issue — the absence of identity for a Negro in the white world. It was an urgent task for McKay to restore the Negro from his inferiority to a normal ontological condition. Cesaire has articulated this urgency felt by many black intellectuals in the late 1920s in his famous interview:

> We lived in an atmosphere of rejection, and we developed an inferiority complex. I have always thought that the black man was searching for his identity. And it has seemed to me that if what we want is to establish this identity, then we must have a concrete consciousness of what we are — that is, of the first fact of our lives: that we are black; and that Negroes were not, as you put it, born yesterday, because there have been beautiful and important black civilizations. At the time we began to write people could write a history of world civilization without devoting a single chapter to Africa, as if Africa had made no contributions to the world. Therefore we affirmed that we were Negroes and that we were proud of it, and that we thought that Africa was not some sort of blank page in the history of humanity; in sum, we asserted that our Negro heritage was worthy of respect, and that this heritage was not relegated to the past, that its values were values that could still make important contributions to the world [76].

This concrete rather than abstract coming to consciousness is Negritude to Cesaire. Without the term, McKay laid the foundation. Essentialism, in this context, to use Gayatri Chakravorty Spivak's term in a different context, is "strategic."

Ray, in spite of his liberal white-oriented education, comes to realize bitterly that he has no place in the Western society. He comes to realize that Western society is rotten to the core by its materialistic values and is destroying other cultures in the name of civilization. He understands that it is his primitive earth-loving race that retained the vitality for life. This explains McKay defining the Negro as a challenge rather than a problem[13] to Western civilization (*BJ* 273). He not only made the primitive, instinctual life of the Negro healthy, but also asserted it as an antidote to the disease of Western materialistic civilization. As the rag is to the bull, he says, so is the composite voice of the Negro — speech, song and laughter — to a bawdy world (*BJ* 314). It is in this context that McKay gave a thinly disguised slap to the "black

Brahmin" W.E.B. Du Bois, who made his contribution to the "problem" by presenting the race behind a veil (*BJ* 272). Turning the tables he says, it was the white people who were the great wearers of veils, shadowing their lives and the lives of other people by them. Rather than hide behind any kind of a veil, Negroes, McKay claimed, are too fond of the sunny open ways of living (*BJ* 273).

Ray/McKay developed this confidence only after meeting the vagabond beach boys and the Africans. Driven to the edge of Europe, Marseilles, and standing on its docks he saw his African roots beckoning. The text portrays Ray's evolution toward pan–African identity with the help of the beach boys and the distant but unifying Africa. In the final revision of his condition, Ray acknowledges the positive feeling of wholesome contact with racial roots that the Africans gave him:

> They made him feel that he was not merely an unfortunate
> accident of birth, but that he belonged definitely to a race
> weighed, tested, poised in the universal scheme [BJ 320].

Ray is finally able to identify emotionally with his race. Only after establishing his roots with "Africa," "the missing term," could the "fragmented" diaspora restore his identity, making *Banjo* one of the early texts of Negritude. Stuart Hall has rightly recognized the significance of these Negritude texts in bringing about "imaginary reunification":

> No one who looks at these textual images now, in the light
> of the history of transportation, slavery and migration, can
> fail to understand how the rift of separation, the "loss of
> identity," which has been integral to the Caribbean experi
> ence only begins to be healed when these forgotten connec
> tions are once more set in place. Such texts restore an
> imaginary fullness or plenitude, to set against the broken
> rubric of our past [Mongia, 112].

He further sees them as resources of resistance and identity to challenge the fragmented and pathological ways in which the unique black experience has been constructed within the dominant regimes of discourse of the West (112). The more Ray mixed in the rude anarchy of the lives of the black boys — loafing, singing, bumming, dancing, loving, working — and came to a realization of how close-linked he was to them in spirit, the more he felt that they represented more than he, or the cultured minority, the irrepressible exuberance and legendary vitality of the black race. However, the thought kept him wondering how that race would fare under the ever tightening mechanical organization of modern life (324). He suggests an answer when he joins Banjo on another bout of vagabondage at the end. Nevertheless, many critics were not convinced of this conclusion. Giles speaks for them:

> But there are other, more important, problems with the ending. The reader is not prepared to accept Ray's assumption of the vagabond life because he has not been shown how Ray can utilize his intellectual powers in such an existence. Finally, Banjo has demonstrated so strongly and so repeatedly the universal, inescapable nature of white oppression and imperialism that one wonders just how the two characters hope to escape by hoboing around the world. Ray has said so often that the corrupt white man has his hands on every square inch of the globe that one believes him; therefore, one is unable to accept the ending as being a valid answer to any of the issues the novel has raised [Giles 93].

Giles' criticism demands answers on two levels, ideological and aesthetic. True, there is no escape from oppression and imperialism, and vagabondage on the fringes of the white society is certainly not a solution. But the narrator did not stop there. He laid the route for decolonization suggesting a solution in the unity of the race across the continents leading to social movements like the freedom struggle of Indians led by Gandhi. However, the frequent musing, probing, and questioning shows that the formula was still exploratory and tentative. The narrator frankly admits in the conclusion that this text is only an exercise of interrogation about the identity of the black man in the modern world. If McKay's three novels constitute a trilogy, it is in *Banana Bottom* that he takes up this theme of the intellectual integrating in the society successfully. He could achieve a viable solution only on his native turf — Jamaica. The quest for identity that started in Jamaica has to travel the full course of the triangle (Caribbean — Euro-America — Africa) for its fulfillment.

On the aesthetic level one can conclude that McKay has achieved what is in traditional parlance called poetic justice. It would not be acceptable if Ray, who was deeply disturbed about the "hand of progress" that "was robbing his people of many primitive and beautiful qualities" find a place like the "educated Negroes" in the respectable bourgeois white society. The questing intellectual Ray who found warmth and a "natural gusto for living" among the Banjoes of his race cannot but take the vagabond way. That is his way of combating the dehumanizing, oppressive white civilization. Moreover, like his author, Ray has already indicated that he will use the vagabond life of the beach boys, which Goosey called "dirt," in his writings (*BJ* 116).

Taking a rebellious stand against racial oppression he not only countered many of the stereotypes associated with his race but asserted that they are indeed signs of a healthy instinctual life. By asserting that his race is very much the healthy part of humanity he provided the much-needed ontological stability to the black race. McKay thus reaches a significant stage — "counter-identification" — in his career paving the way to Negritude, one of the significant historical phases in the struggle of the black man against racial oppression. Benita Parry's spirited defense of Nativity and Negritude is true of McKay's vision:

> Negritude is not a recovery of a pre-existent state, but a tex-
> tually invented history, an identity effected through figura-
> tive operations, and a tropological construction of blackness
> as a sign of the colonised condition and its refusal [94].

However, it appears that McKay soon understood that rebellion is only an important phase in the struggle for racial equality. Though it is useful to restore and affirm the black man's identity, it has its limitations. He knew that in a world dominated by technology and white values the black man cannot turn against the tide of history and go back to the pristine primitive values. He has to come to terms and negotiate his identity with it. It is exactly what he attempted in his next novel *Banana Bottom*, through his female protagonist Bita Plant.

— 6 —

Banana Bottom:
The Return of the Native?

Between *Banana Bottom* and *Banjo*, McKay's short stories, which he submitted to Harper along with *Home to Harlem*, were published as *Gingertown* in 1932. It is a collection of twelve stories written at different points of time with half of them set in Harlem, four of the other half set in Jamaica, and of the remaining two, one set in a Mediterranean port similar to Marseilles and the other in an Arab city resembling Tangier. Like his three novels, they are set in three different locations, serving more as supplement to them, and hence do not demand an exhaustive study of a chapter. Except for the problem of skin color all the Harlem stories resemble *Home to Harlem* in their graphic description of the Harlem life of cabarets, parlor socials and the sexual liaisons of "grass" widows, real and pretended. Notwithstanding the unjustified criticism of his peers that he wrote the short stories to prove he is a man of many moods, they do not focus, except for one or two, on the main theme of his major fictional works — the quest for self-definition. Like some of the tales he wrote for the Russian press set in the American South, they are often melodramatic and lack the strength of his other writings.

The central focus of the stories is the inferiority and self-contempt induced by skin color and the way it shatters the lives of the protagonists. As Giles puts it, "black, brown and yellow skins determine both the social success and the psychological makeup of individual characters" (110). McKay asserted to Eastman that after running "dry on the picaresque stuff" his Harlem stories "go much deeper into

142

the life of the Harlem Negroes than *Home to Harlem* ever did." Yet, the African American critics are rightly unanimous that McKay was out of touch with Harlem as a locale and that "strange West Indianisms" were uttered "from the mouths of American blacks" (Rudolph Fisher 3). Because, even though the problem associated with gradations of color was real, it was rarely oppressing in the United States, unlike in West Indies. Although the stories are set in Harlem in all its "exotic" settings, they did not strike the right chord for commercial success. Nevertheless, they gave McKay, who was never a professed prose stylist, enough training for his novels. The collection illustrates the importance of the short story in the development of his fiction.

The "gleaming coffee" colored Bess is let down by her current black lover Rascoe for another yellow-skinned rival in "Brownskin Blues." Let down by her mulatto husband she sticks to black colored Rascoe as she feels safe in his blackness. Shunned by Rascoe as a "black sow" she turns to skin bleaches. In a final moment of desperation, she concocts a mixture of skin bleaches and applies it to her face and unable to bear the burning sensation, she takes a dose of cocaine. The story ends ironically with Bess being taken care of by a faithful light skinned Jack Newell who convinces her that "it ain't the color that counts" but "it's the stuff" (*GT* 31). Similarly, in "The Prince of Porto Rico," "Mattie and Her Sweetman," "Near-White," and "Highball" the protagonists have to confront the problem of skin color. Either a black man is let down by his lover for a light colored man like in "The Prince of Porto Rico," which leads to jealousy and murder, or a Mattie is turned down by her sweetman calling her a "black woman." It is always the skin color that determines the lives of the protagonists; a near white woman, Angie Dove, gets disgusted in her attempts to pass as white, or Nation Roe, a successful black musician, is spurned by his white wife. It is only Mattie who even though was vulnerable to self-hatred finally stands against the humiliation and asserts her pride as a black woman.

"Truant," the last of the Harlem stories is almost autobiographical in conception, dealing with the theme of self-definition. The story also marks the transition from Harlem to Jamaica. A West Indian immigrant, Barclay Oram, is a university dropout like Ray/McKay and works on the railroad. Though married and with a child, Oram like his author was never at home in Harlem. His memory is always shuttling between the calm-green naturalness of the West Indies and the man-made steel and granite of New York:

> What enchantment had lured him away from the green
> intimate life that clustered round his village — the simple
> African-transplanted life of the West Indian hills? Why had
> he for the hard slabbed streets, the vertical towers, the gray
> complex life of this steel-tempered city? ... He was a slave to
> it. A part of him was in love with this piling grandeur. And
> that was why he was slave to it [*GT* 152–153].

Caught in this conflicting situation he finally decides like McKay and Ray in *Home to Harlem* to leave his family for an "eternal inquietude," a condition shared by all sensitive colonial exiles (*GT* 162). The four Jamaican stories serve as supplements to *Banana Bottom*. "Agricultural Show" is a description of a country exhibition that was graced by the island's governor. By describing Busha Glengley, the white imperialist's rags to riches life and his family's drive for social status, McKay completes the picture of Busha left out in *Banana Bottom*. Of these stories, it is "When I Pounded the Pavement" that is most interesting, as it is the prose version of *Constab Ballads*, dealing with the travails of a black constable in the imperial police force. Two arms of the imperial power, the colonial police force and the church, were exposed in their joint repression of the native's sex life in the "British-spirited" island (*GT* 204). The story is about the narrator constable who is forced to "make a case" against a native (*GT* 205). Like McKay, the constable protagonist who is a "son of peasants" "had in his blood the peasant's instinctive hostility for police people" (*GT* 211). Such was the contempt for the repressive arm of the colonial government that peasants "liked the police less than the thieves" (*GT* 211).

To complete his obligation as full-fledged constable the protagonist is forced to "make a case" against a promising black youth with a political career for sleeping with a servant girl in the outhouse of her white employer. The black youth is contesting for the legislature against a white man who is a relative of the white employer. Hence Mr. Klingler, the white employer, takes unusual pleasure "to get him upon the act" (*GT* 216). The constable is forced to enforce a law made by the colonial legislature that was supported by the church. McKay thus exposes the brutality and hypocrisy of the white imperial power hand in glove with the church in repressing the black man's simple natural passions on the island. In another story, "The Strange Burial of Sue," McKay continues his attack against the church in colonial Jamaica. Sue, a sensuous but humane woman, who died due to complications arising out of adultery, is refused a church burial. When the minister declares, "Sue is gone to hell," it is her husband and lover, pushing aside the priest, that perform her cremation. A more sustained and subtle tirade against the church in colonial Jamaica finds its best artistic expression only in *Banana Bottom*. Together, the Harlem and Jamaican stories demonstrate the difference between McKay's treatment of urban Harlem and rural Jamaican life. Even though the Harlem stories cannot withstand the criticism of being a trifle artificial, his Jamaican stories dealing with less hackneyed subjects are quite authentic in the portrayal of characters and their environment. Indeed, they serve as a prelude to *Banana Bottom*.

If *Home to Harlem* and *Banjo* had ended with the departure of exiles, says Kenneth Ramchand, *Banana Bottom* begins with the return of the native (259). In his classic work *The West Indian Novel and Its Background*, Ramchand rightly located *Banana Bottom* as one of the pioneering texts of West Indian literature. *Banana Bottom*, he asserts, is the first classic of West Indian prose and its protagonist Bita Plant is the first achieved West Indian heroine (259). Relegated to a distant silent background on the periphery, the West Indian peasant character for the first time becomes the central figure of a novel. Hence Ramchand concludes: "Earlier recognition of *Banana Bottom* (1933) as a classic of West Indian prose might have established it as a model for that imaginative fiction built around the lives of the folk towards which the present generation of West Indian writers have only just begun to move" (14–15). After spending a substantial period in France, McKay moved to Tangiers, Morocco, in 1932, where it was the "first and last time" that he felt "comfortably assured of his unique creative genius and fully expressed it" (Giles 94). Capturing the lovely pastoral life of the central Jamaican mountain culture, McKay achieves in this novel artistic and ideological maturity. He reaches Michel Pecheux's third mode characterized as "dis-identification."

The plot is woven around a young native woman's effort to reintegrate into the peasant culture of her youth after a formal education in England for seven years. She was brought under the roof of a local Protestant missionary couple, the Reverend Malcolm Craig and his wife, at the age of twelve after a mentally unstable local musician raped her. The missionary couple takes Bita as an experiment to prove that with formal education and training in English culture, her life could be redeemed for the kind of Christian service they were trying to impose upon the semi-pagan native life. But as the plot develops Bita realizes that she cannot fit into the narrow, self-righteous mold of the Craigs. Encouraged by Squire Gensir, created after McKay's English patron, Walter Jekyll, she rediscovers her natural inclination for the ways of the folk and brings into their rhythms her own awareness and sensibilities as an educated, mature girl. The final break with her foster parents comes when she chooses to marry her father's drayman, Jubban, whose strength and reliability are reinforced by his commitment to farming, instead of Newton Day, who is trained as a priest and to dislike the folk life of the natives.

The interesting aspect of the plot is that McKay could finally overcome the rigid dichotomies and overt lecturing that marked his earlier texts. It is also surprising to note that it is in his native setting that McKay achieved a fine synthesis of form and theme, art and message. However, as *Banana Bottom* and *Gingertown* were published at the heights of the Depression, neither of them sold well. This fact was among others an important reason for its commercial failure. The rural locale in the British colonial Jamaica has little to interest either the primitive-exotic demand of the white reading public or the upliftment-seeking new Negro of the United States. In fact, of all McKay's works *Banana Bottom* was the only text that received very little scholarly critical response in the United States. The reasons are obvious. As Campbell rightly concluded, it did "not fit neatly into the Harlem Renaissance construct" (*Centennial* 17). She quotes Addison Gayle, the militant Afro-American critic, as an example "who dispenses with

McKay's use of Bita as a synthesising agent in his irritation that Bita is neither male nor North American"[1]:

> That the way home would be found by the young sensitive
> woman, instead of by one of McKay's intellectual vagabonds,
> or that the problem of black identity cannot be found in
> America, but outside, is symbolic of McKay's growing confu-
> sion concerning identity himself—a confusion to be obviated
> in but a few years, when he will find his identity in the
> Catholic Church, will surrender the god, Obeah, for the most
> demanding of the Christian Gods [*Centennial* 20].

Even if they evaluated the text, many Afro-American critics did it within the parameters of black consciousness, making true the fears of Allis about non-regional critics. Tillery reads the novel as a successful resolution of the conflict between Jamaican narrative folk values and Western European values, which McKay has started in *Home to Harlem*:

> It was also his last attempt to advance the theme he had
> unsuccessfully begun in *Home to Harlem* and carried through
> *Banjo*: that Western civilization was the Negro's cultural hell
> and should be rejected in favor of the simple values of the
> "folk." It was his most successful effort at dramatizing the
> conviction that neither Puritanism nor the love of money
> nor the dominance of science had wrung out of its soul the
> joy which one may get from merely being one's own self
> [129].

Timothy S. Chin emphasizes that McKay's narrative "is structured around a series of oppositions that include the native vs. the European, Obeah vs. Christianity, the primitive vs. the civilized, instinct vs. intellect, folk culture vs. high culture, spontaneous warmth vs. cultivated refinement, natural growth vs. artificial growth, and so on" (4). So within this schema, concludes Chin, Bita Plant — whose name suggests her rootedness in the "native" soil of Jamaican folk culture — represents the triumph of "indigenous" cultural values over the metropolitan ones that have been imposed upon her by the Craigs' European education (4). Elaine Campbell puts it even more assertively, saying that the struggle between the two halves of Bita's self— the indigenous half and the acquired half—is the substance of *Banana Bottom*[2] (139). Many critics affirmed that the plot of *Banana Bottom* concerns Bita Plant's gradual reassertion of her cultural identity and a rejection of the values, Christian and imperial, that the white missionary couple stood for. Bita, for these critics, has had an education like Ray, but unlike Ray, who is never able to resolve his inner conflicts successfully, she is able to rise above Western civilization and return to her roots. West Indian critic Kenneth Ramchand too reads it as a continuation of McKay's "cultural dualism" theme started in his earlier novels — the difference being the "difference in art" (259). The novel for him depicts the heroine's "final liberation" and "embrace of the folk"—a record of her "increasing sense of rootedness in the Banana Bottom community" (260–272).

A culmination of this school of criticism is found in K. Chellappan's essay "Cultural Dualism in *Banana Bottom*: An Indian Perspective" (*Centennial* 32). The central theme of the novel for him "is the return of the native," i.e., "the return to one's own roots" (*Centennial* 33). Extending the implications of such a "return" to her native culture as "reasserting" her cultural identity he concludes that her "progress is from an acquired or imposed culture, which is only superficial, to an inherited or innate culture, in regaining which she rediscovers her true self" (33). By discovering her authentic past and tradition, Bita has actually reclaimed her cultural identity that was subverted by Priscilla Craig's "experiment." For all these critics the novel dramatizes the clash of two cultures: one that imposes the master's culture which is foreign through systematic education in its national institutions, and the other that reaffirms an innate, stable, coherent culture that can be recovered in its pristine form. Bita Plant for them is a model West Indian heroine who succeeded in rejecting the master's culture by discovering and embracing her folk roots.

There is another school of criticism which argues that *Banana Bottom* is a "blending" or "integrating" of the "innate and the imposed" cultures (George 50). Toomer's *Cane* and McKay's *Banana Bottom*, for Kay R. Van Mol, "deal with the development of a Black consciousness which is envisioned largely in terms of a reconciliation or blending of what might be called the 'intellect' of the Western world and the 'primitivism' of the African heritage" (48). Unlike Toomer and in contrast to his two earlier novels, says Van Mol, McKay's heroine achieves her integrated black consciousness by avoiding the "extremes of primitivism and intellect" (50). Total adherence to either "Voo-doo Obeah" or the "white, materialistic, Christian society of the Craigs" will be subversive to a "true twentieth-century Black consciousness" (Van Mol 51).

Though "blending" or "integrating" of cultures is true in the novel, they arrived at this conclusion not by reading it within the Jamaican colonial context. The text suffered a fate similar to that of other McKay works as it was read within either the Western literary tradition or an Afro-American aesthetic framework. Neither of the schools has read it as a postcolonial text, comprehending the distinct dynamics operating in such a context. Colonial encounters, even if recognized, are placed in a rigid dichotomy by these readings, elaborating monolithic constructions of self and other, disregarding the dialogic subtleties and the discursive, although disjunctive, cultural economy of the dynamics of colonial intimacy. The outcome is that they reinscribe, albeit on an ostensibly native terrain, the colonial idiom of constructing and representing the Other. Except for a few critics in either school, most of them have read it as a conflict, neglecting the fusion of cultures and the creole engendered by imperialism in the West Indian context. Moreover, what Bhabha calls the ambivalence inherent in the ideological construction of otherness that marks the Craig's goal of the "experiment" on Bita is never addressed. Finally, they did not consider the gendering of colonial experience, which McKay foregrounds in the novel.

Yet, the plot and many passages in the novel support what these critics read either as an affirmation of an essential, indigenous, cultural tradition or a fine blending or integrating of both the cultures. The novel opens with Bita Plant's "homecoming" after "seven years of polite upbringing" in "England — the mother country" (*BB* 1). The "only native Negro girl ... who had been brought up abroad," she now returns "a real young lady wearing a long princess gown" with "hair fixed up in style" (*BB* 1). It was the Craigs, the white missionary couple of Jubilee and Banana Bottom who "were responsible for that" (*BB* 1). The Craigs hope to "redeem" Bita from her past (she was raped by Crazy Bow) by a long period of education in England without any contact with Banana Bottom and at the finish she would be English trained and appearing in everything but the color of her skin (*BB* 31). However, on returning to Jamaica, Bita feels culturally and socially alienated due to her foreign education and longs to renew her ties with her family and friends at Banana Bottom. When she visits the village market, Bita mingles in the crowd "feeling the color, the smell, the swell and press of it" and experiences a "surging free big feeling" (*BB* 40). With the noises of the market sweeter in her ears than a symphony, Bita feels as if she has "descended for baptism" (*BB* 40–41). The narration runs as if a sense of connection is reestablished with her folk and she is complete again after her market "baptism" (*BB* 41).

Walking back from the market with Hopping Dick, a less-than-reputable character, is the beginning of asserting her independence from the Craigs. Attending late night tea-meetings that were denounced by the church, dancing to native tunes, showing her eagerness to wear the West Indian peasant's bandanna clothes, taking a bath in her childhood pool, flirting with Hopping Dick are some of the events that marked her yielding to the folk in her while rejecting the Western values embodied in the Craigs (Tillery 130). The dancing scene at the Kojo Jeems tea-meeting is taken as a sign of Bita's innate love for the folk culture:

> And Bita danced freely released, danced as she had never danced since she was a girl at a picnic at Tabletop, wiggling and swaying and sliding along, the memories of her tomboyish girlhood rushing sparkling over her like water cascading over one bathing upon a hot summer's day.... And she danced forgetting herself, forgetting even Jubilee, dancing down the barrier between high breeding and common pleasures under light stamping foot until she was one with the crowd [*BB* 84].

As the novel progresses she prefers Banana Bottom to Jubilee where the atmosphere is one of restraint, repression and self-denial. Bita's increasing sense of her rootedness in the Banana Bottom community is reflected in her deliberate flouting of Mrs. Craig's wishes. The increasing antagonism between Bita and Mrs. Craig is taken as between native and alien cultures. Encouraged by Squire Gensir, the eccentric English exile, she not only questions her recently acquired education and culture but also rediscovers and appreciates the indigenous native values. In an oft-quoted passage, she asserts her black identity to Herald Newton Day, a product of white missionary schooling who is arranged to marry Bita and destined to take charge of the mission after the Craigs:

> Let me tell you right now that a white person is just like any other human being to me. I thank God that although I was brought up and educated among white people, I have never wanted to be anything but myself. I take pride in being colored and different, just as an intelligent white person does in being white. I can't imagine anything more tragic than people torturing themselves to be different from their natural unchangeable selves [*BB* 169].

Many isolated passages like these posit and assert cultural identity as innate, stable, unalterable, constant, fixed, and pre-given. Supported by the superficial impression of the plot it is indeed attractive to conclude that it is an affirmation of the subject's moment of transcendence of imposed culture to a harmonious reunification with the innate, native, indigenous self and thus effectively counter the palimpsestic project of imperialism. The process culminates with her breaking away from the Craigs on the issue of her short lived infatuation with Hopping Dick and finally marrying Jubban, a sturdy black peasant giving the impression that the *Plant* is "grafted" to the "root" in the earth (*BB* 313). So Chellapan concludes that by marrying Jubban, who was in harmony with himself and the environment, she has reestablished her link with her culture and true nature. The integrationist school also based its argument on the same statement: "Her music, her reading, her thinking were the flowers of her intelligence and he the root in the earth upon which she was grafted, both nourished by the same soil" (*BB* 313). By integrating the two opposing cultures Bita has finally become a true twentieth century black consciousness for Van Mol (51).[3]

Integration or rejection of cultures is possible only after stratifying them in rigid dichotomy. The synthesis achieved by rejection of the "alien" culture is possible only by subverting and erasing the disjunctive moments in the construction of Bita's gendered colonial subjectivity. As it did not read the text within the Jamaican colonial context the "integrationist" school's conclusion, though true, is incomplete. The "rejection" school's fault lies in its uncritical affirmation of the teleology of Caribbean folk values and native history determined by an ontological stability. The reunification of Bita's consciousness — split by the colonial education that inscribes its own culture by physically and culturally alienating the native subject — can happen only by omitting discontinuous events in the novel that mark the "return" of the native. Only a close study of the text within the Jamaican colonial context of the late nineteenth century can help focus on how Bita was successful in translating two cultures — the European cultural tradition that she acquires during her seven-year stay in England, and the indigenous cultural tradition that she is born into in Jamaica.

Discussion of cultural identity in a postcolonial context revolves around the twin poles of "authenticity" and "hybridization." "Authenticity" can be defined in terms of a "shared culture," a sort of collective "one true self," hiding inside the many other, more superficial or artificially imposed "selves," which people with a shared history and ancestry hold in common. Giving stable, unchanging and continuous frames of reference and meaning, this cultural essentialist position not only gives a strategic political strength, but also becomes a very powerful and creative force in emergent forms of representation amongst the marginalized. Such a conception of cultural identity played a crucial role in all the postcolonial struggles, which have so profoundly reshaped the world. It is also one significant response to the experience of colonialism and the concomitant denigration of cultural identities. This response is necessary because, as Frantz Fanon puts it, "colonisation is not satisfied merely with holding a people in its grip and emptying the native's brain of all forms and contents. By a kind of perverted logic, it turns to the past of oppressed people, and distorts, disfigures and destroys it" (*Earth* 170). Hence, the idea behind the Negritude movement is to restore the African past giving ontological stability to the fragmented black consciousness. Benita Parry defines it as "not a recovery of pre-existent state" (pre-colonial authenticity) but a "textually invented history" (94). This conception of cultural identity played a successful role in imposing an imaginary coherence on the experience of dispersal and fragmentation, which is the history of all enforced diasporas[4] (Hall 112). Making Africa the center of the matrix begins to heal the "loss of identity" which has been integral to the Caribbean experience. Yet this conception has its limitations and does not comprehend Bita's negotiation of identity.

Binary constructions of self and other, innate and imposed, reason and intuition, the foundational principles of "authenticity" have their appeal for their ability to engage in a discursive counter-politics of opposition. It is in this context that Bita's "homecoming" and rediscovering of the folk is viewed as singularly and productively oppositional. Bita appears to erase the imposed, in this context the "alien" English culture, only by appealing to and affirming an ontological stability of binarisms. In considering the notion of ontology as a basis for constructing a black cultural identity, Frantz Fanon rejects it emphatically: "Every ontology is made unattainable in a colonized and civilized society.... Ontology does not permit us to understand the being of the black man. For not only must the black man be black; he must be black in relation to the white man" (*Black Skin* 109–110). To discover and articulate one's blackness is to find one's self caught up, as it were, in the discursive narratives and discourses of blackness.

Even if blackness is already there, this "thereness" does not mean a pre-given, unalterable identity, which was contaminated by colonial impositions; rather it underscores the relational and textual imbrications of self and other in the ideological construction of whiteness and blackness. Hence, Fanon rejects the "magico-social structure" and organicity of black culture, the "rehabilitation" of the Negro by "ruling the world with his intuition." As the very nature of humanity becomes estranged in the colonial condition, black identity for Fanon, according to Bhabha, emerges not as an assertion of will nor as an evocation of freedom, but as an enigmatic questioning (Bhabha 42). It is this enigma, this state of being poised on the cusp of uncertainty, that marks Bita's dual subjectivity. *Banana Bottom* foregrounds exactly this condition and the process of transformation of its protagonist by translating the two cultures.

Stuart Hall's second view of cultural identity, which is a matter of "becoming" as well as of "being," explains Bita's negotiation of identity in the Caribbean context. Hall emphasizes that it is impossible to speak about "one experience, one identity," without acknowledging its other side — the ruptures and discontinuities which constitute the Caribbean's "uniqueness" (112). He says that, cultural identity

> is not something which already exists, transcending place,
> time, history and culture. Cultural identities come from
> somewhere, have histories. But, like everything which is his-
> torical, they undergo constant transformation. Far from being
> eternally fixed in some essentialised past, they are subject to
> the continuous "play" of history, culture and power. Far from
> being grounded in a mere "recovery" of the past, which is
> waiting to be found, and which, when found, will secure our
> sense of ourselves into eternity, identities are the names we
> give to the different ways we are positioned by, and position
> ourselves within, the narratives of the past [112].

So, for Hall, black Caribbean identities are "framed" by two axes or vectors, simultaneously operative: the vector of similarity and continuity; and the vector of difference and rupture. So Caribbean identities always have to be thought of in terms of the dialogic relationship between these two axes (113). Therefore, to comprehend and reconstruct Bita's identity in these terms requires an understanding of the ambivalence inherent in the civilizing mission of the Craigs, and how Bita has negotiated the pulls of the two opposing cultures.

The Craigs send Bita to England, to train her as an "exhibit" (*BB* 17). Mrs. Craig, particularly, wanted to demonstrate what one such girl might become by careful training (*BB* 17). They take this decision after they come to know about her "rape" by "Crazy" Bow, the wandering village musician. Although the Craigs construe it as "abuse" the narrator informs that it is Bita who initiates the encounter:

> As they romped, Bita got upon Crazy Bow's breast and began
> rubbing her head against his face. Crazy Bow suddenly drew

himself up and rather roughly he pushed Bita away.... And
when he had finished she clambered upon him again and
began kissing his face. Crazy Bow tried to push her off. But
Bita hugged and clung to him passionately. Crazy Bow was
blinded by temptation and lost control of himself and the
deed was done [*BB* 10].

While Crazy Bow was tried and sent to a mad house, Sister Phibby
carried the tale to Priscilla Craig, walking overnight to Jubilee which
was a good fifteen miles from Banana Bottom (15). Although Sister
Phibby, a colored woman, "thought it was a sad thing as a good Christian should, her wide brown face betrayed a kind of primitive satisfaction as in a good thing done early" (*BB* 15). However, the face of the
white missionary Priscilla Craig is evidently perturbed:

> Not so that of Priscilla Craig's. It was a face full of high-class
> anxiety, a face that generations upon generations of North-
> ern training in reserve, restraint and Christian righteousness
> had gone to cultivate, a face fascinating in its thin benevo-
> lent austerity [*BB* 15–16].

It was Priscilla Craig's and her fellow workers in Christ agreed opinion that the natives lacked "restraint." Even though "where the law of
the land was concerned they were quite docile in obedience" they were
generally "so lax" in "moral law":

> It wasn't because these people were oversexed, but simply
> because they seemed to lack that check and control that was
> supposed to be distinguishing of humanity of a higher and
> more complex social order and that they were apparently
> incapable of comprehending the opprobrium of breeding
> bastards in a Christian community [*BB* 16].

Mrs. Craig could imagine what would become of a girl like Bita if she
were just allowed to drift along with the "*stigma*"[5] upon her (*BB* 17).
Hence, the "rescue" of Bita appears to be a moral and social imperative for the Craigs. McKay was quite emphatic in locating this "achievement" of "civilizing" Bita in the grand imperial discourse of bringing

"light" to the "dark" races: "Bita was one precious flowering of a great work. Not only the work of Malcolm and Priscilla Craig. But of the pioneers who had preceded them in that field and whose tradition was the living breath of their work" (*BB* 11–12). The role of the missionaries in the spread of colonialism is underlined here. Fanon echoes McKay in his case against the Church, hand in glove with the colonial government in portraying the native as insensible to ethics. The native "represents not only the absence of values, but also the negation of values, and in this sense he is the absolute evil," and so as Fanon says sarcastically, the Christian religion "wages war on embryonic heresies and instincts, and on evil as yet unborn" (*Earth* 32). Hence, the Church for Fanon in the colonies "is the white man's Church, the foreigner's Church. She does not call the native to God's ways but to the ways of the white man, of the master, of the oppressor" (*Earth* 32).

In viewing the natives as sexual degenerates lacking all cognitive capabilities to grasp the meaning of the high social significance of existence the missionaries are assuming their culture and racial identity as superior. But to view the Craig's experiment solely through the lens of a colonial process of racialization in which the natives' culture and English culture are configured as mutually exclusive and binarily opposed is to be oblivious to two important facts: (i) the gendered and discursive nature of the colonizing impulse inherent in the mission of civilizing Bita, and (ii) the sentimental interest of the Craigs in Banana Bottom and Jordan Plant's family. When Mrs. Craig suggested her husband that they do something for Bita, daughter of Jordan Plant, the preferred friend of Malcolm Craig, it gave him an opportunity to demonstrate in full the measure of the family friendship between the Craigs and the Plants, the white man and the black (*BB* 17). Mrs. Craig had her own personal reasons too. Apart from the fact that she was moved with compassion for the girl, she "could not stand the idea of adopting a boy, with her own son living in a cripple-idiot state.... With a girl it was different. A girl could never arouse in her that inexplicably bitter resentment that a boy would. And besides she was something of a feminist" (*BB* 27). Hence, she rejected her husband's proposal of adopting Herald Newton Day. In fact, Mrs. Craig not only initiated the experiment and provided the necessary funds but also took an active role in its successful completion.

Bita returns, proving the experiment of the Craigs: that with the required exposure and inculcation of English manner, education and sensibility an "African peasant girl" can be "transformed from a brown wildling into a decorous cultivated young lady" (*BB* 11). The transformation of Bita, who functions as a representative of her community, gives an occasion for the Craigs to show the benefit from colonial presence and culture. With seven years of sound education and without any contact with her folk Bita became an exhibit — an embodiment of the productive presence of the missionaries, their religion, values, and culture. Educated in the mother country Bita is not only "redeemed" of her past but at the "finish she would be English trained and appearing in everything but the color of her skin" (*BB* 31). Here lies the ambivalence hidden in their civilizing mission. The color of her skin, this "fact" of blackness, is not merely an external distinctiveness of pigmentation but is a signifier arrested in a closed system of signification. In the imperial discourse the black man is sealed in his blackness and conversely the white man in his whiteness. Black and white thus not only become irreducible signs of difference, but denote what Bhabha says are the "complex strategies of cultural identification and discursive address that function in the name of 'the people' or 'the nation' and make them the immanent subjects of a range of social and literary narratives" (*Culture* 140). In *Banana Bottom*, these irreducible signs of difference are pre-given, producing and operating an array of organizational categories and regimes of signifying systems, which subsume difference and otherness by subjecting them to normalizing judgments of ontology, purity and national identity.

If Bita, in spite of her English education and training, can never become English and one of them, because of her skin color, what then is the purpose of giving Bita "the benefit of a sound national institution" (*BB* 45)? It is exactly in this ambivalence of the civilizing mission that the colonizing hold of the Craigs is located. The ways in which black people, black experiences, were positioned and subjected in the dominant regimes of representation are the effects of a critical exercise of cultural power and normalization. That is, they produce "knowledge" about the Other, and exercise colonial authority.

When Bita defies her authority by attending a tea-meeting,

Priscilla Craig wonders if she had not "overdone things with Bita, demanding and expecting too much of her, considering the girl against the background of her race and its place in the Occidental idea of the universe" (*BB* 93). This "Occidental idea," what Edward Said calls "Orientalism," not only constructs natives as "different" and "other" but maps the terrain of knowledge between barbarism and civility, sexual degeneracy and native ingenuity. Therefore, it was easy "to imagine what would become of a girl like Bita if she were just allowed to drift along with the stigma upon her. The countryside was over run with *runts* of girls who had been wantonly introduced to the ways of womanhood before maturity" (*BB* 17). It is this objectification or fixing of the native through paradoxical modes of representation that authorizes the civilizing mission of the Craigs.

The concept of fixity, says Bhabha, which connotes rigidity and an unchanging order as well as disorder, degeneracy and daemonic repetition is an important feature of colonial discourse. The stereotype, which is its major discursive strategy, "is a form of knowledge and identification that vacillates between what is always 'in place,' already known, and something that must be anxiously repeated ... as if the essential duplicity of the Asiatic or the bestial sexual license of the African that needs no proof, can never really, in discourse, be proved" (Bhabha 66). It is the force of ambivalence, continues Bhabha, that gives the colonial stereotype its currency; ensures its repeatability in changing historical and discursive conjunctures; informs its strategies of individuation and marginalization; produces that effect of probalistic truth and predictability which, for the stereotype, must always be in *excess* of what can be empirically proved or logically construed (Bhabha 66). The stereotype then is a paradoxical mode of representation that arrests the Other while proclaiming its unknowable otherness, its exotic difference. The native/Bita is at once knowable, at once unknowable, at once instructable, at once uninstructable: "Bita was atavistic as was her race. A branch of the same root and the deceptive lovely flower would wither to seed a similar tree" (*BB* 92). Even then, the Craigs take on Bita for "careful training" (*BB* 17). Thus, the ambivalent civilizing mission of the Craigs is marked by colonial rationale.

There is yet another angle to the Craig's civilizing mission. It can be found in Lord Macaulay's infamous Minute of 1835 suggesting the formation of "a class of interpreters ... persons Indian in blood and color, but English in tastes, in opinions, in morals, in intellect" — in other words a mimic man raised through English education (qtd. in Bhabha, *Culture* 87). Such a class already exists in Jamaica. Discussing Bita's prospects with regard to her color McKay observes that "there had been established a tradition by which all the little white-collar jobs were considered the special plums of the light-brown natives who came like a dam between the black masses and imperial authority" (*BB* 254). Some of them were even sent to England for higher education and later brought back to serve in administrative positions. The Craigs's decision to send Bita to England for a "thoroughly English education" is to create an intermediary who possesses "native" characteristics but is educated in English manners and culture: "It was generally understood that Bita would be an *auxiliary*[6] at the mission. Her training had been directed towards that end" (*BB* 34). Thus the ambivalence inherent in the Craigs's experiment works as an effective strategy for controlling a subject people through Bita, the intermediary, not wholly black nor wholly white, by training her in English culture.

The constitution of Bita as pre-defined, pre-determined subject suggesting a fixed, black (sealed in blackness), homogeneous identity, with pigmentation serving as an irreducible sign of ethnic difference does not explain her Caribbean identity, which is marked with hybridity. The pre-determination denies the complex intersection of the three presences — African, European and American, which engenders hybridized cultural and social praxes and identities. Right from the moment of its "discovery" the Caribbean has been a stage for multiple histories embodying complex intercultural, socio-economic intersections due to the fine distillation of the three presences. The infusion over the centuries of peoples and bloods from many different lands of Africa, Europe and Asia has resulted in a highly diverse population, with a broad spectrum of racial and cultural characteristics, problematizing notions of race, ethnicity, and national identity as a priori, stable, and fixed categories to narrate and signify cultural differences and identities. The Negro peasantry, the white and the near white, Chinese, East

Indian coolies and the consequent interracial intimacies transform the island into what McKay calls a "cradle of experiment." Here "unique human types" like the offspring of the Chinese and Negro women (the latest and most striking contribution, says McKay), are all caught, as it were, between opposing cultures, resulting in creole languages, cultures and multiple subjectivities. In this context divisions and differentiations between foreign and indigenous, innate and imposed, are subsumed in the discontinuous and disjunctive play of difference within identity.

This play of *difference* within Caribbean identities is the most significant part (the other is similarity and continuity) of it as it acknowledges the ruptures and discontinuities which constitute precisely the Caribbean's uniqueness. To capture this play of difference within identity, which is not pure otherness, Hall uses Derrida's concept of *difference* and *differance* in language:

> For if signification depends upon the endless repositioning of
> its differential terms, meaning, in any specific instance,
> depends on the contingent and arbitrary stop — the necessary
> and temporary "break" in the infinite semiosis of language.
> This does not detract from the original insight. It only
> threatens to do so if we mistake this "cut" of identity — this
> *positioning,* which makes meaning possible — as a natural and
> permanent, rather than an arbitrary and contingent "end-
> ing"— whereas I understand every such position as "strate-
> gic" and arbitrary, in the sense that there is no permanent
> equivalence between the particular sentence we close, and its
> true meaning, as such [115].

This conception of "difference" calls for a rethinking of positionings and repositionings of Caribbean identities in relation to the three presences — Africa, Europe and America. Africa is the unspoken, unspeakable presence in the every day life of the majority population, in customs, language, religious practices, tales told to children, arts, crafts, proverbs and in music. Though it forms an important aspect of the Caribbean cultural identity as it gives an imaginative coherence, one cannot recover it in its pristine form after four hundred years of traumatic history of displacement and dismemberment. One cannot go "home" again. The next important presence in the Caribbean cultural identity is Europe, associated with power, expropriation, imposition, exclusion and hence the temptation to reject it. But it too is creolized with all the cultural elements intersecting Caribbean life at every point, making it difficult to throw off.

The third and the most important presence is the New World — America — the terrain that witnessed and enriched the fusion. It is the beginning of diaspora, of diversity, of hybridity and difference. It is a recognition of a necessary heterogeneity and diversity; a conception of identity which "lives with and through, not despite, difference; by *hybridity*" (Hall 119–120). These diaspora identities are those that are constantly producing and reproducing themselves anew, through transformation and difference. One can only think here of what is "uniquely — 'essentially' — Caribbean" (Hall 120). In constructing Bita's gendered colonial experience, translating two cultures, McKay arrives at this essential Caribbean identity marked with *hybridity*. In such a context, the cultural play could not be represented, as a simple, binary opposition — "past/present," "them/us." The "play" enables the articulation and formation of identity without denying the local and socio-cultural histories and specificities, which shape and inform processes of cultural translation and transformation.

The novel opens with the "return" of the "native." But that Bita did "return," in the full sense of the term, is doubtful because she feels alienated from her community and culture. It is precisely her attempt to reconnect with the larger village community, to make sense of her uprootedness and to understand and negotiate the tension and pull of different cultures that the novel foregrounds. It is the process of hybridization, which is a translational — as well as in this case a transnational — process of identity formation. Even after she chooses to leave the mission and settles down in Banana Bottom, and after marrying Jubban, she ponders the implications of Marce Arthur's "you are only a nigger girl" and the gesture of the little boy in Blake's poem "The Little Black Boy," who strokes the white boy's "silver" hair and hankers to be like him, in interpreting her identity. In attempting to contextualize her own shuttling movement between two cultures, Bita frequently relies on her Western education — novels, books, photographs, music, language, etc. — to interpret and contextualize her "in-betweeness" and hybridized state of being. The numerous references to the European musicians Chopin, Beethoven, Mozart, and Brahms, and English literary figures like William Blake, Shakespeare and others that she was acquainted with during her English education, only reinforce this argument.

Speaking of identity formation in the social and physical movement of travel and migration, Trinh T. Minh-ha observes that identity "lies at the intersection of dwelling and travelling and is a claim of continuity within discontinuity (and vice-versa)" (14). The migrant subject, as it moves from one place to another, carries with it fragments of other locations. Between home and abroad, another space, a third, is formed. This third, says Minh-ha, "is not merely derivative of First and Second. It is a space of its own. Such a space allows for the emergence of new subjectivities that resist letting themselves be settled in the movement across First and Second. Third is thus formed by the process of hybridization which, rather than simply adding a here to a there, gives rise to an elsewhere-within-here/-there that appears both too recognizable and impossible to contain" (18–19). It is this third space that Bita inhabits. In constructing her passage of return to her community, Bita is compelled to return the terms of social and cultural engagement in Banana Bottom, a returning in which the boundaries that separate foreign and native, authentic and inauthentic cultures are redrawn. Although she returns to Banana Bottom, Bita carries within herself what Minh-ha calls "fragments of other locations," the memories of her stay in England. Swimming in an isolated location of the Cane River of her childhood days, Bita's thoughts

> flitted across her mind like cinema scenes. Of her college days and what some of those white girls she had grown to like were occupied with now. Of a moment in the dinning-room of the pension at Munich with Mrs. Craig when it seemed that all the guests were observing her and commenting, but not offensively. Of the brother of one of her college friends that she had liked a little in England [BB 117].

These memories are constantly evoked, erased, and remembered. Their very evocation or erasure embodies a mode of translation in which identity is constructed. Minh-ha further notes that these memories "can consist in operating a profoundly unsettling inversion of one's identity," because it "allows one to see things differently from what they were, differently from how one has seen them and differently from what one is.... Travelling can thus turn out to be a process whereby the self loses its fixed boundaries — a disturbing yet potentially empowering practice of difference" (23). Bita had never had that big moving feeling as a girl when she visited the native market. She thinks that if she had never gone abroad for a period so long, from which she had become accustomed to viewing her native life in perspective, she might never had had that experience (*BB* 40). The social and cultural implications of these processes of change and inversions of identity that mark Bita's attempts to reconnect and reestablish ties with her community of Banana Bottom has to be charted.

The constant, ongoing negotiation and translation of two cultures — native and English — is evident in the recreation of folk tunes resonating with echoes of Mozart, ruminations over the significance of Pascal's *pensees*, and contemplation of the paradox in Blake's heaven in relation to the construction of black identity. At the dancing party she attends stealthily with Hopping Dick in Jubilee, one can find her adapting what she learned in England to the native beat:

> It was the first time since she left college that she had done
> the dances practised there for physical and esthetic training.
> Now it was for the sheer joy of dancing.... Waltzes,
> mazurkas, schottisches, lancers and all the decorous ballroom
> dances that could never do for a fiddle-and–drum carousal
> on the grass at Tabletop nor in the dust of a crowded palm
> booth. But there on the waxed mahogany floor how delight-
> ful they were! And as Bita stood up to Hopping Dick ... who
> poised in the air and she pirouetting around him to the
> fiddling of the native translation of the minuet, she felt it
> was indeed a happy choice when the native tongue turned
> that name to mintoe [*BB* 196].

Music in the Caribbean was another culture code that is the product of hybridization, which Bita celebrates. Along with Squire Gensir, Bita was excited to know that the melody of a native tune with a little variation of measure was originally Mozart. Identifying with Mozart made her romantic and she felt like a "wistful slave mistress" of a lonely plantation of that region, conjuring that savage and tragic scene with the magic of Mozart (*BB* 124). Such was her love for the European classical music that Bita's first favorite playing was Chopin and the second was the spirituals, which were known in the island as Jubilee songs. Preferring to stay in Banana Bottom, which was often read as a rejection of the missionaries and their English culture, this was how Bita lived: "With a fine piano at her disposal it was as good to her as any place in the world could be. And it charmed her to talk to Squire Gensir and have the run of his library. From long conversations with him and from reading she had become almost an unbeliever. For exercise there was her father's pony and the long walks over the savannah" (*BB* 161). Critics often cite Bita's breaking of her college day photograph as a rejection and despising of her metropolitan education and culture. A close reading shows that it is not education that she despised but the "plan of her education" that proclaimed her a "pet experiment" (*BB* 211–212). In fact, when she feels ashamed of going to the dancing party with Hopping Dick stealthily, not only her "native pride" rose against it, but also her education. It was the "independence of spirit" taught by a code that an imperial proud nation had prepared and authorized for her most favored sons and daughters that made her — an alien child of enslaved people — stand against the missionaries (*BB* 205).

Yet, the process of cultural translation made by Bita is not an unexamined celebration and assimilation of different cultures. Squire Gensir marveled that Bita was devouring his profoundest books on religions and their origins and scientific treatises — the theory of the universe, the beginning of life, the history of civilizations and the physiology of man and nature, and that she did not merely parrot the ideas she picked up but interpreted them intelligently (*BB* 240). Similarly, she is conscious of the normalizing, occluding, and marginalizing impulses of her English education in which African art is nothing but the glorification of the "cult of Ugliness" and mere "caricatures of a poor and miserably fallen humanity abandoned of God" (*BB* 198–199). She is also aware of the exclusion of black culture, literature and identity in the literary tradition of the English, which contained tales of all children, except Negro children, for the little black and brown readers (*BB* 61). Yet she esteemed the little prize books, remembering that it was the stimulation of just such literature that had carried her through the novelists on the mission shelves (*BB* 62). Similarly, rejection of the missionary life did not mean embracing of Obeah. She neither rejects English culture and education outright nor embraces exclusively native cultural tradition, because she can reject English culture and affirm her folk tradition only in so far as she can deny and gloss over her own personal history of travel and displacement. To do so would be to indulge in a form of historical amnesia. Hence, she can be seen as perpetually interpreting and translating the meaning and significance, the social and cultural practices and implications of both cultures. Moreover, it is on Squire Gensir that Bita relies to contextualize and make sense of her attempts to create a new sense of belonging to Jamaica.

It is surprising to note that it is Squire Gensir, a white and not a black man, who helps Bita appreciate her own culture and native traditions. In the author's note, McKay declares that all the characters, as in his previous novels, are imaginary, excepting perhaps Squire Gensir. By creating Squire Gensir after his white patron, Walter Jekyll, McKay has reinscribed the colonial patronage system. Though it is not apparent, Squire Gensir too, though he stands as a contrast to the parochial Craigs, is colonial in his approach to the folk culture. When Bita expresses her revulsion to Obeah as "awful crime," Gensir quickly counters that it is his civilization that made it a crime. Obeah for him is only a form of primitive superstition, just as Christianity is a form of civilized superstition (*BB* 124). Even though both the religions are superstitious to him, Obeah is "*primitive*" and Christianity is "*civilized.*"[7] As he goes on to equate Obeah with the primitive Roman and Greek gods and demi-gods and Nordic Odin, and by valuing Christianity as a civilized superstition, it is implied that it evolved beyond this primitive state. What is important here is not that Gensir defends a relativist position that sees value in "other" cultural forms, but that he does so in language that reinscribes the ideological hierarchizing he is seeking to undermine.

In another instance when he replies to Bab's question as to how he is able to tolerate the manners of the peasantry, he says: "easily and with pleasure," because the peasants were like foreigners to him and so he could not measure them by his code of conduct but rather had to study theirs (*and it was a diversion doing so*), living among them (*BB* 82). For the man coming from the metropolitan center studying the peasants, manners is a diversion. After all, the peasants are so free for Gensir that they don't have any idea of words like freedom and restraint (*BB* 121). Even though he appreciates the peasants' culture collecting their folk songs and Anansi stories, they are still understood in terms of the binary divisions that divide the colonizer and the colonized. The folk culture is not "another" culture but remains an "other" culture that has to be valued. By patterning the Squire after Walter Jekyll, McKay not only indicates his friendship with him but also the problematic nature of the ideological frameworks he uses and whose logic he ultimately fails to contest.

It is in this contradictory and paradoxical sense that the transformative experience of Bita's migrant journey occasions the rearticulation and reproduction of indigenous tradition in the discontinuous and fractal experience of colonial Caribbean life. The foregrounding of the discontinuous moments in Bita's reclamation of personal memory and local history dramatizes cultural identity as an ongoing process of negotiation that articulates the translation of colonial culture as transformative and reinventive experience of the migrant's journey. Here the absolutist narratives of empire, nation, and ethnicity yield to the unraveling and dislocating impulses of hybridized, impure subjectivities which rewrite and reconceptualize strategies of selfhood and communal identification. Bita's transformation and translation of cultures faces its biggest challenge when, after the Craigs, Marse Arthur, himself a bastard near-white son of a wealthy country gentleman, tries to seal Bita into her ethnicity when he says, "youse only a black gal" (*BB* 264). The process through which she interpreted it underlines her hybridized identity:

> She thought how the finest qualities of mind or brain or
> heart were the attributes of only the rarest spirits, who may
> spring like flowers in the commonest as much as the most

exclusive places, in the proud domain as well as the peasant's lot and even in hothouses. How then could any class or people or nation or race claim a monopoly of a thing so precious and so erratic in its manifestations? [*BB* 266].

Questioning thus she undresses and looks at her body, thinking, "Only a nigger gal!" But she was proud of being a Negro girl. No banal ridicule of a ridiculous world could destroy her confidence and pride in herself and make her feel ashamed of that fine body that was the temple of her high spirit (*BB* 266). Then she reached for the book of Blake's poems and turned to "The Little Black Boy." Though she knew that it could not be recommended to an impressionable black child, she still appreciated its aesthetics: "How perfect of music and phrasing, and far-reaching the implication of that thought: When he from white and I from black cloud free..." (*BB* 267–268). In capturing this transformative and translative experience of Bita towards a hybridized state McKay arrived at the "essential" Caribbean identity, not by essence or authenticity, but by the recognition of a necessary heterogeneity and diversity.

Her music, her reading, her thinking were the flowers of her intelligence and he the root in the earth upon which she was grafted, both nourished by the same soil [*BB* 313].

Thus he became one of the early West Indian writers, long before the second generation emigrant writers of the 1950s, to grapple with the most complex and perplexing question that colored West Indians faced — cultural identity. Documenting the embryonic West Indian struggle for identity, the text marks the "dis-identification" stage as it readapts fragments from both the cultures to envision and define identity for the present and future. If identity is constituted not outside but within representation, as Hall concludes, then McKay's text, like Caribbean cinema, is not a second-order mirror held up to reflect what already exists, but is a form of representation which is able to constitute the Caribbean people as new kinds of subjects, and thereby enable them to discover places from which to speak (120). By finding an answer to the question of identity McKay laid the route to decolonization, making *Banana Bottom* one of the early texts of Jamaican nationalism. Benedict Anderson argues in *Imagined Communities* that communities are to be distinguished not by their falsity or genuineness but by the style in which they are imagined (qtd. in Hall 120). In *Banana Bottom*, Ramchand rightly concludes, "Claude McKay imagined a community to which it is possible to belong" (273). The spiritual quest for psychic unity and stability that began with *Home to Harlem* came full circle to rest again in the lost paradise of his pastoral childhood. Read comprehensively, McKay's literary productions make a statement of his quest and achievement as a Third World expatriate, which he explicitly traces in the two autobiographies *My Green Hills of Jamaica* and *A Long Way from Home*.

− 7 −

A Long Way from Home

Ending his long exile in Europe and North Africa McKay returned to the United States in 1934, ill and impoverished. With dismal sales of his last two novels and rejection of another, *Savage Loving*, McKay was in serious financial straits. He was forced to sell his dwelling in Tangiers and implore the help of some white patrons like Eastman in America. Acute financial crisis and the reassurance given by James Weldon Johnson that he could still contribute to black writing in America prompted the drifting writer to think of the United States. Actually, McKay had never intended to return to America. Like many of his fellow West Indian emigrants he never gave up his British citizenship. America for this colonial exile always remained only a potential market, "where I make my living by writing and selling my production to the American public"[1] (qtd. in Tillery 137). Hence, Tillery rightly concludes that McKay "had never expressed any loyalty to, nor interest in, the United States other than as a means of support" (137–138). Harlem, like London and Paris, was another place of temporary residence for the exiled writer who came a long way from home.

Finally, when he did decide on returning to America, it was only with the hope of personally promoting his writings and earning his living on a lecture tour. Moreover, ideologically too, McKay was now better prepared for the American milieu. After resolving his dichotomy regarding identity in his last fictional work *Banana Bottom*, and after his long experiences in Europe and Africa, McKay now advocated a strong group spirit for the black community. His observations abroad convinced him that a strong sense of group consciousness could resist exploitation and repression effectively. Though he was sympathetic to the black cause in America he was quite apprehensive about his prospective relationship with the Negro elite with whose ideological orientation he found fault and whose renaissance he had spurned all those years. Declaring that he should "find a new orientation among the Negro intelligentsia," McKay in a letter to Max Eastman expressed his fears: "They are all so touchy. And if I go back home I'll have to live among them. Fact is I am afraid of the idea of returning for good. For now I can't live like in the days before the *Liberator*. I'll have to find myself among the 'Niggerati' as I hear they call themselves in Harlem" (qtd. in Tillery 136). As the Russian connection made it difficult for McKay to seek an entry into the United States, he had to approach the same Negro literati for help. With Walter White's successful persuasion of the foreign office and Max Eastman's financial help, McKay finally landed in New York in February 1934, in the same penniless condition as he left it a decade before.

Unfortunately, the time McKay landed in New York coincided with the Great Depression. The depression's major casualty was the fragile Harlem Renaissance. By the time McKay returned, it was on its last breath. Dismal economic conditions forced the white establishment to withdraw its patronage to the Harlem vogue. The black metropolis which had a decade before been the celebrated center of Negro arts had now become a place of squalor and violence. The "Renaissance" which the African American elite vigorously promoted never took deep roots. Even W.E.B. Du Bois, supposed to be its patron saint, concluded that it was only a "transplanted and exotic thing," for the "benefit of white people and at the behest of white readers, and started out privately from the white point of view" (181). He felt that it "never had real Negro constituency, and did not grow out of the inmost heart and frank experience of Negroes"[2] (181). Though the Harlem Renaissance had a symbolic significance as a first conscious attempt made by the American Negro people to prove themselves equally talented, it failed for the same reasons Du Bois has pointed out.[3] However, scholars like Arthur Schomburg tried in vain to rescue the Renaissance from a premature death. They tried to promote a black magazine with McKay as its editor. McKay now took on whole-heartedly the task of reviving the Renaissance as it suited his present ideology of race pride and strong group spirit. But the project never took off in spite of McKay's best efforts. He was left without employment and was forced to seek sustenance in a work camp and rehabilitation center called Camp Grey Court.

Unable to bear the wretched life in Grey Court, McKay came out and at the suggestion of James Weldon Johnson applied to the Julius Rosenwald Fund in Chicago for a grant to begin a memoir of his years abroad. The fund helped him produce his first autobiography, *A Long Way from Home*, describing his experiences and evolution as a writer after he left Jamaica and clearing up some of the misapprehensions about his personal and political affiliations. McKay proposed to the fund managers to illustrate through his own experiences and observations abroad, the significance of a group spirit to the American Negro. But his advocacy of racial chauvinism and group spirit at that time was again at odds with spirit of the time. Severely affected by the depression, the black minority was now more concerned with economic problems. Sensing the helpless condition of the black community, the American communists changed their tact and started luring them in large numbers. Indeed many black intellectuals openly advocated radicalism, stressing economic conflict. McKay found himself on the wrong side again in his relationship with black Americans. During his first sojourn in America in late 1910s he advocated radicalism and tried to remain aloof in matters of race. A decade later, when he was advocating racial chauvinism, the black masses were more receptive to radical economic programs. This condition and certain uncomfortable incidents involving suspected radicals, who McKay believed were sabotaging his plans to build a Negro writer's guild, only intensified his bitter enmity with the communists.

McKay's relationship with communism is another controversial chapter in his life. His initial advocacy and later condemnation should also be understood in the light of his exile and ideological evolution. After the First World War, many black militant leaders and thinkers drifted toward the socialist movement, as their aspiration for racial equality was frustrated. Excited by the Bolshevik revolution of 1917 they applauded the ideals of the revolutionary regime, which pledged racial and ethnic equality (at least on paper), and the brotherhood of the working class. McKay was no exception to his times. Moreover, the World War proved to McKay the "real hollowness of nationhood, patriotism, racial pride, and most of the things, which one was taught to respect and reverence"[4] (qtd. in Cooper and Reinders, "Black Briton," 275–6). Iconoclastic and rebellious, McKay was more at home with white radical bohemia that offered him a milieu more compatible with his own temperament. His self-conscious association with the black working class while keeping away from the black intelligentsia led him further toward communism.

From the beginning of his sojourn in Harlem, McKay was attracted to the radical magazines, especially the *Masses* and its later version, the *Liberator*, and its editor Max Eastman. His trip to England deepened his knowledge of Marxism, as the approach in England was more doctrinaire. He collaborated with Sylvia Pankhurst, editor of London's radical *Worker's Dreadnought*, an organ of the working-class movement, and was an active member and almost a celebrity in the International Club. He came to believe that the problems faced by the blacks all over the world were due to the oppressive character of the capitalist system and that a solution could be found when blacks accept a socialist pattern. He went to the extreme position of saying that the problem of blacks was economic and not racial. He even criticized American black organizations like the NAACP for viewing the issue from the narrow confines of race.

In truth many African American leaders from A. Philip Randolph to W.E.B. Du Bois too toyed with socialism, but they believed that the issue of race was too overwhelming to think of a revolutionary approach. As always, McKay's advocacy of socialism was at odds with the African American thinkers. Some white radical leaders who combined radical reform programs with bitter and reactionary hatred of African Americans made the black elite approach socialism cautiously. So even if the socialist line was appealing, these intellectuals advocated the attainment of full civil and political rights under the existing socioeconomic system. Unable to comprehend this truth, the colonial exile failed to recognize that if the socialists were to win the confidence of black workers they needed to analyze the specific problems confronting blacks in terms of their status as a racial minority and not merely in terms of their status as workers. McKay, however, was unable to perceive that because of race, the black American's political and economic orientation was more pragmatic than doctrinaire.

Only a bitter and unforgiving experience he faced at a theatre made McKay rethink about his affiliation with communism. When as coeditor, he went to review Leonid Andreyev's play *He Who Gets Slapped*, McKay discovered with great anguish that the front row seats were to be used only by whites. He was "shunted upstairs" by the theatre manager where he sat "apart, alone, black and shrouded in blackness" (*LW* 144). McKay recollects this incident with great pain in his autobiography. The trauma that McKay underwent due to the incident is quite surprising, because even after witnessing first hand many lynching scenes and race riots in Jim Crow America, he felt personally hurt. No black American in that context would have found the theatre manager's act so shocking. It suggests a sheltered, privileged, distinct region of self from the American milieu, which only an outsider can possess. His alienation from the radical whites began when the incident showed him their true colors in matters of race. The passive dismissal of the incident by his *Liberator* colleagues hurt McKay, forcing him to reconsider his ideas on the relationship between blacks and white radicals. However, this reevaluation did not take McKay closer to the black intelligentsia. Realizing the significance of the issue of race in the class struggle, McKay set out to Russia with the hope of projecting it.

His "magic pilgrimage" to Russia did not help him appreciate communism. Just the opposite happened. Though he was thoroughly lionized by the communists he left Russia highly disappointed. Either the "black icon" lost its propaganda value or McKay disliked the Russians using him as propaganda, but his sudden departure from Russia only strengthened his growing distance from communism. McKay's refusal to take part in any organizational matters after his successful participation in the Fourth Congress of the Third International at the cost of official black American representative only infuriated the American communists. McKay was quick to point out that he could never be a radical agitator. He continued: "For that I was temperamentally unfit. And I could never be a disciplined member of any Communist party, for I was born to be a poet" (*LW* 173). His visit to Russia seems to have been prompted more by his deep personal hurt at the theatre than from a desire to become an integral part of any collective organized revolutionary endeavor. He asserted that he could do something significantly creative as a Negro writer rather than being merely a socialist agitator. Indeed, the idea of class struggle inherent in communism was apparently at variance with his belief in the freedom of the individual and the artistic vision for a harmonious order of the world. McKay's affiliation with communism was only an intellectual association, which had its roots in the dim hope that it would solve the problems of the Negroes. As he described to Max Eastman: "Although I was once sympathetic to their cause I was never a Communist. I had a romantic hope that Communism would usher in a classless society and make human beings happier"[5] (qtd. in Geta LeSeur 229). McKay soon started denouncing the communists for their "personal spite and slander" against his writings, which led to an acrimonious exchange of words that ended only with his death (*LW* 226). One good word on the communist side, says Max Eastman in his biographical note, "would have brought him ease, comfort, contemporary fame and a good income" towards the end of his life (*SP* 9). But McKay chose to live in penury and die in sickness rather than compromise his ideology. He tried to set his record straight with both the communists and the Negro intelligentsia in his autobiography as he traced his expatriate life.

But the book was a disappointment for the American Negro intelligentsia as they tried to locate it within the genealogy of African American autobiographies that invariably address the sociopolitical as well as cultural obstacles that impede the liberation and empowerment of African Americans in the United States. African American scholars trace the roots of African American autobiography to the slave narratives, which were primarily produced to prove their humanity and to claim a historically denied voice.[6] According to William L. Andrews, "the history of black American autobiography begins with the publication of the first discrete narrative text in which an African American recounts a significant portion of his life: *A Narrative of the Uncommon Sufferings and Surprizing Deliverance of Briton Hammon, A Negro Man*" (1760). The intention was clearly political as they not only publicized the horrific experiences of slavery but also expressed their existence.[7] As hundreds of slave narratives were published around the Civil War, they indeed functioned as powerful tools in the fight against slavery. But the tone of the post–Civil War narratives had changed as the purpose was to prove that African Americans had come of age and were ready to participate in the larger American society. With the *Souls of Black Folk,* the most influential text of modern African American cultural consciousness, Du Bois set the agenda for an exploration of the racial identity and the conflicted relationship of "the Negro" to "the American" by coining the term *double consciousness.* Based on the formulations of Du Bois, numerous African American texts were produced, often blurring the distinction between fiction and autobiography to explore the African American's existential struggle in the United States. Thus, the original autobiographical impulse in African American literature is firmly rooted in, and thus emerges from, existentially pertinent historical circumstances and cultural interests of their practitioners.

Though McKay's autobiography too shares the major concerns of other black autobiographies, it is shaped out of his exile and cross-cultural experiences. Tracing his exile life in the United States, England, Russia, France and north Africa, it records his ideological evolution from being a British colonial writer in exile to being a black writer in search of identity. Unable to recognize the different context in which it evolved, many African American scholars considered it a failure. They thought that it "failed to convey the complexity of his life" as it gave only an "account of his travels and his encounters with the great and near-great of international communism and the literary world of Europe and America" (W. Cooper 318).

One of the key terms in the context of Caribbean cultural identity is that of exile, a form of existence characterized by voluntary and involuntary displacement away from home and into another political or cultural context. Caribbean writers have shared with members of all classes and people from all parts of the area the experience of having to leave their home and make a living elsewhere in the hemisphere or in their respective European metropolis. While economic survival has generally been the foremost impulse for majority migrants, the lack of an audience at home, more particularly, figures as a key issue for most writers. For them, educational, artistic and publishing opportunities rather than political oppression or social destitution were major reasons to leave the Caribbean. Exile is a norm for the Caribbean writers, and so topics concerning their exile and cross-cultural experiences form a major focus of their autobiographical acts. Acculturation, finding an audience, evolution in the new terrain, revision of achievements, nostalgia and a comparative study of the adopted milieu are some of the topics that will invariably find place in an autobiography of this nature. McKay's motivation for the autobiographical act came from such a context.

The quest for self-awareness, for the exploration and articulation of the individual and collective, the historical and cultural identity, remains a dominant theme in the literary writings of McKay. Similarly, his "auto/bio/graphy" would also lend itself as the appropriate literary form of self-expression, of rendering the process of such self-reflexive acts as to examine one's origins and determine the cultural and historical influences on the personal and collective life and identity. *A Long Way from Home*, like his other texts, should be read in the context of his exile, search for identity and ideological evolution. It traces the unique but complex and painful experience of reorientation or acculturation and ideological maturity in the cross-currents of different cultural environments. McKay is quite authentic in projecting himself initially as a literary artist, a free independent spirit, and intent on experiencing life directly and extensively in order to communicate the truth of his experience in art. The source of this strong intention can only be traced to the pervasive influence of a colonial education. The colonial subject is in complete identification with the notion of universality in art that he inherited from the British literary tradition. Indeed, he stresses his integrity as a writer safeguarding himself from the temptations of becoming a racial or a radical poet. But as the autobiography progresses one can trace his growing disenchantment with the European values he cherished as a colonial. He finally accepts the inevitable influence of race and the necessity of developing a group soul.

The autobiography begins with the eagerness and excitement of an exiled writer who gets a chance to appear before an American audience. The emphasis McKay gives in meeting the editors at the beginning of his autobiography underlines his sole objective of establishing himself as a writer. He informed Frank Harris that the primary reason for his exile from his home country was the dominant desire to find a bigger audience. Jamaica was too small for high achievement, he says, as one was isolated and cut off from the great currents of life (*LW* 20). The rest of the work not only portrays his travels and travails to achieve his aim in the Euro-American world but also underscores his distinctness from the (African) American writers. He even tries to clear up some of the misapprehensions of his African American peers about his relations with the white people in America. In the third chapter, "White Friends," while asserting that he "had more white than colored friends," he justifies his friendship with them in the context of the Jamaican race relations (*LW* 37).

The second part, the "English Inning," describes the colonial in the mother country. But McKay affirms that after he "had grown up in America" he "wasn't excited anymore" about visiting England except for meeting the leading metropolitan literary figure of that time, Bernard Shaw (*LW* 59). The rest of that part is a description of his involvement in radical politics and a thorough disappointment with the mother country. Though the period saw the publication of a volume of his poetry in the mother country, the trenchant criticism he received as a black writer disillusioned him. Here McKay was thoroughly exposed to a cross-section of colonials from Africa, India and the West Indies, which enhanced his awareness of the color problem as a worldwide phenomenon. He even took up the cause of the race when he attacked E.D. Morel's article against the French use of "primitive" African troops in the Rhineland that were outraging German womanhood. Undoubtedly, the colonial's odyssey to the mother country has seriously weakened his identification with Western white values. But the growing awareness did not bring him closer to the black elite in America or the race problem as they saw it, as he still had hopes in communism. Only after the "Magic Pilgrimage" to Russia ended was his disappointment with communism complete. Race became the central focus of McKay's literary vision after the colonial's disenchantment with England, communism, and Western values had set in. McKay then embarked on a long and torturous search for viable native roots. The search took him to France and later Africa.

This period marks a paradigm shift in McKay's career and ideological outlook. As revealed in his *Banjo*, and the "Cynical Continent" section of his autobiography, McKay was thoroughly disgusted by the imperialistic and hypocritical values of the West that dehumanized the black race. Meeting black expatriates from the West Indian colonies and African countries McKay understood the shared history of their suffering. His description of the "Marseilles Motley," where he met the future proponents of Negritude like Senghor, marks an important milestone in his career. By delineating the common characteristics of his race he espoused a pan–African identity rejecting Western values. As he became more and more aware of the imperial politics of the white nations he headed toward the ideology of black nationalism. By referring to Irish and Indian cultural and nationalist movements McKay was actually looking forward to the civil rights and black nationalism movements that were to rise in the subsequent decades. The last stop in the quest for identity was Africa. The symbolic journey across the black triangle, Caribbean, Euro-America and Africa fulfilled his struggle for identity. The journey for black diaspora, as Hall affirms, is an act of imaginary reunification. It imposed an imaginary coherence on the experience of dispersal and fragmentation (112). It was during this period of peace that he wrote *Banana Bottom*, coming to terms with the perplexing question of identity by proposing a syncretic identity.

At the conclusion of his autobiography McKay takes up the immediate American reality of what "belonging to the minority group" is to him. (*LW* 342–354). Though he had an opportunity to merge into the African American milieu, he clearly shows how distant he was from the Negro intelligentsia in the United States. Even after facing controversy for not addressing the African American concerns in his writings, McKay did not make any amends or project himself as an African American writer confronting the specific problems of black America. His opinion that the Harlem Renaissance was more an "uplift organization and a vehicle to accelerate the pace and progress of smart Negro society" was not expected of an insider. His remarks on prominent Negro intellectuals were far from amiable. His opinion that the members of the Harlem group resented his intrusion from abroad in the Renaissance set-up was unfounded (*LW* 321). In fact they welcomed him and would have been happier had he identified with them. Even when he addressed the issue of race his position was at variance with the Harlem intellectuals. But with his outsider's consciousness he diagnosed the Negro problem in the United States: that the American Negro, the most advanced Negro group in the world, was lacking group spirit. The major hindrance for the American Negroes forming a group soul, McKay diagnosed, was the fear of segregation. They were unable to understand, McKay emphasized, the difference between group segregation and group aggregation (*LW* 350). Arguing that no sane group desires public segregation, McKay notes that it is a historical fact that different groups have won their social rights only when they developed a group spirit and strong group organization (*LW* 350). The most obvious model for blacks was the American Jewish group. He elaborated this idea in his non-fictional work *Harlem: Negro Metropolis*. He further emphasized that the Negro intelligentsia should not neglect the Negro masses. McKay's cosmopolitan views on Negro nationalism were far ahead of his American generation. Little did his peers realize that McKay's insistence on Negroes developing a group soul and becoming a strong community was a prelude to the Black Power movement that shook the 1960s. McKay's vision of black nationalism was quite distinct and more practical than the escapist and separatist brand that his fellow West Indian Garvey advocated and more realistic than the utopian brand that the American communists tried to sell. It was only Du Bois who recognized McKay's argument for group aggregation and urged the black American to accomplish his economic emancipation through a voluntary, determined cooperative effort.

In spite of his best efforts, McKay failed to renew the Renaissance. He tried to organize black writers' guilds that would promote group spirit, but every attempt foundered. One can easily trace the reasons in McKay's difficult personality and in the hard economic times. Many Negro intellectuals agreed with Alain Locke, who openly resented McKay donning the role of a group savior. Moreover, except for Langston Hughes, most of the Harlem writers had dispersed, were dead or had changed their profession due to unfavorable times: Rudolph Fisher and Wallace Thurman died in 1934; Jean Toomer had become a religious mystic finding solace in eastern cults; Nella Larsen became a nurse, while Countee Cullen, Arna Bontemps, and Jessie Fauset concentrated on teaching; Zora Neale Hurston left Harlem for her native South; James Weldon Johnson and Walter White like McKay wrote mostly autobiography and social history. So all attempts to revive the Renaissance had miserably failed. But McKay found the communists responsible for the failure of all his race-conscious projects. Day by day, his enmity with the communists grew. Unlike in his earlier stint in the United States, McKay now openly joined many campaigns against economic discrimination. Nevertheless, the last years of his life, Tillery records, were marked with despair (175). Unable to find literary employment, McKay was forced to take up manual labor in the Federal Shipbuilding Yard in 1943, which further deteriorated his fragile health.

As his illness intensified, McKay found refuge in the Catholic Church. He got appointed as the personal adviser to Bishop Sheil on communism and Negro issues and served as a lecturer in the Sheil School of Social Studies. His conversion to Roman Catholicism is another controversial chapter in his life like his past affiliation with its ideological adversary, communism. Finding fault with the historians' assertion that McKay submitted completely to the Catholic Church, Tillery affirms that McKay's conversion was, at best, "a marriage of convenience and principle" because McKay never identified himself completely with anything or anyone (179). It may be true that the physically and spiritually exhausted writer found some succor and comfort under the protected wings of the Church, but to call his conversion opportunism may be too harsh. McKay defended his conversion in an article "Why I Became a Catholic,"[8] stating that the Catholic church had always been free of racial prejudice and asserting that it was Protestantism that created slavery and dehumanized the black man. McKay's defense may be historically inaccurate regarding the two churches, but his opinion remotely agrees with many scholars who traced slavery and its overt mission of "civilizing the primitive native" in the humanist

perpetual exile. The wanderings and cross-cultural experiences in the Euro-American world thoroughly disenchanted the many idiosyncrasies he acquired as a colonial subject. He understood, though painfully, that race, and not his qualification as a poet, was the determining factor of his life and career. Even radical political ideologies that promised classless and raceless society, he found, were hollow.

In Europe and Africa, he became aware of the shared history of common suffering of the black race. Race and identity then became the central focus of his literary vision. As a member of the dehumanized race, he struggled to restore its ontological status by portraying it as possessing a primitive but healthy, community-oriented, tolerant value-system in contrast to the materialistic, racist, power-hungry, exploitative system of the West. This was not to reject or throw out Western cultural values and propagate a supremacist reverse racism, but the need to expose the hypocrisy of its practitioners and espouse a universal humanism. Hence, it will be hasty to conclude that by rejecting Western values he sought narrow nativist utopian chimeras. In *Banana Bottom*, he finally found home and a solution to his identity question by adapting the best of two cultures. Like his female protagonist Bita, decolonization for McKay did not mean throwing out the masterpieces of Western culture but the need to read and interpret them. His literary productions did not reject Western values outright but like "the great liberationist cultural movements that stood against Western imperialism" sought "liberation within the same universe of discourse inhabited by Western culture" (Said xxv).

If the historical experience of imperialism and colonialism for the black subalterns is subservience and marginalization, McKay's writings contributed to the discourse of black resistance that strove for liberation and inclusion. He thus joins the ranks of great writers that Edward Said lists, Frantz Fanon, C.L.R. James, W.E.B. Du Bois, Walter Rodney, Aime Cesaire, and Jose Marti, "whose intellectual pedigree was often entirely metropolitan but whose work could be characterized as providing an alternative consciousness to that of the mainstream, orthodox, or establishment consciousness prevailing in Europe and the United States" (Said xxvi). Like a typical Third World expatriate, McKay sought to reeducate and decolonize his race through his writings. Hence, his career, though started as a colonial's quest to find market and a meaningful existence for his individual spiritual self, paved the way for many movements like the Black Arts, Negritude and African Nationalist movements. To locate McKay's unique contribution within the narrow limits of the Harlem framework is to limit his influence and vision. A rereading of McKay from the colonial perspective is to recognize his writings as contribution to the global discourse of black and Third World expatriate writing. McKay could thus finally become a "universal" writer, offering a "distilled Poetry" of his "existence," his most cherished aspiration, though not in the terms he left his island colony for (*LW* 354). The highest Jamaican national honor, "the Order of Jamaica" that he was awarded posthumously in 1977, is a fitting tribute to his unique contribution.

Chapter Notes

Introduction

1. See George Lamming's book *The Pleasures of Exile*.

2. United States involvement in the Caribbean started with its occupation of Haiti in the early twentieth century.

3. McKay was the first to signal the beginnings of a black colonial revolt against British imperialism (which was to climax after World War II) and thus became the predecessor of the Hampstead School of African Socialism and the first to argue that socialism and nationalism are interdependent.

4. *Narrative of the Life of Frederick Douglass, An American Slave, Written by Himself*, which is often touted as the definitive African American slave narrative.

5. *A Long Way from Home*, 4.

6. Compare Robert B. Stepto's dictum of the black peoples' "finding of the voice" through texts, beginning with the slave narratives in nineteenth century America: *From Behind the Veil: A Study of Afro-American Narrative* (Urbana: University of Illinois Press, 1979); especially the first chapter titled "I Rose and Found My Voice: Narration, Authentication, and Authorial Control in Four Slave Narratives."

7. Professor Henry Louis Gates, Jr., uses that expression to sum up the ontological function of the slave narratives in the nineteenth century, in his introduction, "The Language of Slavery," to *The Slave's Narrative*, eds. Charles T. Davis and Henry Louis Gates, Jr. (Oxford/New York: Oxford University Press, 1985).

8. Caribbean immigration to the United States is generally classified by sociologists into three phases: the first between 1900 and 1930, the second between the Depression and the 1960s, and the third, current one. McKay, Walrond, etc., belong to the first generation while Paule Marshall, Jamaica Kincaid, Michelle Cliff, etc., belong to the second generation. While second generation writers did receive encouraging critical interest with enough attention paid to their immigrant status, even canonized, first generation writers are grossly neglected.

Chapter 1

1. The Asante trickster figure, Anansi the spider, appears in folktales throughout the English-speaking Caribbean and also in the Dutch-speaking islands of Aruba, Bonaire, and Curaçao. Traces of Asante culture, in spite of their being violently suppressed by the planters, can be found in the Jamaican social life. This was possible because unlike the United States, which came to replenish its enslaved population by natural

reproduction, Latin America and the Caribbean relied upon continuous large African imports up until their various dates of emancipation. Fresh batches of slaves seem to have reinforced certain cultural practices both in habit and in defiance of the master.

2. Italics retained.

3. It is now widely accepted by linguists that the Caribbean mass vernaculars are quite normal forms of speech and cannot be simplistically described as corrupt, "bastardized," ungrammatical derivatives of European languages.

4. Of late creole languages are coming to be viewed as symbols of national identity, but there is still some insecurity about their use and uncertainty about their worthiness.

5. McKay registers his anger against American imperialistic interference in the Caribbean through his double, Ray, in *Home to Harlem*.

6. Even within the Afro-American literary canon, says W. Lawrence Hogue in his *Discourse and the Other: The Production of the Afro-American Text*, criticism has left out of account the way in which ideological pressures dictate the canon. Basing on a Foucauldian concept of literature he traced how Afro-American critical practices are not only silent on the production of Afro-American texts but also ignored the various literary and ideological forces that actually caused certain Afro-American texts to be published, promoted, and certified and others to be subordinated or excluded. He traces how the ruling literary establishment (the dominant white American ideological apparatus), a set of literary practices and institutions, affected the production of Afro-American texts (movements) and Afro-American images prior to the social movements of the 1960s. He shows how Richard Wright's *Native Son*, with its naturalis-

tic themes (conforming to the dominant ideology in that period) of social maladjustment, the individual and his environment, criminals, murder, violence, and death, defined as more worthy and "universal," was accepted, while Hurston's *Their Eyes Were Watching God*, which projected independent assertiveness, quest for identity, personal freedom, free will and happiness, was suppressed. So within the Afro-American literary establishment, bowing to the pressure of the dominant literary establishment or refusing or rejecting it, had its effect on promoting and encouraging or suppressing and ignoring those texts that conformed to or opposed each generation's major themes, like promotion of the black bourgeois during the 1920s and '30s, integration during 1940s and '50s and cultural nationalism during 1960s.

7. Edward Kamau Braithwaite. *Microsoft Encarta Africana, 3d ed.* Microsoft Corporation, 1998–2000. Hereafter *"E.A. 2000."*

8. Ideological state apparatuses in the order in which Althusser listed them, are religious (the system of different churches), educational (the system of different public and private schools), family, legal, political (political system, including different parties), trade unions, communications (press, radio, and television) and cultural (literature, the arts, sports, etc.).

9. Italics in original.

10. Ideological State Apparatuses. Abbreviation retained.

11. Italics retained.

12. Morrison says that there also exists a European Africanism with a counterpart in colonial literature (38).

13. The natural growth of the slave population shaped a distinctive slavery in the American South and hastened the transition among slaves from African to African American.

14. Bertha Mason, the mad wife of Rochester in *Jane Eyre*, is a quadroon or mestee. Though Bronte's presentation of the mad woman had colonial intentions it establishes the fusion of English and mixed breeds of West Indian society.

15. The arrival of different groups after emancipation, East Indian, Chinese, Syrian, caused a certain amount of friction, but it never became intense as the alien groups were at no time strong enough in numbers to constitute a serious economic threat. The whole color-class system is dependent upon the almost complete acceptance by each group of the superiority of the white, and the inferiority of the black.

16. Trumper, the protagonist in Lamming's *In the Castle of My Skin*, only realizes that the confrontation between black and white is merely masked by clever British administrative tactics after he has visited America: "None o' you here on this islan' know what it means to fin' race. An' the white people you have to deal with won't ever let you know. 'Tis a great thing 'bout the English, the know-how. If ever there wus a nation in creation that know how to do an' get thing do, 'tis the English. My friend in the states use to call them administrators. In America I have seen as much as a man get kick down for askin' a question, a simple question. Not here. That couldn't ever happen here. We can talk here where we like if 'tis a public place, an' you've white teachers, an' we speak with white people at all times and in all places. My people here go to their homes an' all that. An' take the clubs, for example. There be clubs which you an' me can't go to, an' non o' my people here, no matter who they be, but they don't tell us we can't. They put up a sign, 'Members only,' knowing full well you ain't got no chance o' becomin' a member. An' although we know from

the start why we can't go, we got the conolation we can't 'cause we aren't members. In America they don't worry with that kind o' scatin' 'bout the bush" (295–296).

17. Unlike in the West Indies, the colonies of intervention and exploitation (Africa and Asia) had traditional, precolonial cultures, which continued to co-exist with the new imperial forms even though the culture of the colonizer is privileged. Perhaps that is the reason why anti-colonial nationalism in these colonies was able to create its own domain of sovereignty regarding "inner" aspects of culture, such as language or religion or elements of personal and family life, well before it began its political battle with the imperial power. This was achieved, according to Partha Chatterjee, by dividing the world of social institutions and practices into two domains—the material and the spiritual. The material being economy, statecraft, science and technology. Here Western superiority was acknowledged and its accomplishements carefully studied and replicated. The spiritual, on the other hand, is an "inner" domain bearing the "essential" marks of cultural identity (6). Hence Chatterjee concludes that the "more nationalism engaged in its contest with the colonial power in the outer domain of politics, the more it insisted on displaying the marks of 'essential' cultural differences so as to keep out the colonizer from that inner domain of national life and to proclaim its sovereignty over it" (26). This condition was absent in the West Indies as a foreign or absent mother culture has always cradled the West Indian's judgment.

Chapter 2

1. Emphasis mine.
2. "Harlem Renaissance: The Vogue of the New Negro," *Microsoft Encarta*

Africana 2000. 1999 Microsoft Corporation.

3. Sarojini Naidu was encouraged to be a "genuine Indian poet of the Deccan, not a clever, machine made imitator of English classics." Edmund Gosse, introduction to *The Broken Wing* by Naidu (London, 1912), p. 5.

4. McKay's dream of visiting England was fulfilled only in 1919, at the age of 30.

5. My italics.

6. A dialect poetess of Jamaica, born in 1919.

Chapter 3

1. Roy Simon Bryce-Laporte in his essay "Black Immigrants: The Experience of Invisibility and Inequality" says that for this particular segment of the society, massive survey statistics and census material are limited and incomplete, and neither precise nor uniformly treated given the invisibility of the immigrant black, as well as the ambiguities in the definition of the terms black, immigrant, and even foreigner. But he says that a cursory explanation shows that of the 45,162,638 aliens who entered the United States between 1820 and 1970 about 1,000,000 (2%) of them were from the West Indies and 76,000 (0.1%) of them were Africans (U.S. Department of Justice, 1970, 1965, 1960).

2. Reid also says that the English-speaking immigrant, upon his arrival in the United States, both possesses in himself and arouses in others a strong sense of inferiority or superiority in social status, which makes his adjustment difficult (106).

3. Tillery quotes McKay's letters to his brother, Theophilious, where he expressed his concern for his daughter Ruth Hope's education and job opportunities in Jamaica as she too was dark complexioned like McKay.

4. Ira Reid says that spiritually and culturally the immigrants' bonds are more closely knit with Spain, France, Portugal and Great Britain than with the United States. Their arrival here is not always a metaphorical hand-washing to out the damned spot of their home land; rather, it is thought of as an effort to preserve that which is regarded as most important in the past and link it with the profits—actual and potential—of this, their promised land (112).

5. Reid lists sixteen stereotypes about the West Indian Negro immigrant in his book *The Negro Immigrant: His Background, Characteristics and Social Adjustment: 1899–1937.*

6. McKay retained his until 1940.

7. Tillery quotes Ellen Tarry who knew firsthand that yellow Negroes headed McKay's list of dislikes. A fair complexioned woman, she herself was upbraided for being yellow, many times by McKay (19).

8. Rhonda Hope (Claude McKay) to Braithwaite, 15 February 1916, Braithwaite papers, Harvard University.

9. Claude McKay's introductory remarks to his reading of "If We Must Die," for Arna Bontemps, ed., *Anthology of Negro Poets* (Folkways Record, FP 91).

10. Two decades ago Senator Henry Cabot Lodge had it read from the same platform into congressional records as evidence of the rising radicalism among black Americans.

11. *Catholic Worker* 12 (October 1945): 4–5.

12. Alain Locke in his *Anthology of the New Negro* altered the title to "White Houses," much to the chagrin of McKay, as he was afraid that it might mean the White House in Washington. McKay complained that this had destroyed the symbolic effect intended by him and pointed out that it was published in the *Liberator* with the original

title. The title "White Houses," he said, "changed the whole symbolic intent and meaning of the poem, making it appear as if the burning ambition of the black malcontent was to enter white houses in general" (*LW* 313–314).

13. Emphasis mine.

14. McKay to Joel E. Spingarn, 9 January 1917; Spingarn papers, New York Public Library.

15. Italics retained.

16. Emphasis retained.

Chapter 4

1. Michel Fabre in his essay "Claude McKay and the Two Faces of France" says that McKay was "more discriminating" and "less superficial" in his evaluation of France and its racism than other black writers. McKay was quite conscious of France's politics and its role in colonizing Africa before he set foot in France. A thorough discussion of this aspect will be taken up when dealing with *Banjo*, set in Marseilles, France.

2. George Lamming points out T.S. Eliot's difficulty in acknowledging Lawrence as first rate writer. Lamming quotes Graham Hough to show that Eliot's estimate of Lawrence is colonial in intention: "A rather hoity-toity concept of culture has been used to show that Lawrence had a hole-and-corner upbringing, and remained therefore an inspired barbarian, ignorant of the grand, calm expanses of properly certified European civilization. But the only people who ever inhabit this kind of European civilization are cultivated Americans like Henry James and T.S. Eliot. Europeans live in Nottingham or Nancy, Paris or Piacenza, Frankfurt or Fenny Stratford, and the actual life of any of these places has always seemed a poor and disappointing affair to visitors from the Platonic New England heights" (Lamming, *Pleasures*, 34).

3. It was the first novel by a black writer to hit the best sellers list, selling around 50,000 copies.

4. The inert and timid hero of T.S. Eliot in the poem "The Love Song of J. Alfred Prufrock," who fails to confront his own self.

5. It was the culmination of a general effort by white writers in the 1920s that made the Afro-American "primal" state an artistic subject. Texts like *Nigger Heaven* (1926), Gertrude Stein's *Three Lives* (1909), Eugene O' Neill's *Emperor Jones* (1920) and *All God's Chillun Got Wings* (1924), E.E. Cummings's *The Enormous Room* (1922), Waldo Frank's *Holiday* (1923), Sherwood Anderson's *Dark Laughter* (1925), and DuBose Heyward's *Porgy* (1925) reproduced the image of the Afro-American as exotic and "naturally" primitive.

6. Zora Neale Hurston, Louise Thompson, Claude McKay and Langston Hughes were all supported by the same elderly Park Avenue matron who had a strong penchant for "primitive" tastes.

7. *Crisis*, August 1926, 193–94.

8. McKay, "A Negro Writer to His Critics," *New York Herald-Tribune Books*, March 6, 1932.

9. Lively concludes that McKay's primitivism, while being a protest in his early novels (*Home to Harlem* and *Banjo*), "is a positive alternative which is integrated with Marxism that had been a part of McKay's intellectual make-up from an early age" in *Banana Bottom* (234).

10. McKay's works were resurrected during the 1960s, when black cultural nationalism was the ruling ideology.

11. See Fielding's description of Tom Jones and Mrs. Waters' rendezvous in Upton inn.

12. His relationship with his first mentor, Walter Jekyll, constitutes one of the most complex chapters in McKay's

life. Many scholars believe that their relationship was homosexual.

13. In his autobiography, *A Long Way from Home*, McKay attacks H.G. Wells' *Outline of History* for its distorted and incomplete history of Africa (121–129).

Chapter 5

1. The French translation of *Banjo*, says Robert P. Smith, Jr., exerted a profound influence on Afro-French and Caribbean-French blacks in Paris. Damas confirmed to Daniel Racine that the book appeared in French in France before being published in English in the United States. He made *Banjo* his bedside reading and readily admitted the influence of Claude McKay (52).

2. McKay to Max Eastman, 27 June 1930, and McKay to Max Eastman, 7 December 1929; *MSS*, Indiana University.

3. The photograph of the beach boys surrounding a guitar player in front of a Vieux Port Café is preserved in the McKay papers at the Yale University Library.

4. Robert Smith Jr. says that there was much mutual interest between Claude McKay and the Francophone blacks whom he had a chance to meet or read about in Europe. Though McKay tried to keep aloof from cults Smith notes McKay's meeting with Paulette Nardal, a remarkable black woman from Martinique who hosted and animated the activities of her literary and artistic salon at 5bis, rue Herbert, in Clamart-sur-Seine, near the gates of Paris. She, along with the Haitian Dr. Leo Sajous, in 1930 started the international bilingual (French-English) periodical *La Revue du Monde Noir*, which was to become an important source for Negritude scholars of the future and whose six issues were at the time unprecedented and audacious. The periodical proposed to serve as a voice for black intellectuals and friends of blacks, to study and make known the cultural richness of Africa and black civilizations, and to create a moral and intellectual bond between blacks throughout the world without distinction of nationality. McKay contributed poetry to the first and third issues of the periodical, and among the international contributors were Dr. Sajous, Dr. Price-Mars, Louis T. Achille, Rene Maran, Felix Eboue, Leo Frobenius, P. Thoby-Marcelin, Etienne Lero, Andree Nardal, Rene Menil and black Americans Walter White, Langston Hughes and Clara Shepard (Smith 49–50).

5. *Opportunity*, July 1929, p. 254.

6. See T.S. Eliot's *Waste Land*, line no. 128 "OOOO that Shakespeherian Rag—."

7. Cesaire in his interview says that the Antilleans were ashamed of being Negroes, and hence they searched for all sorts of euphemisms for Negro: they would say a man of color, a dark-complexioned man, and other idiocies like that. Depestre call this "a case of total alienation" (Cesaire, 73).

8. Italics retained.

9. Italics mine.

10. Surprisingly, McKay's ire against educated Negroes is very much similar to the "clinical study" of Fanon, who quotes and agrees with Professor D. Westermann, in *The African Today*, that the Negroes' inferiority complex is particularly intensified among the most educated, who must struggle with it unceasingly. Their way of doing so, he adds, is frequently naïve: "The wearing of European clothes, whether rags or the most up-to-date style; using European furniture and European forms of social intercourse; adorning the Native language with European expressions; using bombastic phrases in speaking or

writing a European language" (*Black Skin* 25).

11. In the *Discourse on Colonialism*, Depestre and Cesaire acknowledge the importance of African art and its recognition by the French artists and its influence on the Negroes coming to consciousness:

R.D. Do you see a relationship between the interest of European artists and the coming to consciousness of Negroes?
A.C. Certainly. This movement is another factor in the development of our consciousness. Negroes were made fashionable in France by Picasso, Vlaminck, Braque, etc.
R.D. During the same period, art lovers and art historians ... were impressed by the quality of African sculpture. African art ceased to be an exotic curiosity ... [77].

12. McKay as early as in 1920 protested the bourgeois press coverage against the French black troops in Germany, who made a hue and cry about alleged raping of German woman by Negroes. McKay refers to this in *Banjo*: "A big campaign of propaganda was on against them, backed by German-Americans, Negro-breaking Southerners, and your English liberals and socialists. The odd thing about that propaganda was that it said nothing about the exploitation of primitive and ignorant black conscripts to do the dirty work of one victorious civilization over another, but it was all about the sexuality of Negroes" (146). But his protest in 1920s was spiced more by left-wing politics that he was participating in than by the urge to defend the morality of his Negro brethren.

13. Emphasis mine.

Chapter 6

1. During the 1960s, militant Afro-American critics like Addison Gayle, Holt Fuller, and Ron Karenga not only declared war on the social, political, psychological, and cultural institutions and apparatuses within the dominant American ideological apparatus but also devised a theory of literature, the black aesthetic, that exposed the "enemies" and promoted only those texts that presented only positive images of the Afro-American (Hogue 48). So, as Campbell indicts, "Gayle's critique smacks of disappointment over McKay's turn from Harlem back to Jamaica" in this novel (*Centennial* 20).

2. In her essay *The Dichotomized Heroine in West Indian Fiction*, Campbell says that "expressions of cultural dichotomy remain active in the novels of contemporary West Indian writers as in the novels of the older or post–world war generation." Cultural dichotomy for her is emblemized by the novelistic protagonist (often a woman) who is often engaged in weighing the values of conflicting cultural systems (138). She found examples of such dichotomized heroines not only in McKay but in Orlando Patterson's *Die the Long Day*, Lamming's *Season of Adventure* and many other West Indian writings.

3. Van Mol concludes that both *Cane* and *Banana Bottom* are still relevant today as valid literary expressions of a possible way for Western blacks to reconcile the dualism of their two fold cultural heritage and to achieve black consciousness (52).

4. Speaking about the Mexican-American autobiography in the nineteenth century, particularly after the U.S. war against Mexico in 1846–48, Genaro Padilla makes two significant observations: the narrative recreation of a mythic, Edenic past, and the refiguration of an "I" centered narrative "within a collective matrix" which he calls a "filial" act (29). Attempts to create a harmonious past should be read in relation to the socio-historical moment of its enunciation, and in this sense,

Padilla considers them a "strategic narrative activity—conscious of its general implications—for restoring order, sanity, social purpose in the face of political, social, and economic dispossession" (11).

5. Italics mine.
6. Emphasis mine.
7. Italics mine.

Chapter 7

1. McKay to American consul general, 18 January 1929, McKay Papers, James Weldon Johnson Collection.
2. W.E.B. Du Bois, "The Negro College," in *A Reader*, ed. Meyer Weinberg (New York: Harper, 1970).
3. The Renaissance's best achievement can found in other arts: music, theatre and dance.
4. McKay's article, "A Negro Poet Writes,' *Pearson's Magazine* (September 1918), 275–6.
5. McKay, letter to Eastman, 30 June 1944, Lily Library, Indiana University, Bloomington.
6. Indeed, these narratives had a great influence as many of the patterns and images of the narratives were repeated in diverse works of African American literature.
7. Similar narratives were produced in the West Indian context.
8. *Ebony*, March 1946, 32.

Works Consulted

Primary Sources

McKay, Claude. *Banana Bottom*. Chatham, N.J.: Chatham Bookseller, 1970. (*BB*).
_____. *Banjo: A Story Without a Plot*. New York: Harcourt, 1957. (*BJ*).
_____. *The Dialect Poetry of Claude McKay*. Two vols. in one. Vol. 1, *Songs of Jamaica*. Vol. 2, *Constab Ballads*. Freeport, N.Y.: Books for Libraries Press, 1972. (*DP*).
_____. *Gingertown*. 1932. Freeport, N.Y.: Books for Libraries Press, 1972. (*GT*).
_____. *Harlem: Negro Metropolis*. New York: Harcourt Brace Jovanovich, 1968.
_____. *Home to Harlem*. Chatham, N.J.: Chatham Bookseller, 1973. (*HH*).
_____. *A Long Way from Home*. New York: Harcourt, 1970. (*LW*).
_____. *My Green Hills of Jamaica and Five Jamaican Short Stories*. Ed. Mervyn Morris. Kingston, Jamaica: Heinemann Educational Book (Caribbean) Ltd., 1979. (*GH*).
_____. *The Negroes in America*. Trans. by Robert J. Winter. Ed. by Alan J. Mcleod. New York: Kennikat Press, 1979. Originally published as *Negry v Amerike*, USSR, 1923.
_____. *Selected Poems of Claude McKay*. New York: Harcourt, 1953. (*SP*).
_____. *Songs of Jamaica*. Kingston, Jamaica: Aston W. Gardner, 1912.

Secondary Sources

Abrahams, Peter. *Jamaica: An Island Mosaic*. London: Her Majesty's Stationery Office, 1995.
Achebe, Chinua. "Colonialist Criticism." In *Morning Yet on Creation Day*. London: Heinemann, 1975.
Adderley, Roseanne. "African Ethnic Groups in Latin America and the Caribbean." *Microsoft Encarta African 2000*. CD-ROM. U.S.A., 1999.
Allis, Jeannette B. "West Indian Literature: A Case for Regional Criticism," in *Critical Issues in West Indian Literature: Selected Papers from West Indian Literature Conferences 1981–1983*, Ed. Erika Sollish Smilowitz and Roberta Quales Knowles. Parkersburg: Caribbean Books, 1984: 7–18.
Althusser, Louis. *Lenin and Philosophy and Other Essays*. Trans. Ben Brewster. New York: Monthly Review Press, 1971.
Andrews, William L. *To Tell a Free Story. The First Century of Afro-American Autobiography, 1760–1865*. Urbana: University of Illinois Press, 1988.

Andrews, William L., ed. *African American Autobiography: A Collection of Critical Essays.* Englewood Cliffs, N.J.: Prentice Hall, 1993.

Arden, Eugene. "The Early Harlem Novel." *Phylon* 20 (Spring 1959): 25–31.

Aronson, Dan R. "Ethnicity as a Cultural System: An Introductory Essay." In *Ethnicity in the Americas.* Ed. Frances Henry. The Hague: Mouton, 1976. 9–22.

Ashcroft, Bill, Gareth Griffiths, and Helen Tiffin. *The Empire Writes Back: Theory and Practice in Post-Colonial Literatures.* London: Routledge, 1989.

Avi-Ram, Amitai F. "The Unreadable Black Body: 'Conventional' Poetic Form in the Harlem Renaissance." *Genders* 7 (March 1990): 32–46.

Baker, Houston A., Jr. *Modernism and the Harlem Renaissance.* Chicago: University of Chicago Press, 1987.

Bakhtin, Mikhail. "Discourse in the Novel." In *The Dialogic Imagination.* Austin, Texas: University of Texas Press, 1982.

Baldwin, James. *Tell Me How Long the Train's Been Gone.* New York: Dell, 1968.

Balutansky, Kathleen M. "Naming Caribbean Women Writers." *Callaloo* 13.3 (Summer 1990): 539–50.

Barksdale, R.A. "Symbolism and Irony in McKay's *Home to Harlem.*" *CLA* Journal 15 (March 1972): 338–44.

Barthold, Bonnie J. *Black Time: Fiction of Africa, the Caribbean, and the United States.* New Haven: Yale University Press, 1981.

Baugh, Edward. *West Indian Poetry 1900–1970: A Study in Cultural Decolonisation.* Kingston: Savacou, 1971.

Bell, Bernard W. *The Afro-American Novel and Its Tradition.* Amherst: University of Massachusetts Press, 1987.

Bernabe, Jean, Patrick Chamoiseau, and Raphael Confiant. "In Praise of Creoleness." *Callaloo*13.4 (Fall 1990): 886–909.

Bhabha, Homi K. *The Location of Culture.* New York: Routledge, 1994.

Blary, Liliane. "Claude McKay and Black Nationalist Ideologies (1934–1948)." In *Myth and Ideology in American Culture.* Ed. Regis Durand. Lille, France: Publications de l'Universite de Lille III, 1976. 211–31.

Bone, Robert. *Down Home: A History of Afro-American Short Fiction from Its Beginning to the End of the Renaissance.* New York: G.P. Putnam's Sons, 1975.

_____. *The Negro Novel in America.* New Haven: Yale University Press, 1958.

Bonnett, Aubrey W., and G. Llewellyn Watson. *Emerging Perspectives on the Black Diaspora.* Lanham, MD: University Press of America, 1989.

Bontemps, Arna, ed. *The Harlem Renaissance Remembered.* New York: Dodd, 1972.

Brathwaite, Edward Kamau. "The African Presence in Caribbean Literature." In *Slavery, Colonialism and Racism.* Ed. Sidney Mintz. New York: Norton, 1974. 73–110.

_____. "History, the Caribbean Writer and X/Self." In *Crisis and Creativity in the New Literatures in English.* Ed. Geoffrey V. Davis and Hena Maes-Jelinek. Amsterdam: Rodopi, 1990. 23–46.

Braithwaite, Stanley William. "Some Contemporary Poets of the Negro Race." *Crisis*, April 1919, 277.

Brawley, Benjamin. "The Negro Literary Renaissance." *Southern Workman*, April 1927, 28.

Bronze, Stephen. *Roots of Negro Racial Consciousness. The 1920's: Three Harlem Renaissance Authors.* New York: Libra, 1964.

Works Consulted

Brown, Sterling. "The Negro Character as Seen Through White Authors." *Journal of Negro Education*, April 1933, 42–49.

Brown, Sterling A., Arthur Davis, and Ulysses Lee, eds. *The Negro Caravan*. New York: Citadel Press, 1941.

Brown, W. Lloyd. "The American Image in British West Indian Literature." *Caribbean Studies* 11.1 (April 1971): 30–45.

_____. "The Expatriate Consciousness in Black American Literature." *Studies in Black Literature* 3 (Summer 1972): 9–11.

_____. "Introduction: Regional Writers, Regional Critics." In *Critical Issues in West Indian Literature. Selected Papers from West Indian Literature Conferences 1981–1983*. Eds. Erika Sollish Smilowitz and Roberta Quarles Knowles. Parkersburg, Iowa: Caribbean Books, 1984. 1–6.

_____. "The West Indian as an Ethnic Stereotype in Black American Literature." *Negro American Literature Forum* 5.1 (1971): 8–14.

_____. "West Indian Literature: Road to a 'New World' Sensibility." *Journal of Black Studies* 7.4 (June 1977): 411–36.

_____. *West Indian Poetry*. Boston: Twayne, 1978.

Bryce-Laporte, Roy S. "Black Immigrants: The Experience of Invisibility and Inequality." *Journal of Black Studies* 3: 29–56.

_____, and Delores M. Mortimer, eds. *Caribbean Immigration to the United States*. Washington, D.C.: Smithsonian, 1976.

Butcher, Margaret J. *The Negro in American Culture*. New York: Knopf, 1956.

Callahan, John F. "'A Long Way from Home': The Art and Protest of Claude McKay and James Baldwin." *Contemporary-Literature* 34.4 (Winter 1993): 767–76.

Calverton, V.F. "The New Negro." *Current History*, February 1926, 694–98.

Campbell, Elaine. "The Dichotomized Heroine in West Indian Fiction" in *Claude McKay: Centennial Studies*, ed. A.L. McLeod. New Delhi: Sterling, 1992.

_____. "Poetry and Prose of Claude McKay: A Jamaican Return" in *Claude McKay: Centennial Studies*, ed. A.L. McLeod. New Delhi: Sterling, 1992.

Carby, Hazel, V. "Policing the Black Woman's Body in an Urban Context." *Critical-Inquiry* 18.4 (Summer 1992): 738–55.

Carnegie, Charles V. "A Social Psychology of Caribbean Migrations: Strategic Flexibility in the West Indies." In *The Caribbean Exodus*. Ed. Barry B. Levine. New York: Preaeger, 1987. 32–43.

Césaire, Aimé. *Discourse on Colonialism*. Trans. Joan Pinkham. New York: Monthly Review Press, 1972.

Chaney, Elsa M., and Constance R. Sutton, eds. *Caribbean Life in New York City: Sociocultural Dimensions*. New York: Center for Migration Studies, 1987.

Chapman, Abraham. "The Harlem Renaissance in Literary History." *College Language Association* 2 (September 1967): 38–58.

Chatterjee, Partha. *The Nation and Its Fragments: Colonial and Postcolonial Histories*. New Delhi: Oxford University Press, 1993.

Chauhan, P.S. "Rereading Claude McKay." *CLA Journal* 34.1 (September 1990): 68–80.

Chellappan, K. "Cultural Dualism in *Banana Bottom*: an Indian Perspective." *Centennial*. [Missing info.]

Chi, Yuan Wen. "In Search of Black Identity: Claude McKay's *Home to Harlem*." *American Studies (Mei-kuo-yen-chiu)* 21.1 (March 1991): 103–22.

Chin, Timothy S. "'Bullers' and 'Battymen': Contesting Homophobia in Black Popular Culture and Contemporary Caribbean Literature." *Callaloo* 20 (Winter 1997): 127–41.

Christian, Barbara. "The Race for Theory." *Cultural Critique* 6 (Spring 1987): 51–63.

Clayton, Horace, and St. Clair Drake. *Black Metropolis: A Study of Negro Life in a Northern City.* New York: Harcourt, Brace and World, 1945.

Clifford, James, and George Marcus, eds. *Writing Culture: The Poetics and Politics of Ethnography.* Berkeley: University of California Press, 1986.

Collier, Eugenia. "The Four Way Dilemma of Claude McKay." *CLA Journal* 15 (March 1972): 345–53.

Colonialism and Colonies. Microsoft Encarta 2000. CD-ROM. U.S.A., 1999.

Conroy, Sister Mary. "The Vagabond Motif in the Writings of Claude McKay." *Negro American Literature Forum* 5 (1971): 15–23.

Cooper, Carolyn. "Race and the cultural politics of self-representation: A view from the University of the West Indies." *Research in African Literatures* 27 (Winter 1996): 97–105.

Cooper, Wayne F. *Claude McKay: Rebel Sojourner in the Harlem Renaissance.* New York: Schocken, 1987.

_____. "Claude McKay and the New Negro of the 1920s." *Phylon* 25 (1964): 297–306.

_____. *The Passion of Claude McKay: Selected Poetry and Prose, 1912–1948.* New York: Schocken Books, 1973.

_____, and Robert C. Reinders. "A Black Briton Comes Home." *Race* 9 (July 1967): 67–83.

Coulthard, G.R. "The West Indian Novel of Immigration." *Phylon* 20 (Spring 1959): 32–41.

Cowley, Malcolm. *Exile's Return: A Literary Odyssey of the 1920's.* New York: Viking Press, 1951.

Cruse, Harold. *The Crisis of the Negro Intellectual.* 1967. New York: Quill, 1984.

Cudjoe, Selwyn R. *Resistance and Caribbean Literature.* Athens: Ohio University Press, 1980.

Curtin, Philip D. *The Image of Africa.* London: Macmillan, 1965.

_____. *Two Jamaicas: The Role of Ideas in a Tropical Colony, 1830–1865.* Cambridge: Harvard University Press, 1955.

Dabydeen, David, and Nana Wilson-Tagoe. *A Reader's Guide to West Indian and Black British Literature.* Kingston-upon-Thames, Surrey: Danaroo, 1987.

Dash, J. Michael. "In Search of the Lost Body: Redefining the Subject in Caribbean Literature." *Kunapipi* 11.1 (1989): 17–26.

Davis, Arthur. *From the Dark Tower: Afro-American Writers 1900–1960.* Washington, D.C.: Howard University Press, 1974.

Deane, Seasmus. "Imperialism/Nationalism." In *Critical Terms for Literary Study.* Eds. Frank Lentricchia and Thomas McLaughlin. Chicago: University of Chicago Press, 1995. 354–368.

Diawara, Manthia. "Englishness and Blackness: Cricket as Discourse on Colonialism." *Callaloo* 13.3 (Summer 1990): 830–44.

Dixon, Melvin. *Ride Out the Wilderness: Geography and Identity in Afro-American Literature.* Urbana: University of Illinois Press, 1987.

Dorris, Ronald. "Claude McKay's Home to Harlem: A Social Commentary." *McNeese Review* 29 (1982–83): 53–62.

Works Consulted

Drayton, Arthur. "McKay's Human Pity: A Note on His Protest Poetry." *Black Orpheus* 17 (June 1965): 39–48.

Du Bois, W.E.B. "The Browsing Reader." *Crisis* 35 (1928): 202.

_____. "Criteria of Negro Art." *Crisis*, October 1926, 295–96.

_____. *Dusk of Dawn: An Essay toward an Autobiography of a Race Concept*. New York: Harcourt and Brace, 1940.

_____. Review of *Banjo*, by Claude McKay. *Crisis*, July 1929, 234.

_____. Review of *Home to Harlem*, by Claude McKay. *Crisis*, September 1928, 202.

_____. *The Souls of Black Folk*. New York: Penguin Books, 1996.

Dunn, Richard S. *Sugar and Slaves: The Rise of the Planter Class in the English West Indies, 1624–1713*. New York: Norton and Company, 1973.

Elimimian, Isaac I. "Theme and Technique in Claude McKay's Poetry." *College Language Association Journal* 25.2 (1981): 203–211.

Emanuel, James A., and Theodore L. Gross, eds. *Dark Symphony: Negro Literature in America*. New York: Free Press, 1968.

Emerson, O.B. "Cultural Nationalism in Afro-American Literature." In *The Cry of Home: Cultural Nationalism and the Modern Writer*. Ed. Ernest H. Lewald. Knoxville: University of Tennessee Press, 1972. 211–44.

Fabre, Michel. "Aesthetics and Ideology in *Banjo*." In *Myth and Ideology in American Culture*. Ed. Regis Durand. Lille, France: Publications de l'Universite de Lille, 1976. 195–209.

_____. "Claude McKay and the Two Faces of France." In *From Harlem to Paris: Black American Writers in France, 1840–1980*. Urbana: University of Illinois Press, 1991.

Fanon, Frantz. *Black Skin White Masks*. Trans. Charles Lam Markmann. New York: Grove Press, 1967.

_____. *The Wretched of the Earth*. Trans. Constance Farrington. London: Penguin Books, 1967.

Felgar, Robert. "Black Content, White Form." *Studies in Black Literature* 5 (Spring 1974): 28–31.

Ferraro, Thomas J. *Ethnic Passages: Literary Immigrants in Twentieth-Century America*. Chicago: University of Chicago Press, 1993.

Fieldhouse, D.K. *Colonialism 1870–1945: An Introduction*. London: Weidenfeld and Nicholson, 1981.

Fisher, Rudolph. "White, High Yellow, Black [Review of *Ginger Town*]." *New York Herald Tribune Books*, March 27, 1932, 3.

Floyd, Barry. *Jamaica: An Island Microcosm*. New York: St. Martin's Press, 1979.

Foner, Phillip S., and James Allen, eds. *American Communism and Black Americans: A Documentary History, 1919–1929*. Philadelphia: Temple University Press, 1987.

Fox-Genovese, Elizabeth. "Literary Criticism and the Politics of the New Historicism" in *The New Historicism*, H. Aram Veeser, ed. New York: Routledge, 1989.

Franklin, John Hope. *From Slavery to Freedom: A History of Negro Americans*. Rev. 4th ed. New York: Knopf, 1961.

Garvey, Marcus, "*Home to Harlem*, Claude McKay's Damaging Book Should Earn Wholesale Condemnation of Negroes." *Negro World*, 29 September 1928, 1.

Gates, Henry Louis, Jr. *Figures in Black: Words, Signs, and the "Racial" Self.* New York: Oxford University Press, 1987.

_____. *The Signifying Monkey: A Theory of African-American Literary Criticism.* New York: Oxford University Press, 1988.

Gayle, Addison. *Claude McKay: The Black Poet at War.* Detroit: Broadside, 1972.

Gayle, Addison, Jr. *Black Expression: Essays by and about Black Americans in the Creative Arts.* New York: Weybright and Talley, 1969.

_____. *The Way of the New World: The Black Novel in America.* Garden City, N.Y.: Anchor Press/Doubleday, 1976.

George, Kent E. "Claude McKay's Banana Bottom Reappraised." *CLA Journal* 18 December (1974): 222–34.

_____. "The Soulful Way of Claude McKay." *Black World* 20 (1970): 37–50.

Giles, James. *Claude McKay.* Boston: Twayne, 1976.

Gilroy, Paul. *The Black Atlantic: Modernity and Double Consciousness.* Cambridge: Harvard University Press, 1993.

Greenberg, Robert M. "Idealism and Realism in the Fiction of Claude McKay." *College Language Association Journal* 24.3 (1981): 237–261.

Greenblatt, Stephen. "Culture." In *Critical Terms for Literary Study.* Ed. Frank Lentricchia and Thomas McLaughlin. Chicago: University of Chicago Press, 1995. 225–232.

Griffin, Barbara J. "Claude McKay: The Evolution of a Conservative." *CLA Journal* 36.2 (December 1992): 157–70.

_____. "The last word: Claude McKay's unpublished 'Cycle Manuscript.'" *MELUS* 21 (1996): 41–57.

Griffiths, Gareth. *A Double Exile: African and West Indian Writing Between Two Cultures.* London: Boyars, 1978.

_____. "Imitation, Abrogation and Appropriation: The Production of the Post-Colonial Text." *Kunapipi* 9.1 (1987): 13–20.

Hall, Stuart. "Cultural Identity and Diaspora" in *Contemporary Postcolonial Theory.* Ed. Padmini Mongia. London: Arnold, 1996.

Hamalian, Leo. "D.H. Lawrence and Black Writers." *Journal of Modern Literature* 16 (Spring 1990): 579–596.

Harris, Wilson. *The Womb of Space: The Cross-Cultural Imagination.* Westport, Conn.: Greenwood Press, 1983.

Hart, Robert C. "Black-White Literary Relations in the Harlem Renaissance." *American Literature* 44 (January 1973): 612–28.

Helbling, Mark. "Claude McKay: Art and Politics." *Negro American Literature Forum* 7 (Summer 1973): 49–52.

Hellwig, David J. "Black Meets Black: Afro-American Reactions to West Indian Immigrants in the 1920's." *The South Atlantic Quarterly* 77 (1978): 206–224.

Henriques, Fernando. *Family and Color in Jamaica.* London: Macgibbon and Kee, 1953.

Herskovits, Melville J. *The Myth of the Negro Past.* Boston: Beacon Press, 1990.

Hieglar, Charles J. "Claude McKay's 'If We Must Die,' *Home to Harlem,* and the Hog Trope." *A Quarterly Journal of Short Articles, Notes, and Reviews* 8.3 (Summer 1995): 22–26.

Hogue, W. Lawrence. *Discourse and the Other: The Production of the Afro-American Text.* Durham: Duke University Press, 1986.

Works Consulted

Holder, Calvin. "West Indian immigrants in New York City 1900–1952: In conflict with the Promised Land." In *Emerging Perspectives on the Black Diaspora*. Eds. Aubrey W. Bonnett and G. Llewellyn Watson. Lanham, MD: University Press of America, 1990.

Hudson, Brian. "Geography in colonial schools: The classroom experience in West Indian literature." *Geography* 79 (October 1994): 322–329.

Huggins, Nathan Irvin. *Harlem Renaissance*. New York: Oxford University Press, 1971.

Hughes, Langston. "The Negro Artist and the Racial Mountain." *Nation* 122 (June 1926): 692–694.

Hurston, Zora Neale. *Dust Tracks on a Road*. Philadelphia: Lippincott, 1971.

Jackson, Blyden. "Claude McKay and Langston Hughes: The Harlem Renaissance and More." *Pembroke Magazine* 6 (1975): 43–8.

_____. "The Essential McKay." *Phylon* 14 (1953): 216–7.

Johnson, James Weldon. *Along This Way: The Autobiography of James Weldon Johnson*. New York: Viking Press, 1933.

_____. *Black Manhattan*. 1930. Pref. by Allan H. Spear. New York: Atheneum, 1968.

Jones, LeRoi. *Blues People*. New York: William Morrow, 1963.

Kavanagh, James H. "Ideology." In *Critical Terms for Literary Study*. Ed. Frank Lentricchia and Thomas McLaughlin. Chicago: University of Chicago Press, 1995. 306–320.

Kaye, Jacqueline. *Caribbean New York: Black Immigrants and the Politics of Race*. Ithaca, NY: Cornell University Press, 1992.

_____. "Claude McKay's *Banjo*." *Presence Africaine* 73 (1970).

_____. *Earth*. [Missing info.]

Keller, James R. "A chafing savage, down the decent street: The politics of compromise in Claude McKay's protest sonnets." *African American Review* 28 (1994): 447–456.

Kent, George E. "Claude McKay's *Banana Bottom* Reappraised." *CLA Journal* 18 (December 1974): 222–34.

_____. "The Soulful Way of Claude McKay." *Black World* 20 (1970): 37–50.

Kent, G.E. *Blackness and the Adventure of Western Culture*. Chicago: Third World Press, 1972.

King, Bruce, ed. *The Commonwealth Novel since 1960*. London: Macmillan, 1991.

_____. *West Indian Literature*. London: Macmillan, 1979.

Kirpal, Viney. *The Third World Novel of Expatriation: A Study of Émigré Fiction by Indian, West African and Caribbean Writers*. New Delhi: Sterling, 1989.

Lacovia, R.M. "Migration and Transmutation in the Novels of McKay, Marshall, and Clarke." *Journal of Black Studies* 7.4 (June 1977): 437–54.

Lamming, George. *The Castle of My Skin*. Trinidad: Longman Caribbean, 1970.

_____. *The Pleasures of Exile*. London: Allison and Busby, 1984.

Lang, P.M. "Claude McKay: Evidence of a Magic Pilgrimage." *CLA Journal* 16 (June 1973): 475–84.

Lee, Robert A. "Harlem on My Mind: Fictions of a Black Metropolis." In *The American City: Literary and Cultural Perspectives*. Ed. Clarke Graham. New York: St. Martin's, 1988. 223.

_____. "On Claude McKay's 'If We Must Die.'" *CLA Journal* 18 (December 1974): 216–7.

LeSeur, Geta. "Claude McKay's Marxism." In *The Harlem Renaissance: Reevaluations.* Eds. Amritjit Singh, William S. Shiver, and Stanley Brodwin. New York: Garland, 1989. 219–32.

_____. "Claude McKay's Romanticism." *CLA Journal* 32.3 (March 1989): 296–308.

Levine, Bary B., ed. *The Carbbean Exodus.* New York: Praeger, 1987.

Lewald, Ernest H., ed. *The Cry of Home: Cultural Nationalism and the Modern Writer.* Knoxville: University of Tennessee Press, 1972.

Lewis, David Levering. *When Harlem Was in Vogue.* New York: Knopf, 1981.

Lewis, Rupert, and Maureen Lewis. "Claude McKay's Jamaica." *Caribbean Quarterly* 23.2 and 3 (June–September 1977): 38–53.

Lively, Adam. "Continuity and Radicalism in American Black Nationalist Thought, 1914–1929." *Journal of American Studies* 18.2 (August 1984): 207–235.

Locke, Alain, ed. *The New Negro.* 1925. New York: Johnson Reprint Corporation, 1968.

_____, and Bernhard J. Stern, eds. *When Peoples Meet: A Study in Race and Culture Contacts.* New York: Progressive Education Association, 1941.

Lueth, Elmer. "The Scope of Black Life in Claude McKay's Home to Harlem." *Obsidian-II* 5.3 (Winter 1990): 43–52.

Major, Clarence. "Dear Jake and Ray." *American Poetry Review* 4 (1975): 40–2.

Makward, Edris. "Claude McKay: The African Experience," in *Claude McKay: Centennial Studies,* ed. A.L. McLeod. New Delhi: Sterling, 1992.

Mangan, J.A., ed. *"Benefits Bestowed"? Education and British Imperialism.* Manchester: Manchester University Press, 1988.

McLeod, A.L. "Claude McKay, Alain Locke, and the Harlem Renaissance." *Literary Half-Yearly* 27.2 (July 1986): 65–75.

_____. "Claude McKay as Historical Witness." In *Subjects Worthy of Fame: Essays on Commonwealth Literature in Honour of H.H. Anniah Gowda.* Ed. A.L. McLeod. New Delhi: Sterling, 1989.

Memmi, Albert. *The Colonizer and the Colonized.* Boston: Beacon, 1965.

Microsoft Encarta 2000. CD-ROM. U.S.A., 1999.

Microsoft Encarta Africana 2000. CD-ROM. U.S.A., 1999.

Miller, James A. "African-American Writing of the 1930s: A Prologue." In *Radical Revisions: Rereading 1930s Culture.* Eds. Bill Mullen and Sherry Lee Linkon. Urbana: University of Illinois Press, 1996.

Minh-Ha, Trinh T. "Strategies of Displacement for Women, Natives and Their Others: Intra-views with Trinh T. Minh-ha." *Women's Studies Journal,* Vol. 10, no. 1; pp. 5–25; March 1994.

Mintz, Sidney, ed. *Slavery, Colonialism, and Racism.* New York: Norton, 1974.

Mongia, Padmini. *Contemporary Postcolonial Theory: A Reader.* New Delhi: Oxford University Press, 1997.

Montrose, Louis A. "Professing the Renaissance: The Poetics and Politics of Culture" in *The New Historicism,* H. Aram Veeser, ed. New York: Routledge, 1989.

Morrison, Toni. *Playing in the Dark: Whiteness and the Literary Imagination.* Cambridge, Mass.: Harvard University Press, 1992.

Naipaul, V.S. *Finding the Centre: Two Narratives.* London: Deutsch, 1984.

Nelson, Emmanuel S. "Black America and the Anglophone Afro-Caribbean Literary Consciousness." *Journal of American Culture* 12.4 (Winter 1989): 53–8.

Norton Anthology of Poetry. Third ed. Allison et al., eds. New York: Norton, 1983.

Works Consulted

Ngugi Wa Thiong'o. *Homecoming: Essays on African and Caribbean Literature, Culture and Politics.* London: Heinemann, 1972.

Padilla, Genaro, in Mario T. Garcia, *Memories of Chicano History: Life and Narrative of Bert Corona.* University of California Press: Berkeley, 1994.

Park, Robert E. "Human Migration and the Marginal Man." *American Journal of Sociology* 33 (May 1928): 881–93.

Parry, Benita. "Resistance Theory/Theorising Resistance or Two Cheers for Nativism." In *Colonial Discourse/Postcolonial Theory.* Eds. Francis Barker et al. Manchester: Manchester University Press, 1994.

Parry, J.H., and P.M. Sherlock. *A Short History of the West Indies.* London: St. Martin's Press, 1965.

Pecheux, Michel. *Language, Semantics and Ideology.* Harbans Nagpal, trans. New York: St. Martins, 1982.

Pratt, Mary Louise. *Imperial Eyes: Travel Writing and Transculturation.* London and New York: Routledge, 1992.

Preibe, Richard. "The Search for Community in the Novels of Claude McKay." *Studies in Black Literature* 3 (Summer 1972): 22–30.

Prestianni, Vincent. "Bibliographical Scholarship on Three Black Writers." *Obsidian-II* 5.1 (Spring 1990): 75–85.

Pyne-Timothy, Helen. "Perceptions of the Black Woman in the Work of Claude McKay." *CLA Journal* 19.2 (December 1975): 152–64.

Rahming, Melvin B. *The Evolution of the West Indian's Image in the Afro-American Novel.* Millwood, N.Y.: Associated Faculty Press, 1986.

Ramchand, Kenneth. "West Indian Literary History: Literarines, Orality and Periodization." *Callaloo* 11.1 (Winter 1988): 95–110.

_____. *The West Indian Novel and Its Background.* 2nd ed. 1970. London: Heinemann Educational Books, 1983.

Redding, J. Saunders. *To Make a Poet Black.* Chapel Hill: University of North Carolina Press, 1971.

Reid, Ira De Augustine. *The Negro Immigrant: His Background, Characteristics and Social Adjustment, 1899–1937.* 1939. New York: Arno Press and the New York Times, 1969.

Reid, Margaret A. "Langston Hughes: Rhetoric and Protest." *The Langston-Hughes-Review* 3.1 (Spring 1984): 13–20.

Roberts, Kimberley. "The clothes make the woman: The symbolics of prostitution in Nella Larsen's Quicksand and Claude McKay's Home to Harlem." *Tulsa Studies in Women's Literature* 16 (1997): 107–130.

Rosenblatt, Roger. *Black Fiction.* Cambridge, Mass.: Harvard University Press, 1974.

Said, Edward. "Orientalism Reconsidered." *Cultural Critique* 1 (Fall 1985): 89–108.

Sartre, Jean Paul. Preface, trans. by Constance Farrington, to *The Wretched of the Earth* by Frantz Fanon. London: Penguin Books, 1963.

Scruggs, Charles. "'All Dressed Up but No Place to Go': The Black Writer and His Audience During the Harlem Renaissance." *American Literature* 48 (January 1977): 543–63.

Segal, Aaron. "The Caribbean Exodus in a Global Context: Comparative Migration Experiences." In *The Caribbean Exodus.* Ed. Bary B. Levine. New York: Praeger, 1987. 44–66.

Sen, Sarbani. "How 'Red' Is 'Black'? An Analysis of the Relationship of the African-

American Movement with Marxism." In *Literature and Politics in Twentieth Century America*. Ed. J.L. Plakkoottam and Prashant K. Sinha. Hyderabad: American Studies Research Centre, 1993.

Senghor, L.S. *Liberté I: Negritude et Humanisme*. Paris: Seuil, 1964

Shelley, P.B. "To a Skylark." *The Norton Anthology of Poetry*. 3rd ed. New York: Norton, 1983.

Shourie, Usha. "Ideologies and Paradoxes: Claude McKay's Search for Meaning" in *Claude McKay: Centennial Studies*, ed. A.L. McLeod. New Delhi: Sterling, 1992.

Sinfield, Alan. *Fault Lines: Cultural Materialism and the Politics of Dissident Reading*. Los Angeles: University of California Press, 1992.

Singh, Amritjit. *Novels of the Harlem Renaissance: Twelve Black Writers, 1923–1933*. University Park: Pennsylvania State University Press, 1973.

Singh, Amritjit, S. William Shiver, and Stanley Brodwin, eds. *The Harlem Renaissance: Revaluations*. New York: Garland Publishing, 1989.

Smith, Robert P., Jr. "Rereading Banjo, Claude McKay and the French Connection." *CLA Journal* 30.1 (September 1986): 46–58.

Smith, Robert. "Claude McKay: An Essay in Criticism." *Phylon* 9 (1948): 270–273.

Smith, Gary. "The Black Protest Sonnet." *American Poetry* 2.1 (Fall 1984): 2–12.

Solomon, Mark. *Red and Black: Communism and Afro-Americans, 1929–1933*. New York: Garland Publishing, 1988.

Soyinka, Wole. Preface to *Myth, Literature and the African World*. Cambridge: Cambridge University Press, 1976. Vii–xii.

Sprinker, Michael. *Imaginary Relations: Aesthetics and Ideology in the Theory of Historical Materialism*. London: Verso, 1987.

Stein, Gertrude. *Paris France*. New York, 1940. 2.

Stoff, Michael. "Claude McKay and the Cult of Primitivism." In *The Harlem Renaissance Remembered*. Ed. Arna Bontemps. New York: Dodd, Mead, 1972. 124–46.

Story, Ralph D. "Patronage and the Harlem Renaissance: You Get What You Pay For." *CLA Journal* 32.3 (Mar 1989): 284–295.

Street, Brian V. *The Savage in Literature*. London: Routledge and Kegan Paul, 1975.

Sutton, Constance R. "The Caribbeanization of New York City and the Emergence of a Transnational Socio-cultural System." In *Caribbean Life in New York City: Sociocultural Dimensions*. Eds. Elsa M. Chaney and Constance R. Sutton. New York: Center for Migration Studies, 1987. 15–30.

Terdiman, Richard. *Discourse/Counter Discourse: The Theory and Practice of Symbolic Resistance in Nineteenth Century France*. Ithaca, 1985.

Thomas, H. Nigel. "Claude McKay's *Banana Bottom*: A Black Response to Late Nineteenth and Early Twentieth Century White Discourse on the Meaning of Black Reality." In *Nationalism vs. Internationalism: Inter-National Dimensions of Literatures in English*. Wolfgang Zach, ed., preface and introduction; Ken. L. Goodwin, ed. Tubingen, Germany: Stauffenberg, 1996.

Tiffin, Helen M. "Rites of Resistance: Counter-Discourse and West Indian Biography." *Journal of West Indian Literature* 3.1 (1989): 28–45.

Tillery, Tyrone. *Claude McKay: A Black Poet's Struggle for Identity*. Amherst: University of Massachusetts Press, 1992.

Tomlinson, John. *Cultural Imperialism: A Critical Introduction*. Baltimore: Johns Hopkins University Press, 1991.

Van Mol, Kay R. "Primitivism and Intellect in Toomer's Cane and McKay's Banana

Bottom: The Need for an Integrated Black Consciousness." *Negro American Literature Forum* 10 (Summer 1976): 48–52.

Wagner, Jean. *Black Poets of the United States: From Paul Laurence Durbar to Langston Hughes.* Trans. Kenneth Douglas. Urbana: University of Illinois Press, 1973.

Wall, Cheryl. "Paris and Harlem: Two Cultural Capitals." *Phylon* 35 (March 1974): 64–73.

Warren, Stanley. "Claude McKay as an Artist." *Negro History Bulletin* 40.2 (March–April 1977): 685–87.

West, Cornel. "Marxist Theory and the Specificity of Afro-American Oppression." *Marxism and the Interpretation of Culture.* Eds. Cary Nelson and Lawrence Grossberg. London: Macmillan, 1988. 17–33.

White, Hayden. *Tropics of Discourse: Essays in Cultural Criticism.* Baltimore, Md.: Johns Hopkins University Press, 1978.

Wilson, William J. *Power, Racism, and Privilege: Race Relations in Theoretical and Sociohistorical Perspectives.* New York: University of Chicago Press, 1973.

Woods, Gregory. "Gay re-readings of the Harlem Renaissance poets." *Journal of Homosexuality* 26 (1993): 127–142.

Index

INDEX